Coaching Soccer FOR DUMMIES®

by The National Alliance For Youth Sports
with Greg Bach

WILEY

Wiley Publishing, Inc.

Coaching Soccer For Dummies®

Published by
Wiley Publishing, Inc.
111 River St.
Hoboken, NJ 07030-5774
www.wiley.com

WILEY

About the Authors

The **National Alliance For Youth Sports** has been America's leading advocate for positive and safe sports for children for the past 25 years. It serves volunteer coaches, parents with children involved in organized sports, game officials, youth sports administrators, league directors, and the youngsters who participate in organized sports. The Alliance's programs are utilized in more than 3,000 communities nationwide by parks and recreation departments, Boys & Girls Clubs, Police Athletic Leagues, YMCAs/YWCAs, and various independent youth service groups, as well as on military installations worldwide. For more information on the Alliance's programs, which appear in the following list, visit www.nays.org.

National Youth Sports Coaches Association — More than 2 million volunteer coaches have been trained through NYSCA, which provides training, support, and continuing education.

Parents Association for Youth Sports — Parents gain a clear understanding of their roles and responsibilities in youth sports through this sportsmanship training program, which is utilized in more than 500 communities nationwide.

Academy for Youth Sports Administrators — More than 1,500 administrators worldwide have gone through the Academy, which is a 20-hour certification program that raises the professionalism of those delivering youth sport services. A professional faculty presents the information, and participants earn Continuing Education Units (CEUs).

National Youth Sports Administrators Association — The program provides training, information, and resources for volunteer administrators responsible for the planning and implementation of out-of-school sports programs.

National Youth Sports Officials Association — Officials who go through this certification program gain valuable knowledge on skills, fundamentals, and the characteristics that every good official must possess.

Start Smart Sports Development Program — This proven instructional program prepares children for the world of organized sports without the threat of competition or the fear of getting hurt through an innovative approach that promotes parent-child bonding.

Hook A Kid On Golf — Thousands of children of all ages and skill levels tee it up every year in the nation's most comprehensive junior golf development program, which features an array of instructional clinics and tournaments to choose from.

Game On! Youth Sports — This worldwide effort introduces children to actual game experience by giving them the freedom to create and play on their own.

Global Gear Drive — This program puts sports equipment in the hands of children around the world who wish to take part in quality sports activities but are unable to because of equipment shortages. The Alliance collects new and used youth sports equipment from individuals, organizations, and companies that it distributes to impoverished regions of the world.

Greg Bach is the communications director for the National Alliance For Youth Sports, a position he has held since 1993. Before joining NAYS, he worked as the sports editor of the *Huron Daily Tribune* in Bad Axe, Michigan, where he captured numerous writing awards from the Associated Press, Michigan Press Association, and the Hearst Corporation. He has a journalism degree from Michigan State University, which he earned in 1989, and he spends a lot of his free time during football and basketball season cheering for his beloved Spartans. He's an avid sports fan and has coached a variety of youth sports.

Dedication

National Alliance For Youth Sports: This book is dedicated to all the volunteer soccer coaches who give up countless hours of their free time to work with children and ensure that they have positive, safe, and rewarding experiences. We applaud their efforts and commend them for making a difference in the lives of youngsters everywhere.

Greg Bach: This book is dedicated to my mom and dad, the best parents anyone could ever wish for. I am truly lucky and forever grateful for their never-ending love and support.

Authors' Acknowledgments

A successful youth soccer program doesn't just happen. It takes a real commitment from not only dedicated volunteer coaches, but also parents who understand their roles and responsibilities and league directors and administrators who know what it takes to ensure that every child who steps on the soccer field in their community has a safe, fun, and rewarding experience. Soccer plays an important role in the lives of millions of children and provides them with the opportunity to learn the skills of the game and the chance to develop both emotionally and physically as individuals. The National Alliance For Youth Sports extends a heartfelt "Thank you" to every person who makes a positive difference, through soccer, in the life of a child.

This book is the result of a lot of hours of hard work from a lot of great people. A huge "Thank you" goes out to the incredibly talented staff at Wiley, particularly Mike Baker, the project editor of this book, whose editing expertise, insight, and creative touch as we went along from chapter to chapter made an incredible difference in the quality of the book you're holding right now. Thanks also to Stacy Kennedy, the acquisitions editor, whose efforts behind the scenes many months ago in working with the National Alliance For Youth Sports turned this book idea into reality; to Sarah Faulkner, the copy editor, whose touch can be found on every page with her eye for detail and passion for making every sentence perfect; the fabulous effort of the illustrators — Joni Burns, Shelley Norris, Karl Brandt, and Rashell Smith — whose work will be a great point of reference as you teach your team new soccer skills; and Emory Schlake, who provided a wealth of soccer knowledge.

Publisher's Acknowledgments

We're proud of this book; please send us your comments through our Dummies online registration form located at www.dummies.com/register/.

Some of the people who helped bring this book to market include the following:

Acquisitions, Editorial, and Media Development

Project Editor: Mike Baker

Acquisitions Editor: Stacy Kennedy

Copy Editor: Sarah Faulkner

Editorial Program Assistant: Hanna Scott

Technical Reviewer: Emory Schlake

Editorial Manager: Christine Meloy Beck

Editorial Assistant: David Lutton

Cover Photos: © Ken Chernus/Getty Images

Cartoons: Rich Tennant (www.the5thwave.com)

Composition Services

Project Coordinator: Adrienne Martinez

Layout and Graphics: Carl Byers, Andrea Dahl, Heather Ryan

Proofreaders: Leeann Harney, Joe Niesen, TECHBOOKS Production Services

Indexer: TECHBOOKS Production Services

Publishing and Editorial for Consumer Dummies

Diane Graves Steele, Vice President and Publisher, Consumer Dummies

Joyce Pepple, Acquisitions Director, Consumer Dummies

Kristin A. Cocks, Product Development Director, Consumer Dummies

Michael Spring, Vice President and Publisher, Travel

Kelly Regan, Editorial Director, Travel

Publishing for Technology Dummies

Andy Cummings, Vice President and Publisher, Dummies Technology/General User

Composition Services

Gerry Fahey, Vice President of Production Services

Debbie Stailey, Director of Composition Services

Contents at a Glance

Drills at a Glance

Dribbling and Ball Handling

Passing and Receiving

Shooting

Restarts

Defending

Goal Tending

Table of Contents

Introduction

*W*elcome to *Coaching Soccer For Dummies,* a book dedicated to volunteer coaches everywhere who work with kids in the wonderful sport of soccer. We hope you find it informative, entertaining, and — most important of all — useful in helping ensure that every child on your team has a fun, safe, and rewarding experience. After all, that's what it's really all about.

About This Book

We wrote this book for first-time volunteer soccer coaches looking for some guidance before they step on the field, as well as for coaches who've been on the sidelines for a season or two and are interested in gaining more insight on specific areas of the game to benefit their young squads. If you're new to the sport, you may be somewhat nervous or a bit apprehensive about what you're getting yourself into. You can take comfort in knowing that this book will kick those concerns to the curb and fully prepare you to enjoy a rewarding season with your team. Each chapter is filled with useful and straightforward information. The more chapters you knock off, the more knowledgeable you're going to be about this great game and how to teach it.

We also have plenty of information for veterans of the postseason pizza parties who've spent countless evenings at the local soccer fields. We wrote plenty of chapters specifically for you, covering everything from drills you can employ to upgrade individual skills to examining in detail the various systems of play that are available and how to choose the one that best fits your team's talent level.

One of the neat things about this book is that you can jump in anywhere. If you're a rookie coach, you probably have several questions swirling around in your head on everything from how to plan an effective practice to what to say to the team after a loss. Just check out the table of contents or the index for the topic you want to read about and then flip right there to get the scoop. Each chapter is divided into sections, and each section contains information on a specific topic concerning coaching youth soccer.

Conventions Used in This Book

To help you navigate this book, we use the following conventions:

- ✔ *Italic* text is used for emphasis and to highlight new words and terms that we define in the text.

- ✔ **Boldfaced** text is used to indicate keywords in bulleted lists or the action parts of numbered steps.

- ✔ Monofont is used for Web addresses. If you find that a specific address in this book has been changed, try scaling it back by going to the main site — the part of the address that ends in .com, .org, or .edu.

- ✔ Sidebars are shaded gray boxes that contain text that's interesting to know but not necessarily critical to your understanding of the chapter or topic.

We've also packed this book full of diagrams of practice drills and plays that you can work on with your team. The following chart is the key to under-standing all the squiggles and lines:

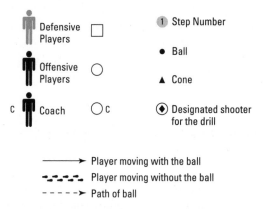

What You're Not to Read

Personally, we would read every word of this book if we were you. That's how good we think it is. But we may be biased, and you may be short on time. So, for your convenience, we're telling you that you don't have to read every-thing. In fact, when you see text marked with the TechnicalStuff icon, feel free to skip it. It isn't integral to your understanding of coaching or soccer. We also include gray-shaded boxes called *sidebars* that we fill with interesting (but totally skippable) information. Read at your own pace, and if you have time, let us know what you think of the book.

Foolish Assumptions

Here are some things that we assume about you:

- ✔ You know that soccer is played primarily with the feet and involves lots of running.

- ✔ You have a son or daughter who's interested in playing soccer this year, but you're unsure how to go about teaching him or her the game.

- ✔ You're a novice youth soccer coach, and you need to get your coaching skills up to speed.

- ✔ You don't have any aspirations of climbing the coaching ladder and overseeing a high school or college soccer team in the near future.

- ✔ You want the basics on things like what to do during the first practice of the season, how to determine who plays where, and whether teaching youngsters how to head a ball is safe.

If any of these descriptions hits the mark, you've come to the right place.

How This Book Is Organized

This book is divided into parts, each one pertaining to a specific aspect of coaching a youth soccer team. Here's a quick rundown.

Part 1: Getting Started Coaching Soccer

Coaching youth soccer can be a real challenge, but what you do before you and your team ever step on the field can make the difference between a smooth-running season and one that dissolves into total chaos and confusion. In this part, you get the scoop on how to develop a coaching philosophy that you're comfortable with and one that your players and their parents will embrace rather than reject. You also discover what all those markings are on the field and get an overview of the rules of the game.

Part 11: Building Your Coaching Skills

Fresh air. Green grass. Colorful uniforms. This is where the real fun — and actual coaching — begins. Before you step on the field, though, this part provides valuable information on how to conduct a preseason parents meeting, an often-overlooked aspect of coaching youth sports that's crucial for open-ing the communication lines, reducing the chances of misunderstandings and hurt feelings, and keeping your sanity. It also answers questions such as:

- How do I create practice plans that aren't the same boring thing week after week?
- How do I work with the uncoordinated kids or the shy youngsters who won't stop staring at the ground?
- What about the kid who doesn't even want to be here?

Plus, we show you the game-day ropes — from pre-game routines to your post-game speech — and help you assess your team and your performance at midseason.

Part III: Beginning and Intermediate Soccer

Teaching kids the basics of the game — from passing and defending to drib-bling and shooting — is crucial for their long-term enjoyment of the sport. This part shares how you can go about teaching by providing a variety of fun-filled drills that are highly effective in teaching skills. Also, when your team has a pretty good handle on some of the basics, check out the chapter devoted to kicking those skills up a notch.

Part IV: Advanced Soccer Strategies

When your players have a pretty good grasp of the basics of the game, they're eager to learn more advanced skills and continue their development. Part IV serves you well in this aspect. You discover more in-depth offensive and defensive techniques — such as outlet passes and counterattacking — while being presented with an assortment of drills that you can use to help your players maximize their development. From indirect free kicks to defend-ing a 2-on-1, this part examines it all.

Part V: The Extra Points

Part V is a smorgasbord of information on several topics that we hope you won't be dealing with much this season, such as recognizing injuries, con-fronting problem parents, and dealing with discipline problems on your team. You also find valuable information on pre- and post-game nutrition that you can share with your team to help maximize performance. And for those coaches looking to coach a travel team, you find all the information you need to help make your transition to a more competitive level of soccer a smooth one.

Part VI: The Part of Tens

It just wouldn't be a *For Dummies* book without the Part of Tens. Here, you find all sorts of precious information that you can put to use to boost the fun and enjoyment your team has playing for you this season. We include information on ways to make the season memorable and fun ways to end on a high note and keep 'em coming back next year.

Icons Used in This Book

This icon signals valuable tips that can really enhance your coaching skills. If you're scanning a chapter, take a moment to read these tips when you come across them and then put them to work.

When you're coaching youth soccer, you have a lot to comprehend. This icon alerts you to key information that's worth revisiting.

Watch out! This icon alerts you to situations that can be dangerous or derail your instruction.

Soccer can be a pretty complex game, particularly at the more competitive levels, so at times throughout this book, we present some rather technical information. You may want to skip some of this information if your young squad isn't ready to get too in-depth in the game.

Where to Go from Here

If this season is your first on the sidelines as a volunteer youth soccer coach, you may be most comfortable digging in with Chapter 1 and moving forward from there. Please note, though, that the book is structured so that you can easily move around from chapter to chapter at your convenience. So if you need answers to some of your most pressing early-season questions, you can scan the table of contents or index for those topics and jump right to those chapters.

Part I

Getting Started Coaching Soccer

"Excellent job defending the ball, Adam, but you can stop now. Practice is over. These balls are coming home with me."

In this part . . .

*B*efore you take the field with your young troops for the first time, do yourself, and your team, a big favor by diving into some behind-the-scenes homework that will lay the foundation for a smooth-running season. The homework includes outlining your coaching philosophy, understanding how your league operates, and learning the basic rules of the sport. You find all the information to get your season headed in the right direction in this part.

Chapter 1

Teaching Soccer to Children

Congratulations on your decision to coach a youth soccer team this season. You're embarking on a wonderful journey that will be filled with many special moments that both you and your players — regardless of their age or skill level — will remember for the rest of your lives.

Before you step on the field, you need to be aware that you're taking on a very important role. How you manage the youngsters on your team, and the way you interact with them during practices and games, affects how they feel about the sport and even themselves for years to come. How you handle the lengthy list of responsibilities that comes with the job either helps them develop an unquenchable passion for the game or drains their interest in ever participating again.

All you need — besides a whistle and clipboard — is some good information to guide you through the season. In this chapter, you find useful, straightforward insight and tips to help you and your team have a safe, fun, and rewarding season.

Doing Your Homework

Whether you volunteered to coach youth soccer this season because you want to spend more time with your child or because the league has a shortage of coaches and you're willing to step forward, you're accepting a responsibility that you can't take lightly. Before you roll out the soccer balls at your first practice, you have plenty of work to do behind the scenes to ensure that the season gets off to a smooth start.

Working with — and not against — parents

The overwhelming majority of parents with children involved in organized youth soccer programs are a supportive and caring group who want only the best for their children. Of course, parents in the minority can turn out to be a source of season-long aggravation that you may be forced to deal with. You can head off many potential problems by gathering the parents together before you begin the season and laying the ground rules on what you expect in terms of behavior during games, as well as their roles and responsibilities.

Coaches and parents finding ways to work together — the adult form of teamwork — is a formula that produces tremendous benefits for the youngsters. Coaches and parents who clash over everything from playing time to why Junior isn't getting to play sweeper spoil the experience for that child, and quite possibly others as well, when the negativity seeps into the team's practice sessions and envelops game day.

With parents, keep the following in mind:

- **Be proactive with them.** Outlining your expectations and coaching methods before the season paints a clear picture to parents about how you plan to handle the season. When parents hear firsthand that you're committed to skill development over winning and that you adhere to the league's equal-playing-time rule, you leave no room for petty squabbles over how much playing time their children receive. If you don't clarify these issues for parents well in advance, you're asking for a heap of trouble — and you'll get it, too. In Chapter 2, we help you develop your coaching philosophy and become familiar with your league so that you can clearly communicate these points to the parents.

- **Involve them.** Parents invest a lot of time and money in their child's soccer experience, and being included (instead of simply watching practice from the car or dropping their youngster off and then running errands) makes it far more worthwhile to them and their child. Parents can do more than bring treats after the game, too. Find ways to involve them at your practices, and recruit the right ones to assist you on game day; doing so helps you turn the season into a rewarding one for everyone involved. Throughout the book, you can find tips on boosting parental involvement, from practice drills that have team parents sticking around (see Chapter 6) to working with parents when you take a step up the coaching ladder and graduate to travel teams (see Chapter 20).

- **Communicate with them.** Besides a preseason parents meeting (which you can read all about in Chapter 4), keep the communication lines open all season long. Talk to the parents about the kids' progress; share your thoughts on where they really make improvements; offer suggestions for things they can do to help their youngsters develop in other areas; and check in from time to time to find out whether their children are having fun playing for you. Including parents in all facets of the season is the right thing to do and the smart thing to ensure that their children have positive experiences. In fact, we suggest that you meet 1-on-1 with each parent as part of your midseason progress review (see Chapter 8).

Despite your best efforts, problems may arise with parents. Our advice is to remain calm and in control of your emotions, and never allow situations to escalate. Check out Chapter 19, where we help you troubleshoot this issue and other problems coaches are most likely to face throughout the season.

Deciphering rules and mastering terminology

You've taken the job of teaching kids the world's most popular sport, and if you're like many volunteer coaches today, chances are pretty good that you never played soccer growing up. Therefore, to fulfill your responsibilities, you have to get a good handle on the basics of the game and be able to explain rules, introduce terminology, and teach strategies to your young players. Sound complicated? It isn't; it just takes a little time and effort on your part to learn some of the quirky rules (like offside) and some of the terms (like corner kicks and indirect free kicks) that are at the heart of this great game. We open up the rulebook in Chapter 3 and cover all the terms that you need to know. And we concentrate on the skills, techniques, and strategies that you need to pass along to your kids throughout Parts II and III of this book. Whether you need to brush up on fundamental skills for a beginning team or work out a defensive formation when you play against that high-octane older squad, we have you covered.

One of the most important steps you can take is find out what special rules your league operates under. Quite often, the rules that leagues utilize vary depending on the age and experience level of the players. Everything from the size of the field to which rules are enforced changes from community to community. Knowing these rules — and sharing them with your players — makes a tremendous difference in your players' enjoyment of the sport.

Taking the Field

Coaching youth soccer is all about the kids, their smiles, and their eagerness to get started learning from you and developing skills under you. What you say and do from day one through the course of the season has a major impact on whether these kids take a great interest in the sport and continue playing it for years to come or choose to turn their backs on it.

Practice planning

The drills you choose to teach kids skills and the manner in which you go about designing your practices influence your team's enjoyment and progress during the season. Practices that kids look forward to with the same enthusiasm as the first day of summer vacation promote learning and skill development. On the other hand, practices that you put together in your car in the parking lot five minutes before the players begin arriving stifle learning and put a roadblock on fun. While working with your team, keep the following thoughts in mind to help squeeze the most out of your sessions:

- ✔ **Be more than a coach.** Although you're teaching your players the basics of the game, you also have the opportunity to impact their lives in other areas. While they warm up, talk to them about the importance of doing well in school, and ask them what their favorite subjects are. Take the time to speak to them about how important it is to listen to what their parents and teachers say and what it means to be a good kid. Your practices can be great times to teach more than how to kick a soccer ball, and the words you deliver may stick with the children for the rest of their lives.

- ✔ **Create a positive atmosphere.** Turn your practices into sessions in which youngsters can make mistakes without the fear of being yelled at in front of their teammates. Letting the kids know from the first practice of the season that making mistakes is part of the learning process allows them to relax and, in the process, helps them learn skills quicker and perform better.

Choose drills that keep kids moving at all times and are challenging enough to hold their interest. Drills that force kids to stand in line awaiting turns are not only boring, but also dramatically cut down on the number of touches of the ball each child receives, which minimizes learning. Check out Chapters 10, 14, and 17, where we provide all sorts of drills and ideas for beginning, intermediate, and advanced players.

Game day

Coaching is about constantly adapting to ever-changing conditions, and that's most evident on game day, when you're challenged to make all sorts of decisions in a short period of time. With younger kids just starting out in the sport, you want to make sure you rotate them around to all the different positions so they can experience the sport from a variety of perspectives. With the older kids, you may find yourself making halftime adjustments and determining whether a more aggressive approach serves the team best in the second half or whether a more defense-oriented style of play is warranted. But don't worry; we help you handle it all in Chapter 7.

Game day provides many great teachable moments for the kids. It gives you a chance to reinforce some of the points you talk about all week during practice, such as the importance of working as a team, displaying good sportsmanship toward the opposing team and the officials, abiding by the rules, doing your best at all times, and having fun regardless of what the scoreboard reads.

Balancing Parenting and Coaching

We certainly don't have to tell you that being a parent is a difficult job, but here's what we can share with you: Coaching your son or daughter's soccer team is equally tricky. After you step inside the white lines, and your child straps on the shin guards, you're likely to encounter an assortment of issues. We hope most of them are minor, but some may be problems that you never even dreamed of dealing with before. Don't panic! Although coaching your child can be complex and confusing, it can also be, if handled properly, an extremely rewarding experience for both of you. Sure, you'll probably experience occasional bumps along the way, but if the two of you work together, you'll enjoy some very special memories to savor for a lifetime.

And take comfort in the fact that you're not alone. Approximately 85 percent of all volunteer soccer coaches have their own sons or daughters on the team, so you're venturing into common parenting territory.

Kicking around the decision with your kid

Before you decide to grab the whistle and clipboard and assume the role of soccer coach, sit down with your child and gauge how she feels about you overseeing the team this season. If you don't ask her how she feels, you'll never know. Many youngsters are thrilled to have their dad or mom as coach, and if you see that sparkle in your child's eyes when you bring the subject up, that makes all the time and effort you put into the season well worth it.

On the other hand, some children — for whatever reason — aren't going to feel comfortable with the idea and would prefer that their parents don't coach the teams. Take your child's wishes into account before making the decision to step forward.

Here are a few tips to help you reach the right decision on whether you and your child are ready for you to pick up the coaching whistle:

- ✔ **With your child's help, put together a list of all the positives and negatives about being the coach.** On the positive side, you may list that the two of you will be spending more time together than before and that, as the coach, you'll ensure that your child and the rest of the team have fun as they learn new skills. Resolve the negatives by working with your child to develop solutions. For instance, your child may expect to play a certain position simply because you're his parent. Explain that you must be fair to everyone and can't show favoritism and that your child and his teammates will have an equal chance to play different positions.

- ✔ **Examine your motivations.** Don't take on the task of coaching your son or daughter if your goal is to make your child a star. You must be willing to do whatever is best for your child's overall development, and harboring thoughts of college scholarships and athletic stardom is simply a blueprint for trouble.

- ✔ **Explain to your child that being the coach is a great honor.** The fact that he's "sharing" you with the other kids during games and practice sessions doesn't mean you love him any less. Explain to him that your responsibility is to help all the players on the team. Taking the time to explain your role to your child helps promote better understanding and reduces the chance of problems arising after the season gets under way.

After the two of you talk things through, take your child's thoughts seriously. If he still isn't comfortable with the idea, push your coaching aspirations to the side for the time being. You can revisit the subject with him the following season to measure his feelings. Just because he isn't ready this season doesn't mean he won't want you guiding his team next season or at some point in the future. The last thing you want to do is turn your child off to the sport and make him uncomfortable.

Focusing on family-friendly field rules

If you and your child agree that having you grab the coaching reins is a good move, keep these tips in mind as you navigate through the season:

- ✔ **Remember that you're still the parent.** Whether the team wins or loses, you have to step out of coaching mode and remember that first and foremost, you're a parent — and that means asking your child whether she had fun and praising her for doing her best and displaying good sportsmanship. Take your child out for that post-game ice cream or pizza whether she scored a goal or tripped over the ball on a breakaway.

- ✔ **Keep talking.** To effectively monitor how the season is going, you want your child to understand that she can come to you with a concern or problem at any time. Just because you're the coach doesn't mean that certain topics are now off limits.

- ✔ **Don't push practice at home.** If your child has a bad practice, you may be tempted to work with her on specific skills as soon as you get home. Never push your child in this direction. In casual conversation, ask her whether she wants to spend a few extra minutes practicing a certain skill that may be giving her a bit of trouble. If she does, that's great, but if not, let it go. Pushing your child to perform extra repetitions can drain her interest in the sport.

✔ **Never compare siblings.** Let your child develop at her own rate. She should never feel burdened by your expectations to control or kick a soccer ball as well as her brother did at his age. This type of comparison can crush her self-esteem and smother her confidence.

✔ **Praise, praise, praise!** Be sure to praise your child's willingness, understanding, and cooperation in this special venture. Coaching your child can be one of the most rewarding experiences you ever have, but it isn't always easy.

✔ **Be careful with car conversations.** A lot of adults have the natural tendency to replay the game on the drive home, and that's perfectly okay if the youngster is an enthusiastic participant in the discussion. But if the game didn't go as well as you planned, refrain from dissecting every mistake, and don't spend the ride probing the youngster for reasons why the team lost or why she didn't perform up to the best of her ability.

✔ **Refrain from pushing too hard.** All parents naturally want their kids to excel, no matter what the activity. In a sport like soccer, sometimes parents go overboard and take their newfound coaching position to the extreme by viewing the position as a chance to control their child's destiny. When this happens, the youngster's experience is unfairly compromised because the parent typically pushes her harder than the other kids, demands more from her, and piles on criticism when she's unable to fulfill the unfair expectations. When parents lose sight of the big picture of what youth soccer is all about, problems materialize that impact the child's emotional well-being, as well as her interest in learning and playing soccer.

Coaching your kid can be a great experience for both of you, but the job can feel a bit like walking a tightrope at times as you try to avoid two common traps that many coaches (especially coaches who are unfamiliar with their roles) tend to fall into. Ideally, your behavior should fit somewhere between these two extremes:

✔ **Providing preferential treatment:** Parents naturally lean toward showing preferential treatment to their own children, whether they realize it or not. Typically, they give their children extra playing time; shower them with more attention during practices and games; and assign them special duties, such as team captain. Showing favoritism throws your child into a difficult spot with her teammates and weakens team camaraderie.

✔ **Overcompensating to avoid the preferential-treatment label:** Coaches can also go too far out of their way to ensure that no one thinks they're giving preferential treatment to their children. Quite often, the coach will reduce his child's playing time or give his child less 1-on-1 instruction during practices. Taking away playing time from your child to steer clear of the favoritism issue does, in effect, create a negative atmosphere for your child. She will question why you're punishing her unfairly.

Game-day questions to ask your child

Ideally, your child is looking forward to game day. Keep in mind that the conversations you have with your child on game day — whether at the breakfast table or in the minivan on the drive to the game — have the power to either minimize nervousness and ensure a fun and relaxed demeanor or to fuel stress and hamper your child's ability to perform. Here are a few questions that result in positive game-day discussions:

✔ **What are you most looking forward to about the game?** Your child's response speaks volumes about his state of mind and often provides valuable insight on the mood of the entire team. If your youngster seems overly uptight, the rest of the team may be as well. Perhaps this apprehension stems from the extra emphasis you're unknowingly putting on this game or the way you've been interacting with the kids during practices recently. Listen to your child's response, but also pay attention to the tone of his voice and his body language.

✔ **What have you enjoyed the most about the season?** The answer to this question provides some valuable information. If your child mentions a particular drill that you used way back in the second week of the season but haven't used since, it may be something worth using at one of your upcoming practices because several other kids likely feel the same way.

✔ **How about trying that new skill today, if you get a chance? I'm looking forward to seeing it.** Genuinely and enthusiastically letting your child know that you can't wait to see her put her new skill to use is a real confidence-booster. This comment shows your child that you're pleased with how she's picked up the skill, and it gives her that little extra impetus to want to use it during the game.

Chapter 2

Getting Organized

Coaching a squad of young soccer players involves more than showing up with a whistle, a roster, and a trunk filled with soccer balls. In order to be one of those coaches whom kids look up to and look forward to seeing all season long, you have to do a lot of preparation prior to the first practice of the season.

First, think about why you got involved this season, what you hope to accomplish, and what your approach is going to be to help your team get there. Have you assumed the coaching role because you genuinely want to help kids learn and develop skills in a fun and safe environment, or because you want to make a run for the league title? What's your take on playing time, motivating players, and creating a positive atmosphere?

This chapter considers those aspects, and many others, which form the basis of your coaching philosophy. Having a philosophy in place and sticking to it as best you can sets the tone for a good season. The league you're coaching in also dictates a portion of your philosophy, which is why gathering as much information as you can about the league's policies before you step on the field is important. Being involved in a league that promotes values that you want to impart to your team is critical for everyone's enjoyment.

Developing a Coaching Philosophy

Creating a coaching philosophy is fairly simple. Living up to it all season long is the tricky part. What's a coaching philosophy? Basically, it reflects the standards you set for yourself and your team, and it's the foundation of your coaching values and beliefs.

Entering the season without a coaching philosophy is like driving across the country without a road map. Sure, you eventually arrive at your destination, but not without wasting a lot of time and energy with wrong turns and dealing with unnecessary problems and aggravation along the way. A thoughtful coaching philosophy keeps you on the right track as you negotiate your way through the season. In the sections that follow, we introduce the various components to consider when developing a philosophy that stresses respect, sportsmanship, skill development, and safety.

Even with a carefully planned philosophy firmly in place, adhering to it at all times can be difficult. Challenges show themselves when Billy's mom confronts you halfway through the season about why the team isn't winning more games or when Jennifer's dad questions why the lesser-skilled kids are receiving as much playing time as the team's best players. (Explaining your coaching philosophy to the parents before the season gets under way, which we discuss in Chapter 4, helps you steer clear of many of these potential headaches.)

Your coaching philosophy speaks volumes about you — not only as a coach, but also as a person. Take the time to put some real thought into it; you'll be glad you did. Lead your players in the direction you know is right. Strive to instill in them the values that you want your own kids to exhibit throughout their lives. Accomplish this goal, and regardless of how many games you win this season, you and your team will be winners in the truest sense.

Tailoring your philosophy to your age group

Although each child has his own unique strengths and weaknesses, all youngsters possess general characteristics that are dictated by age. Children are continually changing, and part of your responsibility as a coach is to know what to expect both physically and emotionally from youngsters at various age levels.

Being fully aware of the general age-related differences we cover in the following pages enhances your coaching skills and your ability to relate to your team. It also ensures that you don't favor the players on your squad who are more mature and skilled at the expense of players who are less skilled and developed.

No matter what the age or skill level of your players, always be supportive and enthusiastic. Pile on the praise, and never stop encouraging them. This approach builds their confidence and self-esteem, and whether they're 6 or 16, you give a gift that will last for years to come.

Ages 6 and under

Children in the 6-and-under age bracket have probably never played soccer
before, and this season may be their first experience in an organized team
setting. Your job is to introduce them to some of soccer's most basic elements and whet their appetite for future participation. (We cover the fundamentals that you can focus on with this age group and the next in Chapter 9.)
Children at this age generally aren't concerned about how their soccer skills
compare with those of the others on their team; they're primarily interested
in being with friends and having fun learning and playing the sport. Competition
is usually the furthest thing from their mind, which is why most beginner soccer
leagues don't keep game scores or standings for this age group.

Ages 7 to 9

Youngsters in the 7-to-9 age bracket start focusing on mastering some of the
basics of the sport. They crave feedback from coaches and parents on how
they're performing certain skills and how they're progressing with new ones.
They begin noticing their teammates' abilities and skill levels. When coaches
verbally recognize one of their peers for properly executing a skill, the kids
want to earn that same feedback. The desire to compete carries much more
prominence for some youngsters in this age range than others. Children who
have older siblings may be particularly competitive because they've watched
their brothers and sisters compete in soccer or other sports, and now it's
finally their turn to display their skills.

Ages 10 to 12

More than likely, children ages 10 to 12 have had some experience playing
soccer in the past and are continuing with it because the sport has piqued
their interest. Keep the positive momentum going by adding to their foundation of skills. Fuel their desire to continue playing by conducting practices
that are both challenging and fun.

Quite often, sports take on added importance at this juncture in their life, and
they really want to do well. (For more on skills and drills with this age group,
see Chapters 11 through 14.) As children hit this age range, many become
more competitive, and winning and losing take on more importance in their
lives. They begin embracing the challenge of putting their skills to the test
and trying to outperform other kids their age. When they help the team prevail, they feel immense satisfaction accompanied by a unique feeling of
accomplishment that can be attained only through the wonderful world of
playing youth soccer.

Ages 13 and 14

Welcome to the challenging world of the teenager! Kids ages 13 and 14 have
already developed many of the basic skills needed to play the sport, and now
they want to improve on them. Children at this age are typically searching
for their own personal identities as well, so try getting to know them on a

personal level by learning who their favorite soccer players or their favorite soccer teams are. Of course, this tip is great for building special coach–player bonds with kids of all ages. (Feel free to turn to Part IV, where we cover offensive and defensive sets for older kids and drills that will challenge them.)

Ages 15 and above

Gaining the respect of your players is always important to your coaching success, and that's particularly true for kids ages 15 and older. These teens have developed a real passion for the sport. They attend soccer camps, perhaps play in leagues year-round, and, in some cases, may actually be more knowledgeable in some areas of the sport than you are.

If you volunteer or get recruited to coach this age group, don't be scared! You don't need to panic. Instead, welcome the chance to enhance your coaching abilities, and embrace the opportunity to coach kids who have a deep-rooted love for the game. Be sure to let them know that you value their opinions, suggestions, and input regarding the team. A youngster's passion for soccer is wonderful, and it actually helps make your job easier.

Focusing on fun and skill development

As a youth soccer coach, don't let your vision of what's best for your players become blurred by trying to win every game, grab the league title, and show off the shiny first-place trophy on your mantel at home. Your team's win–loss record at the end of the season (if you're coaching in a league that keeps standings) doesn't define your success as a coach. For the true barometer of what type of coach you are, look at whether the kids learn skills, have fun doing so, and want to play for you again next season.

Certainly, at the more advanced levels of play, winning takes on a more prominent role, and you shouldn't sweep the concept aside because it's a part of playing soccer. After all, doing well on a test in school is a form of winning. So is beating out ten other people for a job you really want. Winning is something that we all must attain in order to achieve some level of success in everyday life.

But youth soccer coaches must exercise great caution. Children are highly impressionable. If they get a sense that winning is *all* that really matters to you, having fun and developing skills suddenly become secondary in their minds, and the season begins a downward spiral. After this descent begins, altering the season's course and getting everything back on track becomes really difficult. When you're coaching younger and less experienced children, focus less on wins and losses and more on teaching skills and ensuring that the kids are having fun playing and learning.

Children's short attention spans can make coaching difficult at times, but they can also work to your advantage. Many youngsters just beginning in the sport usually forget the score of the last game pretty quickly and direct their attention to something else. So, even if you happen to lose 9-0, praise the kids for their effort, and congratulate them on how well they passed the ball, which gives them a boost of confidence and a sense of accomplishment that they're making strides in their play.

Never let scoreboards or opposing teams define how much fun you have on the soccer field or impede your team's progress in learning the game. The skill-development process is ongoing and occurs throughout the season. Use every practice and game as a building block to learning, and never forget to have fun along the way. With the right approach, your team will surely enjoy this journey with you every kick of the way.

Emphasizing teamwork and building bonds

Although soccer is a sport that allows individuals plenty of opportunities to create and maneuver on their own, you and your team are much better off if you can get everyone to work together as a cohesive unit on the field. Of course, this is easier said than done.

Imagine having ten kids in front of you, and you have one really cool toy that they're all eyeing. You give the toy to one child and ask her to share it with everyone. Tough to pull off, eh? The same goes for soccer. You have one soccer ball that the children all have to share in order for the team to be successful. So how do you get the team to that point?

Finding a surefire route to teaching the essence of teamwork among your players is difficult. Try to get your players to see the enormous benefits that accompany working as a team (rather than as a bunch of individuals) with the following pointers:

- ✔ **Praise team efforts.** During practices, recognize the efforts of the team whenever possible. For example, if you're conducting a 3-on-1 drill, and the offensive players score a goal, there's a natural tendency to applaud the end result and acknowledge the youngster who delivered the kick at the expense of the others involved in the drill. But be sure to recognize the perfectly executed pass that began the play or the pass that found the open player who scored the goal. If you spread your admiration among all the players who played a role in the goal, players begin to understand that assists are just as important as goals in the team framework.

- ✔ **Get the kids to praise one another.** Encourage the kids who score goals to acknowledge the passes from their teammates. If you get kids in the habit of giving one another high-fives or telling one another "great pass," you forge bonds for the benefit of the team.

✔ **Promote sideline support.** Encourage players who aren't in the game to stay involved by cheering and supporting their teammates. This role keeps them involved in the action so they aren't glancing over to see what their parents are doing or what kind of food their friends are buying at the concession stand.

✔ **Allow individual freedom — at times.** Although you should allow players individual freedom to create plays on their own, it must be done within the confines of the team setting. At some point during the game, a player's 1-on-1 moves to work the ball down the field may be called for, and that's part of the game. But when that player ignores teammates and isn't willing to give up the ball, the team chemistry is threatened. Remind that player that he has teammates for a reason and to look out for them. (We cover dealing with a player who isn't willing to give up the ball in Chapter 19.)

✔ **Avoid the captain syndrome.** Continually relying on two or three players to serve as team captains throughout the season puts them on a platform above the rest of the squad. Giving every player the opportunity to lead warm-ups in practice or head a drill infuses the team with the sense that everyone is equal. In most youth soccer programs, "official" team captains aren't required until around the age of 14 or until kids join travel teams (discussed in Chapter 20), when the competition becomes more intense and the players become more passionate about the game. At the younger levels, captains aren't necessary, but they are another tool that you can use to build self-esteem and team bonds.

Creating a team environment in which children are comfortable and genuinely feel that they're valued and contributing members is imperative for any learning and skill development to take place during the season. Building team bonds also ensures that the kids give you their best effort all season long — and have fun doing so.

Here are a few ways you can help emphasize team spirit:

✔ **Listen to the young voices.** Let the kids regularly make some choices. Letting them select a favorite drill to run during practice and choose the team snack at the next game are great ways to involve everyone and make them a part of what's going on this season. If the league allows it, you can even let the players choose the team name and the color of the uniforms. Or, to help promote team unity, you can let players pick what color t-shirt everyone wears to the next practice.

✔ **Play the name game.** Let players choose nicknames for themselves. If you feel daring, you can even let the team come up with a nickname for you.

✔ **Come up with a team cheer.** Work with everyone to come up with a clever team cheer that can be used before games to help remind players that they're taking the field as a team and working together as one.

✔ **Hold an early-season pizza party.** You can't go wrong with pizza, and there's no rule that says you have to wait until the season is over to gather the team for a pizza party. Having a team party or other type of group activity early in the season helps build camaraderie among the players and forges friendships. The benefits will spill over to the field as the players work more closely together.

Making every kid count

REMEMBER

All team members should feel prized, respected, and accepted. As the coach, your job is to work with, and play close attention to, all the youngsters on your team, regardless of how fast they run or how hard they kick a ball. Sometimes, this evenhandedness is a lot more difficult than it sounds. After all, becoming enamored with kids who are more athletically gifted than the rest of the team is easy, and you may end up showering them with all the attention, accolades, and praise. Spreading the encouraging words around equally takes real focus and effort. Making sure that each child — no matter how big or small his actual contributions are during games and practices — feels valued and appreciated for his efforts is the cornerstone of good coaching.

Providing *immediate* feedback and continually recognizing *all* players for their various contributions are the most effective ways to boost their self-confidence and fuel their interest in giving their best effort all season long. Consider these points:

✔ **Acknowledge all on-the-field contributions.** The kids who score goals during games hear the gratifying applause from the stands, and they should hear praise from you, too, but you should also take the time to acknowledge the efforts that led to the goals. For instance, recognizing the youngster who delivered the pass that began the play, or applauding your defender who swiped the ball to regain possession for your team, goes a long way toward making each child truly feel appreciated and a part of the team. After all, without the effort of all the children, no one scores a goal, and it's well worth mentioning to the team to reinforce that wins, losses, and goals are never the result of one player but of the total team.

✔ **Seek out less tangible contributions.** Applaud good attitudes and strong work ethics as much as you applaud properly executed passes or good defensive plays. Even lesser-skilled youngsters struggling to contribute during games can be recognized in a number of ways that will inflate their self-esteem and maintain their interest in participating. Applaud their hustle chasing after the ball, acknowledge their team spirit and enthusiasm, and point out to the rest of the squad the example of good sportsmanship that they display during games. These attributes are what youngsters carry with them the rest of their lives, long after they have put their shin guards away.

✔ **Cheer when mistakes are made.** Yes, you should cheer even when a child makes a mistake or fails to do a skill the way you just demonstrated it. Making mistakes is a part of playing soccer, and the team needs to be reminded of that. Praising the effort rather than criticizing the result frees the child to keep trying until she gets it. She won't fear making a mistake, because she knows she won't receive negative backlash from you. This approach opens the door to all sorts of learning this season.

✔ **Provide awards for all.** Many coaches enjoy handing out awards at the end of the season to their players. If you elect to do so, make sure you come up with something for every player on the team instead of taking the old Most Valuable Player route. In Chapter 22, we discuss this idea in detail and provide some fun ideas that you can use to recognize the contributions of each team member.

Modeling good sportsmanship

Teaching good sportsmanship to youngsters can be tricky, especially because they're bombarded with images on television of professional athletes trash-talking, showboating, and disrespecting opponents. Good sportsmanship is one of the healthiest and most important ideals you can instill in your young players. Here are a few ways you can help cultivate good sportsmanship and make your squad one of the most liked and respected teams in the league:

✔ **Continually stress the importance of being a good sport at all times.** While your players are going through warm-ups before practice or a game, discuss a game on TV that they saw, and ask them whether they saw a player display good sportsmanship. Subtle reinforcement goes a long way toward instilling good sportsmanship in your players.

✔ **Set the tone before each game by crossing the field to shake the opposing coach's hand.** The players, fans, and opposing coaches will notice your gesture of sportsmanship, and it will make a difference.

✔ **Be a model of good sportsmanship at all times.** That means no yelling at officials or questioning calls that you're sure should have gone your team's way. If you aren't a model of good sportsmanship at all times, you can't expect your players to be. Players are going to take their cue from you, so if you rant and rave about a call to an official, expecting your players to show respect for the officials is hardly fair.

✔ **During your post-game talk, recognize players who displayed good sportsmanship.** Perhaps one of your players went out of her way after the game to congratulate an opposing player who scored a goal or made a good play during the course of the game. By recognizing these displays, your players gradually learn that their behavior on the field is important.

✔ **Insist on a post-game handshake.** Regardless of the game's outcome, have your players line up and shake hands with the opposing team and its coaches. If your team won, your players should acknowledge that their opponents played a good game, and if your squad lost, your players should congratulate the opposition. It's also a classy move for your players to shake the referee's hand following the contest.

✔ **Deal with problems.** During the season, you may encounter a win-at-all-costs coach who prowls the sidelines yelling and berating his team or an out-of-control parent who spends the entire game shouting instructions at his child or argues every call that doesn't go his way. In Chapter 19, we present tips on how to handle this type of inappropriate behavior, which has no place in youth soccer.

Motivating players

Regardless of their ages or experience levels, your players will arrive at the field with vastly different motivations for playing the game. Although some are strongly motivated individuals and real gems to work with, others may benefit from your inspiring words.

Some players respond positively to challenges you issue, such as seeing whether they can deliver ten accurate passes in a row. With others, that approach may actually detract from their motivation to participate. Each youngster you come in contact with is different, and you have to discover for yourself what motivational tool works for each child.

Here are a few general tips you can employ to help your players become the best they can be:

✔ **Love what you're doing.** If you have a sincere passion for soccer and for teaching it to children, your excitement and enthusiasm will rub off on the team.

✔ **Set attainable goals for youngsters.** Having reasonable expectations for the kids you're coaching and setting goals that are within their reach encourages them to keep working. If a child senses that your expectations are impossibly far-fetched, he wonders what's the point of even trying, and his play on the field will suffer tremendously.

✔ **Recognize the good things happening on the field.** Stop practice to point out when a player does something really well, not when a player makes a mistake. Being positive is simply one of the best motivational tools around. Think about it. If your boss tells you that you did a great job on a presentation in front of your co-workers, you're going to give even more effort on your next presentation. The same goes for kids performing skills on a soccer field.

✔ **Don't motivate through fear or threats.** Making a child run a lap for failing to perform at an expected level has no place in youth soccer. This type of approach typically handcuffs a youngster's ability to perform, because he's now afraid of making a mistake that's going to translate into punishment. Children have to feel free to make mistakes in order to improve. Plus, this motivation-through-fear tactic has the strong chance of chasing members of your team away from the sport in the future.

Getting to Know the League You're In

Youth soccer leagues around the country are as different as the millions of kids who strap on shin guards to play in them. You can find outdoor and indoor leagues. Numbers go from 4-on-4 to 11-on-11 leagues. Ages fluctuate from 5-and-under leagues to 17-and-under leagues. You even have the option of same-sex leagues or coed leagues.

Along with this diversity comes the smorgasbord of rules that are a part of each league. Some adhere strictly to the official rules of the sport and allow no modifications. The majority of programs, however, alter the rules to fit the age and experience level of the kids.

Brushing up on the rules

Reading a soccer rulebook isn't as exciting as reading a Stephen King novel or a John Grisham thriller, but it should be bedside reading for you. To be successful at coaching, you have to know the rules of soccer, as well as the particular rules your league is enforcing this season, and be able to teach them to your players. Even if you have an extensive knowledge of soccer and perhaps even played at the high school or college level, take a look at the league's rulebook. Consider it a refresher before you take the field. Chances are good that the league is using some rules that were never applied in the same way when you played as a youngster. If you don't know and understand the rules, you can't expect your team to, either. And if the youngsters don't know the rules, playing soccer can be a pretty frustrating experience.

Don't plunge in and attempt to memorize all the rules in a single sitting. Review a few pages every night prior to the season's start until you're pretty comfortable with them. (For a quick primer on the rules of soccer, check out Chapter 3.)

Don't assume that older kids have a firm grasp on all the rules simply because they've played the sport for years. If no one took the time to explain certain rules that may be somewhat confusing, the kids may not have ever learned them. And as kids progress from league to league, they encounter new rules that may not have been enforced the previous season. It's up to you to know which rules are in place and to share that information with the team before the season gets under way.

Rainy days and make-up games

Some days Mother Nature just isn't going to be on your side, and she's going to wreak havoc on your season. Rainy weather often forces you to reschedule or call off practices. Inclement weather on game days may result in the games moving to days that you normally don't play on or in total cancellation. Some leagues may even have a week set aside at the end of the season specifically for make-up games. Being aware of the league policy regarding cancellations alleviates a lot of the confusion with parents and team members when bad weather arrives.

Exercise great caution with approaching storms. Waiting for the first sign of lightning before canceling practice or stopping a game is flirting with serious trouble. Get your players off the field before lightning threatens the area. (Check out Chapter 18 for more information on dealing with the weather.)

Practices, practices, practices

The age of your team generally dictates how much time you spend conducting practices during the season. With most beginner leagues, you have just one practice a week. Many leagues restrict the number of practices a coach can hold, so be aware of this rule before you put together your practice plans.

Quite often, leagues set the practice schedule for the entire season based on the number of fields that are available and what other programs they have going on. This helps eliminate a lot of scheduling headaches on your part. So, for example, during the season, your team may practice every Tuesday from 5:30 to 6:30.

The time you spend with your team during practice sessions is critical for its success. Practice isn't a social hour when you roll some balls out on the field and have the kids knock them around while you stand on the sidelines watching. You have to carefully plan these sessions and be actively involved in them at all times. Kids may not even recall a game they played in, but they may fondly recall a practice and what you said to them or a drill that was so much fun they couldn't wait to tell their parents about it. Turn to Chapter 6 to get some in-depth tips on running a great practice.

Focusing on fun or first place

The two distinct classifications that exist for soccer programs are recreational and competitive. Each type requires a vastly different approach to coaching. Do you know what type of league you're coaching in this season? Before agreeing to volunteer, check with the recreation director to learn more about the league and make sure it's the right fit for you.

Recreational leagues

If you're coaching soccer for the first time, chances are good that you're involved in a recreational league. This type of program focuses on teaching kids the basic skills of the game. Generally, the program has rules in place regarding equal playing time.

Often, with kids ages 8 and under, the league scales teams down to 4-on-4 and has them play games on much smaller fields to allow each child plenty of touches with the ball. Usually, these teams have no goaltender. Because the players are so young and are just learning the skills, having a child positioned as the goaltender would result in an enormous amount of standing around and very little action for the youngster. Typically, pylons (orange cones) are set up at each end of the field to serve as the goals.

Recreational leagues also feature rules that have been altered to meet the needs of the age and experience level of the kids. In the younger divisions, you don't see corner kicks, indirect kicks, or penalty kicks (all terms that we cover in detail in Chapter 3, when we address the basics of the game). Referees don't call offsides; there won't be throw-ins; and a child touching the ball with his hands often isn't whistled for an infraction but is gently reminded that the action is a no-no.

Another trademark of a recreational program is that coaches are allowed on the field during games with the youngest kids. Usually, the league allows a coach from each team to stand on each half of the field, giving coaches a chance to talk to their players during the course of play and to provide positive feedback and encouragement.

When meeting with the opposing coach before the game, encourage him to provide positive feedback to your players when the action is at his end of the field, and let him know that you'll do the same when the play takes place near you. At this level, you just want kids running around and getting a feel for kicking the ball and being with their teammates.

As kids become older and stay involved in the sport longer, they naturally become more competitive. Winning takes on a more prominent role with a lot of kids around the age of 10 or 12. If these kids still play in a recreational program, some of the emphasis will shift to winning, but not at the expense of league policies regarding equal playing time.

Competitive leagues

Children whose thirst for competition can't be quenched in their local recreational program can turn to the avalanche of competitive leagues that exist. These leagues are typically referred to as select or travel teams, which we examine in greater detail in Chapter 20.

This type of program is for youngsters who have demonstrated higher skill levels than many other kids their age. These elite programs give kids the chance to compete against others of similar ability in their state or region. Usually, kids involved in these programs have their eyes on long-term advancement in the sport, such as playing at the collegiate level (or, as is often the case, their parents are thinking college scholarships and have pushed the children into this highly competitive environment).

Coaches of select or travel teams have an array of issues to deal with that the recreational volunteer coach doesn't face. For example, you have to orchestrate tryouts; make cuts; and, at the oldest levels, make game tapes to send to prospective college coaches.

Your schedule is crammed with practices and is typically tournament heavy, with lots of travel and weekends away from home. The environment is entirely different because victories in tournaments push the team into the national spotlight and garner lots of attention for the players involved. Coaches are given the reins of a select or travel team only if they have a strong coaching background and have proved through their experience to be well versed in all areas of the game.

 If you're in a highly competitive league that you don't believe you're adequately prepared for, notify the league director immediately. Let him know that in the best interests of the kids, you would prefer to coach a less experienced team in a less competitive league. Do what you're better suited for at this time in your coaching career.

Chapter 3

Getting Up to Speed with the Basics

Soccer is a truly amazing, wonderfully complex, and sometimes even mysterious sport. If you never played it as a child or have little experience coaching it as an adult, the rulebook may seem more difficult to learn than a foreign language, and the markings on the field may look pretty imposing. But you have nothing to worry about. In this chapter, we take you on a tour of the field; explain all those lines, rectangles, and arcs; and let you in on a little secret: The rules really aren't as difficult to comprehend as you may think.

In this chapter, we talk about the various positions and the skills required to play them. We also guide you through the maze of hand signals that referees and linesmen use during the course of games that you need to be familiar with in order to provide your team with the best possible coaching at all times.

Surveying the Field

At first glance, all the markings on a soccer field may look intimidating or confusing, but when you can easily identify them, you see that each serves a specific purpose. Just like the markings on a basketball court or hockey rink, they're part of the foundation of the game.

In many sports, the size of the field or court never changes. But soccer is a different story. The size and shape of a regulation soccer field can vary in length from 100 to 130 yards, and its width can be anywhere from 50 to 100 yards. In international matches, games are generally contested on fields that are 120 yards long and 80 yards wide. (Take a look at the markings on a soccer field in Figure 3-1.)

Of course, in youth soccer, the field size is scaled down considerably to account for the small bodies (see the "Reduced field size" section, later in this chapter). Often, one regulation soccer field can accommodate at least a half-dozen youth games at one time. Field sizes vary greatly from community to community and are often dictated by a combination of how much space is available and the number of participants.

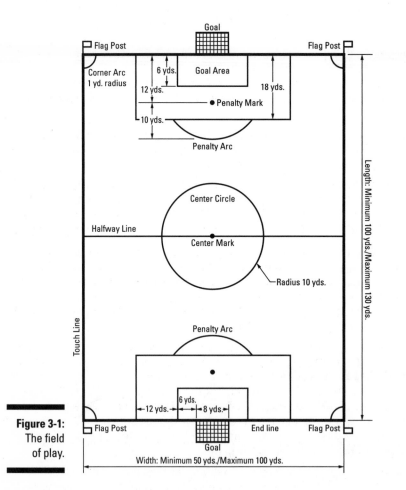

Figure 3-1:
The field
of play.

The soccer field includes the following elements:

✔ **Touch lines:** These are the "sidelines" of the field. Balls that cross over these lines can be picked up (touched) by players in order to put them back into play.

✔ **Goal lines:** These are the lines at both ends of the field, also referred to as the end lines, and the goals are positioned directly atop the lines.

✔ **Corner areas:** A quarter-circle with a radius of 1 yard marks off four small corner areas to indicate exactly where the ball must be placed for corner kicks.

✔ **Halfway markings:** The *halfway line* runs across the center of the field and is primarily used for the opening kickoff. During kickoffs, each team is required to stay on its half of the field. The middle of the halfway line is marked by the *center mark,* which is where the ball is placed for kick-offs. Surrounding the center mark is the *center circle.* When a team is kicking off from here, opponents must stay outside the center circle. The other purpose of the halfway line is determining offside violations, because a player can't be called offside when he's on his team's side of the halfway line. (We get into deeper detail on the topic of offside later in this chapter.)

✔ **Goals:** The goals at each end of the field are 8 feet high and 24 feet wide in a regulation international soccer match, such as the World Cup or the Olympics.

✔ **Goal areas:** These rectangles are directly in front of each goal and measure 6 by 20 yards in regulation soccer. Besides indicating where the ball is placed for goal kicks, it's the area of the field where goalies have some shelter and are partially protected from collisions with opposing players.

✔ **Penalty areas:** This area is the larger rectangle that surrounds each goal area, and it measures 18 by 44 yards in regulation soccer and includes the goal area within it. The goalie can handle the ball when it's inside his penalty area or goal area. The lines marking the sides of the penalty areas closest to midfield in regulation soccer are 18 yards from the goal lines and are referred to as the *18-yard lines.*

✔ **Penalty kick marks:** These marks in regulation soccer are 12 yards from each goal and are centered between the goal posts. If a team commits a major foul within its own penalty area, the referee awards a penalty kick that's taken from the *penalty mark* in that penalty area. The ball is placed on the penalty kick mark. When a penalty kick is taking place, only the goalie is allowed to defend 1-on-1 against the shooter.

✔ **Penalty arcs:** This semicircular arc extends from each penalty area. During a penalty kick, all the players except the person delivering the kick and the goalie must remain outside the penalty arc, as well as the penalty area. Referees don't award penalty kicks for fouls committed within these arcs, and goalies can't touch the ball with their hands within them either.

Taking Up Positions

In soccer, the basic playing positions on the field are goalie, sweeper, full-back, halfback, and forward. In a typical full-scale soccer game of 11 versus 11, you have a goalie, sweeper, three fullbacks, three halfbacks, and three forwards (see Figure 3-2). As the coach, you can modify your line-up and use all sorts of different formations, which we detail in Chapter 15.

Each position on the soccer field carries its own specific set of responsibilities. The positions are as different as the kids under your care who will be manning them this season. Starting from your own goal and working out, the following sections outline each position. (For tips on assigning children to various positions, see Chapter 5.)

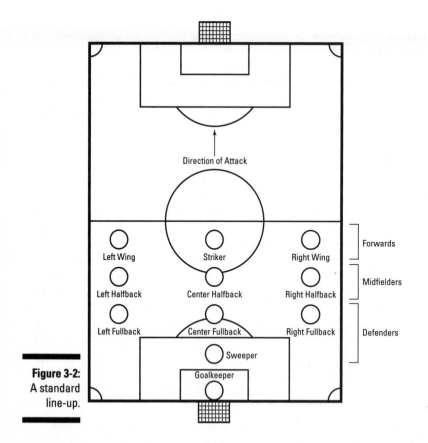

Figure 3-2:
A standard
line-up.

Direction of Attack

Left Wing   Striker   Right Wing   Forwards

Left Halfback   Center Halfback   Right Halfback   Midfielders

Left Fullback   Center Fullback   Right Fullback   Defenders

Sweeper

Goalkeeper

Goalie

This player positions himself between the goal posts and usually stands a few yards out from the goal line. His number-one responsibility is to defend your team's goal and prevent the ball from going into the net.

Any time the ball is within the goalie's own penalty area, which includes the goal area, he's allowed to touch it with any part of his body. So he can scoop the ball up with his hands, hold it, or simply kick it away. When the goalie strays outside his own penalty area, he's just like any other player on the field and can't touch the ball with his hands or arms. Although he's allowed to wander all over the field, doing so is a strategy usually not recommended under any circumstance. You always want him stationed in front of your net and ready to make a save when called upon.

When a goalie is positioned inside his goal area, he receives special protection from opposing players. When the goalie has the ball in his hands or arms, opposing players aren't allowed to kick at it or interfere with the goalie's throw. Only minor and incidental body contact by opposing players is allowed during a play for the ball in this area. Although the rules in this area of the game are generally left to the discretion of each individual referee, most goalies are allowed the privilege of not being interfered with while they're grabbing the ball.

But goalies do have some limitations that they must adhere to, which include the following:

- ✔ **The ticking clock:** A goalie who secures possession of the ball can't stand and hold it for an extended length of time while his team gets set to begin an attack. The goalie has six seconds to put the ball into play. If he delays the game by holding onto it longer than that, he can draw a penalty and forfeit possession for his team.

- ✔ **Doubly possessed:** When a goalie has possession of the ball with his hands, and he sends the ball back into play, he can't touch the ball again with his hands until an opposing player makes contact with the ball anywhere on the field or one of his teammates plays it outside the penalty area. This rule doesn't enter into play when the goalie is playing the ball with his feet. He can dribble or kick the ball just like any other player on the field, whether or not he touches it with his hands. So he can stop the ball with his hands, put it on the ground, and kick it to a teammate. He can even gain possession of the ball with his feet, dribble it, and then scoop it up if he chooses to do so. He can't possess the ball twice with his hands, though. A ball played back to the goalkeeper by a player on his team can't be picked up if the other player plays it back with her feet.

Sweeper

This player holds down the position in front of the goalie and rarely strays from the goal-scoring area. The sweeper's top priority is to make sure that no ball gets behind her. As the last line of defense before the goalie, the sweeper has the responsibility of "sweeping" the ball out of the goal-scoring area. Sweepers must always be aware where the opposing players are near the goal and guard them very tightly when they're positioned to get a shot on goal. A sweeper usually doesn't leave the goal area unless a teammate is available to provide back-up while the sweeper steps out to defend another offensive threat. Or if her team is pushing the ball downfield, she moves forward to provide support for the midfielders and eliminate any gaps in the field that can be exploited by the opposition if it regains possession of the ball and begins a counterattack.

Fullbacks

These players play in front of the sweeper and provide primarily defensive help. The primary responsibility of the fullbacks is to help ensure that players from the opposing team don't get close enough to take quality shots. Youngsters who play these positions are also sometimes referred to as *stoppers,* because you rely on them to stop the opposing team's attack when it's converging on the goal.

The left and right fullbacks, as their names suggest, play to the left and right of the center fullback. These players have the task of containing the other team's forwards, who are playing opposite them. While the forwards' jobs are to penetrate the defense by attacking the corners of the field and distributing the ball to the center forward (or *striker*), the left and right fullbacks must be focused on stopping that penetration, or at least slowing it down and making sure that the opponents don't get off a quality centering pass. In most cases, the center fullback is responsible for picking up the striker when he poses an offensive threat.

Because the fullbacks play in the shadow of their own goal, coaches generally don't want them taking any unnecessary chances with the ball that can put their team at risk. That means they don't spend a lot of time dribbling; instead, their focus is on getting the ball away from their goal and out of danger as quickly as possible. Fullbacks typically send clearing passes to the sidelines to avoid turning the ball over to the opponent in that dangerous middle-of-the-field area, where an attacking player has a lot of options.

Rarely do fullbacks have any type of offensive responsibilities, although they can spark offensive attacks from time to time. So the team benefits if they're as skilled at handling and passing the ball as their teammates are and can get attacks going.

Halfbacks

Halfbacks play between the fullbacks and the forwards, and provide both offensive and defensive support. When it comes to having success in soccer, your team's effectiveness is determined, to a large extent, by which team controls the middle of the field the best. During games, the center of the field is where a big chunk of the action usually takes place.

And that's where the halfbacks enter the picture. These players, also referred to as *midfielders,* are stationed in the middle of the team's formation. Their top priority is to gain possession of the ball and get attacks under way by dribbling the ball upfield or getting the ball to the forwards with accurate passes. It's no secret that the team that maintains possession of the ball the longest is the team that probably generates more quality scoring chances and likely winds up scoring more goals, too.

The essential job of the halfback is to control the ball, distribute it to teammates, and move the ball upfield if he's unable to spot an open teammate. Halfbacks also handle a lot of the throw-in responsibilities (see the "Rules of the Game" section, later in the chapter), which can be a valuable offensive weapon at the opponent's end of the field. Sound throw-ins are also important at your end of the field, because an inaccurate throw can quickly turn into a great scoring opportunity for the other team.

The center halfback has additional roles beyond those of the left and right halfbacks. When on the attack, this player often joins the action as a second *striker* and is counted on to deliver shots on goal from a little farther out than her teammates on the front line, who usually work in much closer around the net. She also serves as a trailer on a lot of attacks and can be effective in taking advantage of any rebounds the goalie may give up. All the halfbacks have defensive responsibilities as well and must provide support whenever the opposing team has possession of the ball.

Forwards

These players are counted on to score goals for the team. When the team has possession of the ball, these players move forward and look to receive passes from the halfbacks that they can use to deliver quality shots on goal. Soccer actually has two types of forwards:

- **Striker:** The center forward, whose primary focus is scoring goals. The striker is clearly an important piece of your offensive puzzle. But his skills will be suffocated and his ability to score greatly reduced if you don't have halfbacks who can get the ball to the wingers (see the next bullet) and wingers who can push the ball upfield and into the corner areas. The bottom line is that the center forward is going to be only as effective as his teammates allow him to be. After all, soccer is the ultimate team game.

✔ **Wingers:** The forwards to the left and right of the striker, who look to create shots for themselves from the outside or deliver passes to the striker in the middle of the field. The left and right forwards' primary responsibility is to dribble the ball down the sideline, work their way as close to the end line as possible, and then look to center the ball back to the striker for a shot on goal. A lot of the team's success in the opponent's half of the field is dictated by how effective the left and right forwards are at getting the ball to the striker in positions that produce quality scoring chances.

The wingers are also responsible for taking a large number of corner kicks (see the "Rules of the Game" section, later in the chapter), because a lot of their play happens in that area of the field when they're attacking with the ball.

Rules of the Game

Soccer is a complex game, and it involves all sorts of rules. Some are basic and easy to understand, and some may initially leave you scratching your head. If you're not familiar with a lot of the rules of soccer, becoming overwhelmed by them (and all the little nuances that are attached to many of them) is easy. First of all, don't panic, and don't try to learn every single rule in one sitting. Focus on learning two or three rules each night and how they're applied, and build from there. You can't possibly expect your young players to learn every single rule during the first week of the season, so don't put that kind of pressure on yourself either. Learn the rules one at a time; build on them; and before you know it, you'll be rules savvy — and so will your team. So grab a beverage and a snack, and get comfortable. It's time to dig into the rules of soccer.

Getting started

The goal of soccer is to . . . well, score as many goals as possible within the allotted time by kicking the ball into the opposing team's . . . uh, goal. A regulation soccer game consists of two 45-minute halves, with a 5-minute halftime. At the youth level, games are much shorter and sometimes are even broken into four quarters. In regulation soccer matches, the teams have no timeouts, but again, at the youth level, leagues often allow coaches to call timeouts to help reorganize their players and provide valuable instruction.

The referee keeps the official time of the match on her watch, and time doesn't stop for minor interruptions in play, such as balls that roll out of bounds, penalties, or any type of minor injuries. Referees can stop the clock for major interruptions in play, which include substitutions and serious injuries.

To make up for the time used up by these short stoppages in play during which the clock keeps ticking, the referee may add *extra time* (also called *injury time*) to the end of each half. The amount of time that's added in order to make up for these incidents is left up to the ref's discretion. This addition usually occurs only at the more advanced and competitive levels of soccer. At the younger levels, the kids play for a set period of time without extra time even if you had a stoppage for an injury or you had to run on the field and delay the game to tie a child's shoe.

The game ends at the exact moment when time expires (regulation time plus whatever extra time the ref adds). So if a ball is in midair and headed for the net, but doesn't cross the goal line before the referee blows her whistle to signify that time has run out, the goal doesn't count. A half may end while a ball is out of play and the action is stopped. However, time can't run out when a team is lining up to deliver a penalty kick. If the referee calls a foul right before time expires, the team is entitled to a penalty kick, and the referee extends the time in order for the kick to take place (see the "Avoiding penalty calls — and their results" section, later in the chapter, for more on penalty kicks).

A simple flip of the coin is generally used to determine which team will kick off. The team that wins the coin toss has the option of kicking off or choosing which end of the field it prefers to defend. *Kickoffs* are used to begin games, second halves, and overtimes, as well as to start play again after a goal has been scored. Each team must remain on its side of the center line until the ball is kicked. Players on the opposing team must stay at least 10 yards from the ball until it's kicked, and this distance is conveniently marked by the center circle (see Figure 3-1).

Keeping the ball in play

The ball is *in play* as long as any part of it is touching the field of play. The goal lines and touch lines are considered part of the field of play (see Figure 3-1), so the *entire ball* must pass *completely beyond the outside edge of these lines* for the ball to be called out of bounds. Also, once a ball is out of bounds, it can't roll back in bounds and be played. So if the ball rolls out of bounds, hits a rock, and ricochets back into play, it's a dead ball.

The opponents of the team that last touched the ball before it went out of play get to put the ball back into play. For example, if a player from the blue team kicks the ball, and it hits a player from the red team in the knee and bounces out of bounds, the blue team puts the ball into play, because the player in red was the last to touch it.

A ball that makes contact with a referee or linesman on the field is still in play unless, of course, it bounces out of bounds after hitting him.

The three methods that a team can use to put the ball back into play after it rolls out of bounds are the throw-in, corner kick, and goal kick. In the following sections, we provide you with the rules; check out Chapter 13 for more information on instruction and drills concerning the actual techniques.

Throw-ins

A *throw-in* is the method of putting the ball into play after it rolls out of bounds over a touch line. The referee signals out-of-bounds balls by pointing in the attacking direction of the team that gets to put the ball back into play. Players need to put the ball back into play immediately so they don't delay the game.

A player makes a throw-in from within about a yard of the spot where the ball crosses the touch line, while standing out of bounds. Anyone on the team may take the throw-in. The thrower's teammates, as well as the opposing players, may position themselves anywhere they want on the playing field. The only thing the opposing players can't do is attempt to distract the thrower.

When a player executes a throw-in, he must be facing the field and standing with both feet on the ground, and he must throw the ball over his head with both hands. At least parts of both feet have to be touching the touch line or the grass outside the touch line. The ball must enter the field through the air; it can't be rolled in or bounced along the ground. After the player delivers the throw-in, which can be of any distance, he can't touch the ball again until another player does so first.

If the player makes an illegal throw, such as not having both feet on the ground, the opposing team is awarded the ball and delivers the throw-in at the same spot.

The ball can't be thrown directly into the goal on a throw-in; it must touch another player before your team can take a shot. And although you have to watch for an illegal throw, you don't have to worry about being called for off-side on a throw-in if you're the offensive team (see the "Staying onsides" section, later in this chapter).

Corner kicks

When a ball rolls out of bounds over the goal line, either a corner kick or goal kick gets the ball back into play. You use *corner kicks* when a player knocks the ball out of bounds over his own goal line. So when a player from the blue team knocks the ball over the goal line that her goalie is defending, the red team is awarded a corner kick in whichever of the two corners is closer to where the ball went out of play. (We cover goal kicks in the next section.)

After the referee indicates which corner you're taking the kick from, any player can set the ball down so that it's entirely within the corner area (see

Figure 3-1). Also, any player on the team may take the kick. Other things to keep in mind during a corner kick include the following:

✔ **Position of defense:** The opposing players must stay at least 10 yards away from the ball until it's kicked, while teammates of the kicker may position themselves anywhere on the field.

✔ **Corner flags stay put:** Some of your players may be tempted to move the flags, but they can't move them in order to clear out some extra space and make the kick a little easier.

✔ **Direct goal:** Players can score a goal directly from a corner kick, because another player doesn't have to touch the ball before it goes into the net.

✔ **In play:** When the player puts the corner kick into play, she can't touch the ball again until contact has been made by another player.

Goal kicks

Goal kicks are used when a player knocks the ball out of bounds over the opponent's goal line. If a player on the red team takes a shot on the blue team's goal but misses, and the ball sails over the goal line without anyone touching it, the blue team takes possession of the ball in its own end with a goal kick.

After the referee points to the goal area, indicating that he has called for a goal kick, any player from the team is allowed to place the ball at any spot within the goal area. The following are some other key points to keep in mind regarding this type of kick:

✔ **Position of defense:** Players on the opposing team must stay outside the goal area until the ball clears the penalty area. Meanwhile, the players on the goal-kicking team may stand anywhere on the field, but they can't touch the ball until it leaves the penalty area.

If a player from the opposing team steps into the penalty area before the ball leaves the area, the referee has the option of whistling the play dead and allowing the team to re-kick or allowing the play to continue if it didn't impact the kicking team.

✔ **There's no time like the present:** When the referee awards the kick, the players don't have to wait for their opponents to get into position before delivering the kick.

✔ **Any direction:** The kick may be delivered in any direction and is in play as soon as it leaves the penalty area.

✔ **No goal:** A player can't score a goal directly off a goal kick, because another player must touch the ball first.

✔ **Don't touch:** After the ball is put into play, the player who kicked it may not touch it again until another player touches it.

Staying onsides

In addition to your team's quest to keep the ball in play, move it downfield, and score goals, you have to stay onside at all times. The most perplexing and misunderstood rule in all of soccer is the offside rule. One of the most frustrating things in soccer is seeing one of your players break free with the ball, ready to unload a shot on goal, only to have the referee whistle the youngster offside. What is it? How does it occur? How can you help your players learn this confusing rule?

Remember playing basketball with your friends? One player always stayed at one end of the court, hoping for easy baskets, while everyone else was at the other end. He was called a *cherry picker* for camping out down there. Soccer players aren't allowed to do that without being called for offside.

The basic idea surrounding the offside rule is that attacking players can't position themselves ahead of the ball. The rule is in the books to ensure that players on the attacking team don't linger around the opponent's goal when the ball is nowhere near them in hopes of getting an easy score if the ball is turned over somewhere on the field.

For a player to be *onside,* at least two defenders (including the goalie) must be between him and the goal the moment the ball is played by a teammate. Offside can be called anywhere in the attacking half of the field. A player is *offside* when he's closer to the opponent's goal line than two defensive players, including the goalie (see Figure 3-3). When the referee whistles a player for being offside, the opposing team is given an indirect free kick from the spot where the offside violation occurred.

Here's an easier way to explain the offside rule to your team (or understand it yourself, if it's still hazy): A player is offside when she gets behind the last defender before the ball is played by a teammate. (You can just leave out the whole goalie-as-the-second-defender thing.) Tell your players to stay a couple steps behind the last defender so they'll be less likely to be caught offside.

In addition to not keeping two defenders between her and the goal line when a pass is received, in order for a player to be called *offside* (see Figure 3-3), two things have to happen:

> ✔ **Beat the ball:** The attacker must be ahead of the ball in the play. In other words, to be whistled for offside, the attacker must be between the ball and the defending team's goal line. Being dead even with the ball is perfectly okay, but being even a half-step ahead is cause for the referee to nab the player for the offense.

✔ **Be in the play:** The attacking player must be actively involved in the game at the exact moment the ball is either passed or shot by his team-mate. This rule represents one of those tricky areas in soccer where the referee has a lot of wiggle room for interpretation. Offside is usually called whenever the attacker in the offside position is moving to receive a pass, attempting to play the ball before a defender can get to it, or blocking the vision of the goalie, among many other examples.

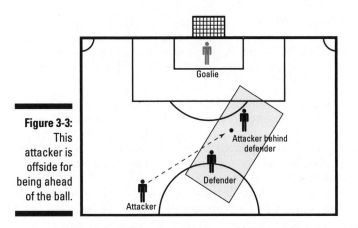

Figure 3-3:
This attacker is offside for being ahead of the ball.

As we stated, the referee doesn't call offside if at least two defenders are between the attacker and the goal line. When an attacker is even with the last defender before the goalie, he's still considered to have two defenders between him and the goal, which puts him onside (see Figure 3-4). Remember, we said the rule was a little tricky. Stay with us, because there's a little bit more to the rule.

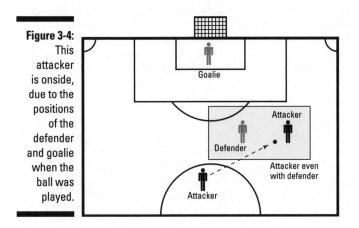

Figure 3-4:
This attacker is onside, due to the positions of the defender and goalie when the ball was played.

Offside doesn't apply to goal kicks, throw-ins, or corner kicks (though it does apply to direct and indirect free kicks, penalty kicks, and goalie clearing kicks and throws). And offside is never called at the defensive end of the field. Your players can be whistled for this infraction only when they're on the opponent's half of the field.

The following are some other examples of when offside isn't called against your team:

✔ **Played by opponent:** Offside isn't called when the ball was last touched by an opposing player. A ball that ricochets off an opponent isn't considered to have been played by him. Now, if the kick that produced the rebound was delivered by a teammate of the offside player, the referee whistles the play.

✔ **Stepping out of bounds:** Offside isn't called when the attacking player steps off the field before the ball is played and he isn't a factor in how the opponent is able to play the ball. This happens to be one of those exceptions to the rule mentioned earlier in this chapter that players are allowed to leave the field of play only when they have permission from the referee. When the player steps out of the field of play to avoid the offside call, he can't return until his team loses possession of the ball or until a natural stoppage in play happens.

✔ **Defensive trickery:** Offside isn't called if the attacker is put into an offside position by a defender who intentionally runs off the field and leaves fewer than two defenders between the attacker and the goal line.

Avoiding penalty calls — and their results

In the sections that follow, we give you all the information you need to keep your team on the straight and narrow — or at least interpret the results when fouls or other violations occur. Soccer has both major and minor fouls that result in the opposing team taking an indirect free kick, direct free kick, or penalty kick. Don't worry — we cover each of the categories and kicks in the sections that follow, and help you get a handle on those pesky yellow and red cards.

Outlining the major fouls

Nine major fouls result in the opposing team receiving a direct free kick. These major fouls are especially troublesome when committed within the penalty area, because the resulting penalty kick is a shot on goal with only the goalie defending (see the "Paying the price for fouls" section, later in the chapter for more on penalty kicks). Take a look at the major fouls:

✔ **Handball:** Soccer is played primarily with the head, chest, legs, and feet — not the hands. This rule is one of the most basic rules of soccer. Besides the goalie, who is able to use his hands within the confines of the penalty area, no other players are allowed to touch the ball with their hands in the field of play. Any player, not counting the goaltender, who intentionally touches the ball with her hand or arm to gain control of the ball is whistled for a handball, and the opposing team takes possession of the ball.

✔ **Kicking:** Kicking an opponent, or attempting to kick him, is a big no-no.

✔ **Tripping:** The referee often calls this foul after a player fails to make a successful tackle (see Chapter 12) and takes out the attacking player's legs instead of knocking the ball away.

✔ **Jumping:** This infraction involves jumping or lunging at a player and most often is called when an opposing player or the goalie is in the air making a play on the ball.

✔ **Charging:** Referees signal charging when a player charges into an opponent with an intent to harm. If the player makes a play on the ball and the contact is incidental, charging doesn't apply.

✔ **Charging from behind:** A player may never knock an opponent to the ground by charging from behind.

✔ **Striking:** Any attempt to strike, or the actual striking of an opponent, is never allowed. This includes intentionally throwing the ball at an opposing player.

✔ **Holding:** Players can't grab an opponent's jersey to slow her down or stick out their arms to obstruct the player's movement in any way.

✔ **Pushing:** Players can't push, shove, or nudge an opponent in an effort to gain any type of advantage.

Detailing minor fouls and violations

Referees penalize minor fouls and rules violations by awarding indirect free kicks to the team that was fouled (see the "Paying the price for fouls" section, later in the chapter). Here are some of the most common minor fouls and violations that you come across:

✔ **Obstruction:** The referee whistles an obstruction infraction if the player's primary intent is to block the other player. A player using his body to block an opponent's route to the ball is okay, but only if the ball happens to be in range where he can make a play on it. If the ball is obviously not within the player's reach, an infraction has occurred. If a player uses his arms or simply stands in an opponent's way, those are deemed obstruction violations. Obstruction can also be called on a player who disrupts a goalie's attempt to put the ball back into play after gaining possession of it.

✔ **Dangerous play:** Players who put themselves or an opponent in danger are whistled for this infraction. Some examples of dangerous play are swinging a leg near a player's head to kick the ball or diving low to head a ball that opposing players are attempting to kick at the same time. Even if the foul is completely accidental, it can still be called.

✔ **Charging:** Legally charging an opponent is possible, such as when two players are going for the ball, and shoulder-to-shoulder contact results. But penalties occur when players use violent or excessive force to gain an advantage, such as knocking into the opponent to get her off balance, disrupting her dribbling of the ball, or unfairly impeding her progress down the field.

✔ **Charging the goalie:** Goalies do receive a thin veil of protection within their own penalty areas; opposing players can't run into them and attempt to dislodge the ball from their possession.

✔ **Offside:** Although the rule is pretty straightforward, it usually is one of the most difficult and controversial for referees to enforce during games, especially at the more advanced levels, where the speed of play is quicker. The rule exists so players don't hide behind defenders at one end of the field, hoping for an unguarded shot on goal.

✔ **Double play:** When a player puts the ball into play, he can't touch it again until another player from either his team or the opposing team makes contact with it.

Paying the price for fouls

Three types of penalties can result from fouls. Here, we provide you with the rules and regulations for these three kicks. Check out Chapter 13 for instructions and drills on the actual techniques.

✔ **Indirect free kicks:** These kicks are awarded to the nonfouling team and result in a free kick from the point of the foul. A player can't score a goal on an indirect free kick because the ball must first touch another player.

✔ **Direct free kicks:** The referee awards these kicks for fouls she considers careless or reckless. These kicks don't have to touch another player before a goal can be scored. The kick takes place where the penalty is committed unless it occurs within the penalty area. In that case, it results in a penalty kick.

✔ **Penalty kicks:** Players look forward to penalty kicks as much as they do the first day of summer vacation. It's the chance to score a goal for their team, going 1-on-1 against the goalie. These kicks are awarded for fouls occurring inside the penalty box. The ball is placed on the penalty spot, which is 12 yards from the front of the goal on a regulation soccer field. On a smaller-scale field for younger players, the spot is much closer.

During the kick, all the other players must remain outside the penalty area. The offensive player gets only one shot. The goalie must stand stationary in the goal with his feet on the goal line. He's allowed to shift his weight, but he can't make any distracting gestures or wave his arms while awaiting the kick. The kicker, who can be anyone you choose from your team, must wait for the signal from the referee before she can proceed with the kick. She's allowed to take a running start at the ball, but she must make the kick in one continuous motion. She can't fake the kick, step over the ball, or stop to pause to try to outsmart the goalie.

Determining what's in the cards

The referee breaks out yellow and red cards at the more advanced levels of soccer to signal minor and major infractions. Use this list to help you understand what they mean:

- ✔ **Yellow card:** The referee issues this card when a minor rules violation occurs. A common scenario that warrants a yellow card includes players entering or exiting the field without prior permission from the referee. Players are allowed to temporarily go out of bounds for corner kicks, free kicks, and throw-ins or to play the ball near the edge of the out-of-bounds line, for example. Virtually any other time, they need permission from the referee. Yellow cards are also usually issued when players argue with the referee over a call.

- ✔ **Red card:** Referees issue red cards for major violations, such as being overly physical during the course of play. Players who commit a particularly violent foul, such as intentionally tripping an opponent who has an obvious scoring opportunity or using their hands to stop a ball on a shot that has a good chance of going in the net, usually get the red card. When the referee issues a red card, the player is immediately ejected from the game, and he can't be replaced, so his team plays short-handed the remainder of the game.

Interpreting the ref's hand signals

Perhaps no other sport leaves such a wide margin for individual interpretation of the rules than the sport of soccer. Knowing what a referee signals during the game and understanding why he makes that particular call are essential for fulfilling your coaching responsibilities and helping your players learn and grow. Take a look at the most commonly used hand signals you'll see in your contests this season. In some cases, the referee may look like he's involved in an intense game of charades. You can check out these signals in Figure 3-5:

- ✔ **Indirect free kick:** The referee initially points in the attacking direction of the team taking the kick. Then he holds one hand up in the air until the ball is kicked and touched by another player or until it goes out of the field of play.

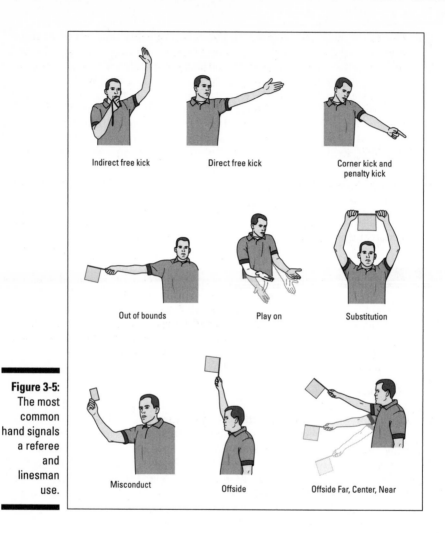

Indirect free kick

Direct free kick

Corner kick and penalty kick

Out of bounds

Play on

Substitution

Misconduct

Offside

Offside Far, Center, Near

Figure 3-5:
The most common hand signals a referee and linesman use.

✔ **Drop ball:** This rarely happens during the course of a game, but every once in a while, the referee may have to stop the game for some reason, such as a small child running onto the field of play during a game or a ball from a nearby field rolling onto the playing field. To restart the game, she goes with the drop ball. The drop ball is used at the spot where the ball was when play stopped. The referee holds the ball out at waist level and drops it to the ground between two opposing players. She can drop the ball at any time without any type of warning, though she typically holds the ball until both teams are ready. Players aren't allowed to touch the ball until it hits the ground.

✔ **Corner kick:** When the referee awards a corner kick, he points briefly to the proper area.

✔ **Out of bounds:** The more advanced levels of youth soccer have a linesman as well as a referee. When a ball rolls over a touch line, the linesman uses her flag to point in the attacking direction of the team that's putting the ball back into play.

✔ **Play on:** Sometimes during the course of play, one team commits a penalty, but the other team maintains an advantage. In this case, the referee may allow play to continue. To indicate that he's making this call, he extends his hands with his palms facing up to indicate that he wants play to continue.

✔ **Direct free kick:** The referee points briefly in the attacking direction of the team taking the kick.

✔ **Substitutions:** When a team wants to make a substitution, the linesman holds both ends of her flag above her head to signal to the referee.

✔ **Misconduct:** The referee displays a yellow card when issuing a caution to a player and a red card when ejecting the player.

✔ **Offside:** The linesman raises his flag quickly to indicate offside and then sticks his arm straight out with the flag if the infraction occurred in roughly the center of the field. He raises his arm at an angle when the offside takes place at the far side of the field, and he lowers his arm at an angle when the offside occurs on his side of the field.

Examining Common Considerations for Younger Kids: League Specials

One of the great things about soccer is that the game can easily be modified to fit the age, experience, and skill level of the players participating. At the beginning levels of youth soccer, it's all about teaching kids the basics of the game, not adhering to the rulebook that's used in the upper ranks of organized soccer. In the sections that follow, we outline adjustments to the rules, field, and equipment that are common in youth leagues.

Reduced field size

Typically in youth soccer, the younger the kids, the smaller the field. If you throw kids on a large field for a game, they huff and puff, and are out of breath and too tired to do anything with the ball when they finally get to it. Depending on how much field space a recreation agency has, the size of a youth soccer field varies from community to community. A 4-on-4 game with beginning players can easily be played on a field measuring just 30 yards long and 15 yards wide. Keeping beginning players confined in a small playing area allows them lots of touches of the ball instead of spending all their time aimlessly running around in a wide-open area. As players get older, they can expect to play on fields that are 60 to 100 yards long and 35 to 50 yards wide.

Smaller balls

We don't throw a classic novel at a child just learning how to read, so giving a youngster just starting out in the sport (or even one who has a year or two under his belt) a regulation soccer ball makes little sense. A child's small foot can't control a soccer ball that's intended for an adult, and forcing a regulation ball on a child just learning the game doesn't speed his learning and development. To build confidence in the sport, a child must continually experience success and notice improvement, and that can happen only if he's learning with the appropriate-size ball for his age. Take a look at the different-size balls that are available for kids to use these days:

- **Size 3:** These balls are typically used for kids ages 7 and under.

- **Size 4:** These balls are generally for kids ages 7–11.

- **Size 5:** Youngsters ages 12 and up are usually ready to handle these balls, which are standard at all other levels of soccer.

No-goalie games

At the beginning levels of youth soccer, most leagues don't have goalies. Because the kids don't have a lot of skills at this point and are in the infant stages of learning the basics of the game, putting a kid in front of the net really doesn't make a whole lot of sense — she'll probably see more butterflies during the course of the game than shots on goal. And even if another kid does take a shot on goal, the goalie will probably be playing with a bug in the grass or waving to her mom in the bleachers instead of defending the shot.

In beginning soccer leagues, you typically set up a couple pylons a few yards apart to help the youngsters get the concept of moving the ball downfield and putting it into the goal. At these early stages of youth soccer, you simply want to introduce the kids to kicking the ball, running after it, and kicking it again. Executing passes, headers, and throw-ins all come later, as does dealing with a goaltender.

Fewer players on the field

Although a regulation soccer game features 11 players on the field for each team, the younger the children are, the fewer you have on the field at any one time. The idea at the youngest age levels is to introduce them to the game by giving them lots of touches of the ball, and that can happen only with a handful of players on the field at one time. Just imagine having a full squad of 6-year-olds on the field at once. The players would be lucky to touch the ball a couple times during the game, which isn't going to be any fun at all.

That's why games of 4-on-4 and 5-on-5 are quite common nationwide. These scaled-down games are great for promoting an interest in the game, because the kids are experiencing the thrill of kicking a ball in a team environment and being actively involved in the action. This type of approach stirs interest in the sport and opens kids' eyes to how much fun playing this great game can be. Positioning takes a backseat at this level, because you just want the kids to learn to go after the ball, begin building some foot–eye coordination skills in making contact with the ball, and get the ball to go in the general direction that they intended.

Special substitution rules

In a regulation soccer game, only two substitutions are allowed, and any player that you substituted for can't return to action. In youth soccer, the substitution rules in place are far more lenient, and with good reason. If you have a squad of 10 players, and your team plays in a 5-on-5 league, you have to be able to interchange players every few minutes to keep their excitement and interest levels high.

In the youngest age groups, coaches typically have the luxury to swap players in and out at any point during the game. In fact, a lot of leagues allow coaches to switch players during the actual game instead of waiting for a stoppage in play. As the kids get a little bit older, the rules on substituting become a little more strict. Also, in virtually all youth programs, the players you substitute for can return to the game; you can substitute players several times, and they're allowed to continually reenter the game.

When you start coaching in leagues with kids who are 8 years old and above, substituting players becomes more formal and is done following the proper procedures, which includes securing the referee's permission before sending a new player out onto the field. Substitutions can generally be made during the following times in a youth soccer game:

✔ **Prior to a throw-in:** If your team has possession of the ball, you can usually make a line-up change at this time.

✔ **Before a goal kick:** Usually, both teams can make player switches when the referee signals one of these kicks.

✔ **Following a goal:** This is one of the most convenient times to change out players, because you have a little cushion of time before everyone is set up and ready to resume play again.

✔ **Injury stoppage:** When a player suffers a minor injury, and the referee halts play so the injured youngster can be helped to the sideline, both teams can use the break to send in a substitution.

✔ **Halftime:** This is another of those convenient times to make a line-up switch.

✔ **Following a caution:** When the referee stops play to issue a caution to the player, removing that player is a good idea. You can use the opportunity to bring the youngster to the sideline to go over what he did wrong and make sure he clearly understands the ruling so that it doesn't happen again later in the season.

Part II
Building Your Coaching Skills

The 5th Wave   By Rich Tennant

"We covered the basics today –
dribbling, passing, and why I have
hair growing out my nose."

In this part . . .

Parents can be a help or hindrance when it comes to their children and organized sports. In this part, we share secrets on how you can get parents on your side — and keep them there all season long. We also delve into what it takes to conduct practices that develop skills and keep your players excited about attending. Finally, we offer some tips to help game day go smoothly.

Chapter 4

Meet the Parents

. . . .

. . . .

A preseason parents meeting is a perfect starting point for the new soccer season. You can get everyone pulling in the same direction — rather than pulling against one another — for the benefit of the children. It's largely up to you to guide the parents, advise them, set a positive tone, and outline your expectations for their children — and them — during the season. The preseason parents meeting provides a forum for you to explain your coaching philosophy and discuss your goals and expectations for the upcoming season, as well as answer all the questions the parents are sure to have on everything from shin guards to post-game snacks.

The parents meeting also lays the framework for a smooth-running season, opens the lines of communication on a positive note, and encourages season-long dialogue among all parties. Plus, for many parents, this season is their first experience having a child involved in a sports program, and they may find themselves in unfamiliar territory. The preseason meeting can help put their minds at ease.

Failing to hold this meeting invites all sorts of problems that can be prevented. Without this meeting, you may have an irate father screaming instructions to his child on the sideline during the first game of the season because he doesn't know that parents aren't allowed to do that. You may have a mother questioning why her child didn't get to play half the game, even though you haven't seen him at practice in three weeks — a situation you can easily avoid if you let parents know about your rule requiring attendance at practice in order to play in games. You don't want to risk opening the door to these uncomfortable scenarios, or others, by not scheduling a parents meeting prior to the first practice of the season. It's simply not worth it.

Your meeting is the springboard to a fun-filled season. In this chapter, you find tips on planning the meeting, making a great first impression, and getting the parents to work with you all season long.

Introducing Yourself

How you interact with your young players — and their parents — has a pretty significant impact on how smoothly your season runs. The preseason parents meeting is your chance to explain all the team rules in a relaxed setting. Young athletes need to receive clear and consistent messages from their coaches and parents on everything from how much emphasis is going to be placed on winning this season to how important displaying good sportsmanship is. If the team sees mixed signals between you and the parents, your message is going to be lost, and that's going to lead to unnecessary problems. Disciplining a child during the season for a team violation that you never discussed with the parents beforehand, for example, isn't fair and can turn into a catastrophe.

You should approach the preseason meeting with the same effort and enthusiasm you display when going for a job interview. Your first impression leaves a lasting imprint on the parents. No one expects you to be a professional speaker, but being able to clearly explain your thoughts on the topics you're covering demonstrates how deeply you care about the upcoming season and reinforces your commitment to each child on the team. Parents appreciate your initiative, recognize your caring, and feel much more at ease turning their children over to your coaching this season. (Check out the "Overcoming anxiety when speaking in public" sidebar in this chapter for a few tips.)

Overcoming anxiety when speaking in public

Public speaking strikes fear into everyone at some point. Being properly prepared is the best antidote for conquering speaking nerves. Practice what you want to say to the group in the mirror in the days leading up to the parents meeting. If you sense that you're really going to be uncomfortable, rehearse what you want to say in front of your spouse, a family member, or a friend. Bring your notepad that contains everything you want to say to the meeting. Referring to it often throughout the meeting isn't a sign of weakness — it's an indication that you want to make sure you cover everything for the benefit of the parents. You can also bring a flip chart with key points highlighted on it. A chart gives you something to divert your eyes toward to ease some of your nervousness throughout your presentation. The parents will also direct their attention to it, so they won't be watching you the entire time, which increases your comfort level.

Aside from getting your shtick together, you need to consider a few of the nuts-and-bolts meeting-planning details:

- ✔ **Location:** You can hold the meeting at your home or at the recreation department. If you let the league director know that you want to meet with the parents of your team, he or she can make arrangements to reserve a room for you. Libraries may also have meeting rooms available.

- ✔ **Timing:** Most parents juggle chaotic schedules these days, so finding time to get together with everyone can be difficult. After you receive your team roster from the league, contact each child's parents to briefly introduce yourself as the coach and let them know the date, time, and location of the parents meeting. Giving parents as much notice as possible may help them rearrange their schedules in order to make your meeting. Plan on spending at least a half hour, and no more than an hour, with this meeting.

- ✔ **Contingency plan:** Ideally, you want all parents to show up on your designated night, so stress the importance of everyone attending. If that isn't possible, you may want to have a contingency plan. Consider holding a second meeting on a backup night; going over everything on the phone some evening; or, if all else fails, making arrangements to meet with the parents following the first practice of the season.

We spend the remainder of this chapter covering the subjects that you may want to discuss with the parents. As you can see, you have a lot of information to cover, but try to keep the parents actively involved, and let them get to know you and one another. To accomplish this goal, include some time for

- ✔ **Introductions:** At some point during the meeting, have the parents introduce themselves and say who their children are, too. Although some of the parents may know one another, introductions are a good ice-breaker for everyone. Parents need to start socializing because they'll be seeing quite a bit of one another during the season.

- ✔ **1-on-1 discussions:** The more comfortable the parents are with you, the stronger your relationship will be both with them and with their children. If you have time following the meeting, talk to the parents individually, and get to know a little about them.

Explaining your coaching philosophy

The most important topic you can address with parents is winning — more specifically, what your stance is on this very sensitive issue. Winning can be defined in a lot of ways. For young children involved in soccer for the first time, what the scoreboard says at the end of the game isn't nearly as important as having fun with their friends, getting some exercise, enjoying the experience of participating in the sport, and using some of their newly developed skills. Countless studies indicate that children are far less concerned about winning — especially at the younger levels — than their parents are.

Your goal is to introduce the kids to the basic concepts of the game — like dribbling and shooting. You want to make it fun enough for them that they can't wait to get to practice to work on their skills and they look forward to putting that colorful jersey on when game day arrives.

By letting parents know your philosophy and how you're going to approach the season ahead of time, you give them ample time to find out whether this team is the appropriate setting or has the appropriate level of competitiveness for their child. This approach works out well for all concerned.

Emphasizing good sportsmanship

Children are easily influenced by the behavior of their parents and other adults at their athletic events. Youngsters who see parents yelling and criticizing officials and opposing coaches or even other players on the field begin to learn that this type of behavior is acceptable. Part of your role is to stress the importance of good sportsmanship by your players at all times — and the same goes for parents.

If you get the parents to understand the importance of being models of good sportsmanship at all times — before, during, and after games — the youngsters will follow in their footsteps. Clearly explain that all comments to all participants (children, including opposing players; coaches; officials; and other parents) should be positive and encouraging, never negative or insulting.

A positive approach can be extremely difficult for some parents to follow. For many of these parents, this season is their first time back at an athletic field since their high school or college playing days, and all sorts of competitive juices and emotions can begin surging through them. Toss into the equation the fact that they're watching their own flesh and blood competing against other children, and it can become a pretty combustible mixture. In addition, many parents, without even being aware of it, perceive how well their child performs on the soccer field as a reflection of how good they are as parents. So, the more successful the child, the more impressive the parent looks in the eyes of other parents. (We discuss this mindset in greater detail in Chapter 19.)

Just as you want to clarify the need for positive feedback, you want to be extremely clear with parents on what type of behavior you won't tolerate:

- ✔ **Criticism of any sort directed at kids.** Soccer isn't fun when parents criticize their children for giving up a goal or making a mistake. This league isn't the professional ranks, and negative comments infringe on the kids' enjoyment and detract from their ability to perform at their best.

- ✔ **Shouted instructions.** All the coaching needs to be left up to you. Remind parents that children are easily distracted and don't perform as well — or have as much fun — when they're being screamed at to go get the ball.

- ✔ **Arguing with coaches.** You, as well as the coaches on the opposing sideline, have enormous responsibilities to fulfill during the game and can't be bothered with criticisms regarding playing time or game strategy. If parents have a problem with you, they can arrange to speak with you privately after the game.

- ✔ **Abuse of officials.** Officials for the younger age groups are usually teenagers who, despite doing the best they can, are probably going to make plenty of mistakes. Yelling at a referee, no matter how bad the call is or is perceived to be, is totally unacceptable at all times. Let parents know that dealing with calls that go against your team is simply part of playing sports. Remind them that over the course of a season, the calls certainly balance out, and your team will receive its share of favorable rulings as well. If the parents don't make a big deal about a call, the kids won't even remember it by the end of the game.

Let parents know that you never want to reach the point where you have to have them removed from the stands for inappropriate behavior, but that you won't hesitate to do so if you feel they're negatively affecting the game. Many leagues have policies in place for the removal of spectators, and you need to be aware of what those policies entail. (We talk about the importance of knowing your league's policies and offer solutions on how to deal with problem parents in Chapter 19.)

Detailing how you determine playing time

Playing time can be a major source of grief for a soccer coach — if you aren't prepared. If you clearly spell out to parents your policies regarding this area of the game, you drastically reduce the chances of conflicts occurring during the season.

Dividing time equally

No one likes to sit on the bench, but it's part of the game. A big part of your job, though, is to make sure that no youngster's fanny is stuck on that bench more than any of his teammates'. At the higher ages of youth soccer — typically, 14 and above — the bulk of the playing time is divvied up among the team's best players. (That's also the case with competitive travel teams that, depending on the community, sometimes offer kids as young as 10 years old the opportunity to play. See Chapter 20 for details.) But for youngsters just learning the sport or kids who have only a season or two of experience under their belts, stick to spreading around the playing time as equally as you can. In the long run, everyone benefits from this approach, which is why most rec leagues have equal-playing-time policies in place. These policies ensure that every child who straps on shin guards, regardless of his skill level, receives as much playing time as his teammates do.

Most parents will be comforted to know that you're doing your best to distribute playing time equally throughout the season, regardless of each child's skill level. At young age levels, a child who can kick a ball harder or run faster doesn't merit more playing time than another child who isn't nearly as skilled. Some parents may grumble upon hearing this news, especially if they believe that they have a budding superstar on their hands and that you're hampering their child's development by surrendering his playing time to a less-skilled teammate.

Rewarding players who practice

Frequent and unaccounted-for absences can create chaos when you're trying to put a team together to work cohesively as a unit. When you meet with the parents, stress how important it is that their child regularly attends practice and that having children going AWOL during the week can create havoc with your practice plan and wreck the team unity you're trying to build.

In some situations during the course of the season, children are going to miss practices during the week but show up on game day ready for action. Let parents know that you adhere to a strict policy: Players who regularly attend practices receive equal playing time during games, but youngsters who show up for practice only occasionally receive limited playing time.

A child's playing time shouldn't be affected by valid reasons for missing practice, however. Let the parents know that the following reasons don't jeopardize the child's standing with the team, and encourage the parents to call and let you know ahead of time when their child isn't able to attend practice:

✔ **Injury or sickness:** Certainly, if a child is dealing with an injury (whether he suffered it during a practice, a game, or some other activity), his standing with the team won't be affected when he can return to play. A child who misses practice because of sickness shouldn't face any ramifications either.

✔ **Family vacation:** Parents typically have vacations planned well in advance, and they need to inform you of the dates their child isn't available as soon as possible. The last thing you want to do is show up for a game in the middle of the season only to find out that the three kids who play goalie are all on vacation. Consequently, you're left scrambling to fill that slot with a child who could have practiced the position for weeks if you'd known those parents' schedules ahead of time.

✔ **Family emergency:** Unfortunately, some instances are simply out of the parents' control. A death in the family or some other family emergency may not allow them to contact you ahead of time. They may come up to you the following week at practice and explain the situation. Be understanding in these types of situations, and don't penalize the child for something that was out of everyone's control.

Be very clear when presenting your rules. Players who practice will play, and players who don't practice for unexcused reasons will see reduced playing time. You can be friendly — but firm — while presenting the rules. Let parents know that there are no exceptions, because it just isn't fair to the rest of the squad, and be willing to stand by your policy during the season. At some point, a parent will probably test you on your policy, and if you give in, you'll have to give in to everyone. Suddenly, your rules and policies carry no weight — and you're giving the indication that you have no control of the team.

"Who's playing goalie?" and other potentially sticky positioning situations

In introductory or beginning-level soccer programs, the playing field is smaller, the number of players per team is trimmed down, and the rules are modified. Often, games feature 4-on-4 or 5-on-5, which helps ensure that each youngster gets plenty of touches with the ball. This alternative is better than being stuck on a regulation field with ten other teammates where a child is lucky to kick the ball once during the game. At this level, soccer is often more about simply playing than positioning. Make sure that the parents receive this message at your initial meeting.

New players, regardless of their age, need to gain experience playing all the positions. Take the time to help them develop their skills so they can confidently play these positions during games. Specialization is only for older children, ages 15 and above, who have been playing soccer for years and are involved in highly competitive leagues. These kids hone their skills in one or perhaps two positions that they excel at. Don't treat your young players like the older, more experienced players.

By moving children around the field, you not only give them a complete introduction to the game, but also keep their interest and enthusiasm level high. If people do the same things day after day in their jobs, with nothing new to look forward to, they become stagnant and disinterested. New challenges create excitement and boost interest levels, and the kids reap the benefits.

The positions on a soccer team are as different as the youngsters who play them. Many of the positions require different skills, abilities, and personality traits than others. Although you want to introduce players to a variety of positions, don't force a child into playing a position that she isn't ready for. (For example, at the first game of the season, you don't want to stick an extra-shy child at the goalie position, where having all eyes focused on him may be traumatic.) Also, never position your young players with the intent of fielding a line-up that gives you the best chance of winning while forsaking the kids' development. If you focus on each player's progress rather than the team's win–loss record, everyone on your team ends up winning in the long run.

Let parents know that you're going to change the line-ups in order to acclimate all youngsters to the different positions on the field. That means that even though the team worked really well together last week, you're not going to lock in and use that exact same line-up the rest of the season.

Putting Together the Paperwork

Virtually every soccer league requires that parents sign a series of permission-related forms before their child is allowed to participate in the program. Sometimes parents fill out these forms during registration, and other times the coaches have to secure the proper paperwork. Beyond the league paperwork, you can make your job easier and keep your sanity intact by distributing your own team packet of information to parents, including lists of rules and contact information.

League paperwork

The following forms are often included in the league-wide parent's packet that you may have to hand out or secure. Although the content and style can vary from form to form, the purpose is generally the same:

- **Parental/guardian consent form:** This form states that there is a risk of the child getting hurt during practices or games and that the league isn't responsible in the event of an injury.

Most programs carry insurance against possible litigation. Be sure you ask about the league's coverage and your own status under the policy. Many coaching organizations provide insurance policies for completing training programs, which serves as a valuable layer of protection when you take the field. In the unfortunate event that an incident occurs in which a child is injured, and his parents sue, you want to be able to demonstrate in a court of law that you went through a training program and did everything possible to properly prepare yourself for your responsibilities. Even if your league doesn't encourage coaches to complete a training program, we strongly recommend that you complete one before taking the sidelines.

✔ **Medical evaluation form:** This form, signed by the child's physician, basically states that the youngster is physically healthy and is able to participate in the sport. If the child has a certain condition, such as asthma or diabetes, it's listed on this sheet. (See the "Meeting Players' Special Needs" section, later in the chapter, for information on working with kids who require special consideration.)

✔ **Emergency-treatment authorization form:** The child's parent or guardian signs this form, which lists the names of (usually) three people to contact in instances where the child is injured and requires emergency medical treatment. The form may give the coach or other league personnel the authority to seek medical treatment for the child if no one can be reached.

Team packets

Distributing a team packet not only provides parents with convenient access to all the information they need this season, but also makes another great impression. Coaches who put in this much effort and go to such great lengths to include parents in every step of the season are rewarded with the parents' respect, admiration, and assistance along the way. Include a page in the front that reinforces your coaching philosophy and reminds parents that they must be models of good behavior in order to help you ensure that every child has a rewarding experience this season. In addition to that first page, include the following elements in your team packets:

✔ **A rules primer for parents:** Most parents aren't going to be as familiar with the rules and terminology of soccer as they are with those of other sports. You — and they — simply don't have enough time to go over the rules of the game in a lot of detail on parents' night without the meeting dragging into all hours of the night.

Having a handy guide at their disposal greatly enhances each parent's understanding and enjoyment of the game. This guide doesn't have to be one of those research papers you dreaded writing in high school or college. Just put together a couple of pages on some of the basics of the game. Include a rough sketch of the field, and indicate where each player is positioned; throw in a page on some basic terms that are used often during the season and what they mean; and include a page of the officials' hand signals and what they mean (we include one in Chapter 3).

✔ **Special rules:** Be sure to include a page noting any special rules in effect in the league. Maybe the league has instructed officials not to call offside on the kids to keep the game moving. Perhaps throw-ins aren't utilized at this level, and when the ball goes out of bounds, the official simply tosses it back into the field of play. Briefly alerting parents to any special modifications of the rules during your parents meeting — and detailing them again in this packet — greatly reduces confusion at games and allows parents to fully understand what's taking place on the field.

✔ **Team roster and contact information:** A sheet with all the kids' names, their parents' names, and their telephone numbers can be a pretty handy tool for parents. In the "Defining supporting roles" section, later in this chapter, we suggest that you have the parents form a "phone tree" to quickly spread last-minute weather and scheduling updates for practices and games. And at some point during the season, parents may need to get in touch with another parent to arrange a ride to practice for their child.

Assembling Your Parent Posse

Coaching youth soccer is an enormous undertaking, but you can make the job less stressful and time consuming by recruiting some parents to lend a hand. They invest a lot of time and energy in making their child's soccer experience a rewarding one, and you'll find that they're usually more than willing to pitch in to help make the season run smoothly. Sure, occasionally parents drop their children off and use you as a baby-sitting service for an hour or so, and some parents are more comfortable staying in the background, watching practices or games from the car. But for the most part, if you let parents know that you want them to be actively involved — and provide them with areas where they can lend a helping hand — they'll gladly do so.

Choosing assistant coaches

To help ease your coaching workload, choose a couple of parents to serve as assistant coaches. With all those kids on the field, a few extra sets of eyes and ears to help direct the action are extremely beneficial to you and your squad. At practice, assistant coaches can

- ✔ Run drills, which maximizes your time on the field by allowing the kids to get extra repetitions and additional instruction

- ✔ Serve as goalies during shooting drills or defenders during attacking drills

- ✔ Perform a variety of helpful tasks, such as chasing down loose balls during drills to keep practices moving, which is vital to keeping your sessions fun and productive

Your assistant coaches can also be invaluable resources on game day. They can help

- ✔ Monitor your substitution rotation to ensure that all youngsters receive an equal amount of playing time

- ✔ Oversee warm-ups to make sure that each child stretches properly

- ✔ Orchestrate the pre-game exercises while you're meeting with the opposing coach and officials

- ✔ Alert you to any unsportsmanlike behavior being displayed that you may not catch while fulfilling your other responsibilities during the course of the game

- ✔ Gather your players and speak to them in a calm, relaxed tone when you're tending to an injured child

Choosing your assistant coaches is one of the most important decisions you make during the season, so do your homework before filling these key positions. You want to select parents who are best suited to support your philosophy and emphasize the fun and learning you want to stress.

If you don't know most of the parents very well, proceed carefully before asking who's interested in filling coaching positions. You may want to take a little time to get to know the parents as the first few practices of the season unfold. You don't want to make the mistake, for example, of choosing an apparently laid-back dad at your preseason parents meeting who turns out to be a yeller with a poor disposition when he arrives at the field. Pay close attention to see how parents interact with their children at practices and maybe even the first game of the season, and gauge their interest in and enthusiasm for the sport.

Also, try to find a balance when seeking assistant coaches. Some overzealous parents may try to take over your practice and impose their own ideals, techniques, and philosophies on the youngsters. Meanwhile, others may require so much mentoring and assistance that it may actually detract from your valuable practice time, which negatively impacts the children.

Defining supporting roles

Some parents may not feel comfortable being on the soccer field providing instruction, but that doesn't mean they can't help in a number of other areas. Many parents want to be involved in their child's experience, and they can fill a number of roles to ease your stress and add to everyone's enjoyment of the season.

 During your parents meeting, you can circulate a list of jobs and responsibilities, which we cover in the following pages, and have parents jot down their names next to those duties they're comfortable helping with. If five parents express an interest in being the team parent, do your best not to turn down their help and make them feel that you really don't need them after all. In this instance, have them all work together as a committee, or if no one signs up to be the fundraising coordinator, mention to them that you appreciate their willingness to help out, and see if anyone is willing to fill that role instead.

Team parent

A great way to wrap up a practice session or game is to gather the troops for a refreshing beverage or tasty snack. Choosing a team parent allows you to keep your focus on teaching and skill development. The team parent can put together a schedule to let parents know which game or practice to bring snacks to. This role can also include organizing an end-of-season pizza party or making arrangements to take the entire team to watch a local high school, college, or professional soccer game.

Telephone-tree coordinator

When it rains all day, and an hour before your practice the sun pops out, parents are going to wonder whether practice is still on. If you decide to cancel practice, it can be extremely time consuming to call every parent. A telephone-tree coordinator is the parent in charge of putting together the phone list for such situations. In this scenario, you let your telephone-tree coordinator know that you've canceled practice and when you've rescheduled it for. The telephone-tree coordinator calls two parents on the phone list, those two parents each call two parents, and so on. In a matter of minutes, everyone knows that the practice has been postponed.

Concession-stand worker

Many leagues require each team to provide a parent or two to work the league's concession stand a couple of times a season. Check with the league director to find out what dates you need to fill, and see which of your parents are willing to help out on those days.

Photo coordinator

Team photos are great keepsakes for the children, who years from now will get — excuse the pun — a real kick out of seeing themselves and their friends all decked out in their colorful uniforms. Often, the league works directly with a local photography company; other times, team photos are left up to the discretion of the coach. In either case, having a parent fulfill the photo-coordinator position can be extremely helpful. Besides working with you to select a convenient time for the team photo, the photo coordinator can look into the possibility of having the photographer come out for a game or two to take action shots of the kids. At the end of the season, providing each child a shot of himself or herself during a game is a great touch. (We go into greater detail on fun ways to conclude the season in Chapter 22.)

Fundraising coordinator

Depending on the age and skill level of the kids on your team, opportunities may exist to participate in local tournaments that may or may not be a part of the league. These tournaments typically have registration fees. Team fundraisers can offset these additional costs. Fundraisers can include the usual car washes, candy sales, magazine subscriptions, spaghetti dinners, or other fun activities that the coordinator comes up with.

Team trainer

During the course of the season, children get bumps and bruises and get knocked down on occasion. Having a parent who's properly trained in first aid and has experience dealing with these sorts of problems is a big benefit for your team. Although all coaches need to be trained in CPR and familiar with basic first aid, having parents who are skilled in these important areas is a real comfort not only to you, but also to the other parents.

Trophy coordinator

Some leagues present trophies to the first-place team; some hand out participation trophies or certificates to every child; and others may not have the financial resources to do anything. Depending upon what type of league you're coaching in, you may want to consider assigning a trophy coordinator, who can arrange to have small trophies or plaques to present to each child at the end of the season for their participation. (We explain this idea in greater detail in Chapter 22.)

Game officials

Some starter leagues rely on parents to fill roles as officials. Often, each team is required to provide one parent to serve as a goal judge or simply to monitor a part of the field for any type of major infraction. If this requirement applies in your league (see Chapter 2), be sure to mention it during your meeting. Find out which parents are willing to fill these positions, if needed. Having these names jotted down eliminates one worry on game day. You don't want to be scrambling around minutes before your game looking for a parent volunteer when you could be spending the time getting your team ready.

Travel coordinator

The travel-coordinator position is appropriate only for an older and more experienced team that may be participating in a lot of weekend tournaments or All-Star events throughout the state or region. The person handling this position is involved in locating the most cost-effective and convenient hotels for the team to stay in and arranging a team bus or coordinating car pools for the actual road trip itself. Occasionally, a parent may fill this position at the younger levels if the team advances through several rounds of a local or regional tournament and qualifies to compete against other teams in a statewide tournament.

Going Over Equipment

Injuries are as much a part of soccer as grass-stained uniforms and post-game treats, and no matter the age or skill level, every player who steps on the field is at risk of getting hurt. Although eliminating the threat of injury is impossible, you can minimize the number of injuries that occur — and their severity — by making sure that each child wears the proper equipment.

Don't let a child on the field unless he has the following equipment:

- ✔ **Shin guards:** These guards significantly reduce the risk of injury to the child's lower leg, which is the third-most-common area of the body injured in soccer, after the ankle and the knee. Encourage parents to purchase shin guards with padding that extends to cover the ankle bone, as well as socks long enough to cover the shin guards.

- ✔ **Mouth guards:** Soccer is the second-leading cause of facial and dental injuries in sports. Collisions with other players are quite common, and the risk of a player getting hit in the face with a ball always exists. Furthermore, youngsters with braces face an even greater risk of suffering injuries to the mouth. Although mouth guards can be difficult for youngsters to get used to wearing, they're vital to protect the teeth and mouth. Fortunately, wonderful advancements have been made, so the guards aren't as uncomfortable as you may remember from your playing days.

  You can make a mouth guard a fun piece of equipment by encouraging everyone to wear the same color, because the guards now come in a variety of styles and colors that are appealing to children. Besides promoting team unity, you promote safety.

- ✔ **Water bottles:** One of your team rules may be that all children bring their own water bottles to practice and games; otherwise, they don't get to play. Keeping kids hydrated is extremely important; not doing so can lead to serious health consequences and place the kids in unnecessary danger. Keep a large cooler of water on hand at all times so that the kids can refill their bottles. Remind parents to write their child's name on the bottle, too.

✔ **Sunscreen:** Encourage parents to apply sunscreen to their children before they arrive for practices and games. Let them know that you'll do your best to avoid practicing between the peak sun hours of 10 a.m. and 2 p.m. to minimize the team's exposure to the sun.

✔ **Sports bras and protective cups:** Although you may not be entirely comfortable discussing these areas, they do need to be covered. Younger children don't need sports bras and protective cups, but as children mature, they should be strongly encouraged to wear them. Have parents check with a reputable local sporting-goods retailer for additional information on proper fitting.

In addition to the must-have equipment players take to the field, other pieces of equipment you should briefly review with the parents are

✔ **Uniforms:** Some leagues provide uniforms, but the parents are responsible for keeping them clean and in good condition before turning them in at the end of the season. In other leagues, parents are required to purchase the uniforms. If your team has to purchase its own uniforms, try to get some sample sizes ahead of time from the company to help parents determine what best fits their young players.

✔ **Cleats:** If your league allows cleats, make sure the children wear regular shoes to the game and switch into the cleats after they get to the field. Parking lots and sidewalks can quickly wear down the cleats. Most leagues have restrictions on what types of cleats children can wear during games. Make sure you know what the league outlaws (see Chapter 2 on league policies) so you can pass this information on to the parents before they go out and spend a big chunk of money on cleats that aren't allowed on the field. Children just starting out in the sport are fine wearing a pair of comfortable tennis shoes.

To keep participation costs down, you can gain big bonus points with your parents by suggesting that their children wear regular sneakers to practices and games. Mentioning this suggestion now may save problems later when one child shows up in fancy, top-of-the-line cleats and the rest of the team is wearing regular shoes. The shoes can make that child feel uncomfortable because he stands out, and the other team members may suddenly feel that they're missing out on something.

✔ **Soccer balls:** Many leagues distribute only a couple of balls to each team for practices, so you can ask the parents to have their child bring a ball to practice if they have one. Have the children put their names or initials on the balls so you can figure out who owns the balls at the end of practice.

Meeting Players' Special Needs

You may wonder whether you have what it takes to coach a child who has special needs. The answer is most certainly yes! Think about it. Every child on your team is remarkably different, and you'll be adapting in all sorts of ways and making countless adjustments to meet their needs. It's certainly no different when it comes to a child who may have a vision or hearing problem; who may have attention deficit disorder; or who may suffer from asthma, diabetes, or epilepsy. We discuss some of the conditions that your players may have in greater detail in Chapter 5.

During your parents meeting, make sure to find out whether any of the children under your care this season have a medical condition that you need to be aware of, as well as whether you need to make any special accommodations. Often, a parent may not feel comfortable divulging that type of personal information in front of all the other parents, which is why setting aside time at the end of the meeting for 1-on-1 discussions is always a good idea.

Answering Parents' Questions

During the course of your meeting, the parents are probably going to ask you a variety of questions — and that's a good sign. You want active participation and interest throughout your meeting. Fielding questions throughout your discussion is a great indicator that the parents are deeply concerned about their children's well-being and genuinely enthusiastic about helping them enjoy a rewarding season.

Be sure to set aside time at the end of the meeting to address any additional questions or concerns. Perhaps parents have questions that they're more comfortable asking 1-on-1 after the meeting concludes, so let them know that you're available to chat with them after the meeting or by phone at a time that's convenient for both of you. Also, if any parents ask questions that you can't answer during your presentation, be sure to make a note of them, and let the parents know that you'll find out that information as soon as possible and get back to them with the answers.

Chapter 5

Getting to Know Your Team

Successful business leaders understand the strengths and weaknesses of their employees and utilize their employees' talents for the betterment of the companies they run. The same type of approach applies to coaching a youth soccer team. True, your youth soccer coaching experience isn't like the cutthroat world of big business, but understanding the talent level of your squad and molding and cultivating it to the best of your ability helps define what type of coach you are and how much success your team enjoys this season. Understanding what areas of the game your kids excel in, and in which areas they can really use your helping hand, makes the difference in whether your season is punctuated by kids progressing at dazzling rates or struggling to find their niche on the team.

Your success in this endeavor is also determined by your ability to relate to the kids — all your kids. You're going to have youngsters on your team with enormously different ability levels, diverse characteristics, and wide-ranging wants and needs. In this chapter, we take a look at how you can relate to them, evaluate them, and get them to work together as a team.

The Art of Evaluation

In order to maximize your effectiveness as a youth soccer coach and propel your players to reach their maximum potential, being proficient in the art of evaluating their skills is imperative. Initially, you may have no clue how talented your team is. Most leagues give you a group of kids, and you have no idea what their strengths or weaknesses are. This lack of information poses its own set of unique challenges and requires real focus from you during the first few practices of the season. Be prepared to begin evaluating and understanding your players the first time you get together with them. If you're in a league that allows you to draft players, you head into the season with at least some understanding of the talent level of your squad, and you can arrive at your first practice with a plan that meets the appropriate skill and experience level. Being able to accurately analyze what areas of the team's game need some bolstering, or even just a little fine tuning, is vital for long-term success and helping your players fully enjoy the sport.

Evaluating your players' skills

Evaluating young soccer players can be challenging. After all, soccer is a complex sport that requires a wide range of individual skills and the ability to utilize them in a manner that benefits the team. Being able to properly assess a player's strengths and weaknesses is essential for determining which areas of her game need additional work and instruction and what steps you can take to help remedy any areas she's having difficulty in. Although evaluating players and making adjustments in your coaching approach to fit their progress is critical all season long, it takes on added importance during those first few practices of the season. You risk having kids quit out of frustration if you evaluate them improperly and force them into drills that are too difficult for their skill levels. Take the time to evaluate all players, and then help them strengthen the areas of their game that are lacking.

A practice drill offers a glimpse of a player's ability in a specific area of the game, but the drill provides a rather limited view of the player's overall skills and abilities. When evaluating the skills of younger players, small-sided games of 3-on-3 or 4-on-4 are ideal. These types of scrimmages are great for gauging all aspects of their game and determining their strengths and weaknesses. Players get to touch the ball a lot, are forced to handle the ball in a variety of situations, and have to continually jump back and forth between an offensive and defensive mode. In the following sections, we cover a few tips to keep in mind when putting together evaluations of your players. (For information on evaluating players during competitive travel-team tryouts, flip on over to Chapter 20.)

Don't fall into the trap of being absolutely enamored with goal scorers. If a child is your team's leading goal scorer and regularly notches goals, that doesn't necessarily mean that he's a well-developed, all-around player. His goal-scoring prowess may be attributed to several underlying factors: His teammates are great passers who always feed him the ball when he's open, or perhaps he has a more powerful leg than the other kids and his kicks are too difficult to stop. Remember that even if his offensive skills are well honed, he may have severe deficiencies in the defensive aspects of his play.

On the move

Soccer is a game of continuous movement and reaction. Players who are flat-footed or prone to standing still for any amount of time are less likely to take advantage of opportunities to attack when their team regains possession of the ball. Or they may be defensive liabilities when the team turns the ball over and they suddenly have to assume a defensive position. When evaluating a player's movement, take several factors into account to get a true sense of her ability. Is she involved in all facets of the game? After she delivers a shot on goal, does she stand there and admire her shot, or does she aggressively move forward in case the ball rebounds or the goalie misplays the ball? When she distributes a pass to a teammate, does she immediately become a statue afterward, watching to see whether the ball is on target, or does she move downfield with the action and look to get open to receive a pass in return?

Comfort zone

How players respond to defensive pressure is a key factor to consider. Is the player able to maintain control of the ball when an opposing player charges toward him? Can he maneuver the ball in traffic? When he receives a pass, does he look to gather the ball under control and move with it downfield, or does he immediately look to give it back to a teammate because he isn't comfortable dribbling it?

Capitalizing on opportunities

In the more advanced levels of youth soccer, the number of chances a team has to score a goal during the course of a game dwindles, because many of the players are more developed and highly skilled. With fewer opportunities to score goals, the ability to beat a player 1-on-1 is critical for your team's success. Do your players have the skills to negotiate their way past a defender and get a quality shot on goal? Can they work the ball with both feet, or do they rely too often on their dominant feet? (Relying on your dominant foot makes you easier to defend.) When they take shots on goal, are they getting full force behind their shots, or are the shots dribbling toward the net? Are the shots getting too much air under them and sailing way over the net? Does the ball go where the players are aiming, or, in the excitement of being able to get a shot on net, do the players neglect some of the basic techniques of shooting?

Defensive tenacity

The true mark of a well-rounded player is her ability to excel both offensively and defensively. A one-dimensional player who's good only when the ball is on her foot and she's attacking will have her defensive deficiencies exposed at some point, especially if she continues in future levels of competition. Be on the lookout to see if your player attempts to make steals to regain possession of the ball for her team when she's forced to play defense, or if she tends to pull back and rely on her teammates to take a more aggressive defensive approach. Continually reinforce to your players that whenever they lose possession of the ball, their top priority must be to regain control.

Between the ears

How much impact a player has on the game is influenced, to a great extent, by his mindset. Does he give you his best effort at all times? Or does he droop his head, sag his shoulders, and move slower when things aren't going his way or when the team is losing? Does he handle constructive criticism well and embrace your instruction and suggestions to improve his play, or does he withdraw and take your comments negatively?

Influence on the team

What type of teammate a child is speaks volumes about what type of player she is. Is she a positive influence on the squad? Does she pump her teammates up when things aren't going well? Are her comments positive and supportive? Does she boost confidence levels, or does she drain the team's enthusiasm? When she isn't in the game, is she a vocal cheerleader who supports her teammates, offering encouragement and providing useful guidance? Or does she tend to sulk when she isn't in the game or simply refuse to pay attention to what her teammates are doing on the field?

Situational strengths and weaknesses

A youngster may be a great practice player, but if he can't transfer those abilities to the field during games, he isn't going to derive as much enjoyment from the sport. For example, you may have a truly gifted player who happens to be an incredible ball handler. He's one of those players who can work the soccer ball with both feet equally well, and he impresses teammates during practice with his dribbling skills. But when game day arrives, he turns into a different player. The impressive practice skills he demonstrates are long gone. Now what? By evaluating the player and watching him carefully, you may discover that problems arise for him as soon as a defender puts any type of pressure on him. If you work with this player on some 1-on-1 exercises and get him accustomed to dribbling with a defender in front of him all the time, his ball-handling skills will come to the forefront, and he'll become a better player because of your evaluation.

Identifying your team's strengths and weaknesses

During the course of the season, your team is going to be learning and developing skills, as well as making great progress in how effectively they work together on the field. But regardless of how talented your players are or how experienced they may be, all teams struggle with their play at some point along the way. Perhaps you'll go through a scoring drought, encounter problems working as a cohesive unit on defense, or lose confidence in the team's abilities after suffering a couple of close setbacks in a row.

Being able to identify your team's strengths and weaknesses helps you mold your players and get the most out of them. For example, if your team is struggling to score goals, you may decide that you need to spend more time during practice working on shooting exercises, when in reality that isn't the best solution. Perhaps the underlying problem is that your team has difficulty passing the ball out of your end of the field, which translates into more time spent on defense and, consequently, fewer scoring opportunities. One way to remedy the situation may be to shift your focus in practice to some passing exercises that involve your defensive players. This subtle change may be all you need to erase some of your scoring woes.

In order to get a better perspective on your team and where its strengths and weaknesses lie, consider these helpful hints:

✔ **Videotape:** Consider having an assistant coach or parent videotape one of your games from one end of the field or up high in the bleachers. Because you have so many responsibilities going on during the course of a game, being able to see everything that takes place on the field is virtually impossible. Plus, at the more advanced levels of youth soccer, when the playing area is quite large, your view from the sidelines may be obstructed by the maze of players that you're forced to look through. If the game is videotaped from the end line or from up above, you have an entirely different vantage point than you're normally accustomed to, which gives you a fresh perspective on the team's play.

If you tape a game, use it for your own private viewing. Don't adopt a professional coaching mentality and use it to make your players watch footage of their games. Children involved in organized soccer need to be on the field working on skills, not in front of a screen watching video.

✔ **Solicit outside advice:** If you have a friend or acquaintance who happens to have more experience coaching soccer than you do or who coaches in a league where the players are more experienced, ask him to watch one of your practices. Another set of eyes is always helpful, and he can probably provide some valuable feedback on areas of the game he believes you need to spend additional time on with your team. Assistant coaches are a big help in this regard as well.

Setting early-season goals

One of the best ways to ensure that your players enjoy playing for you is to set goals at the start of the season for each of them — and then begin working to help them reach those goals. Setting and reaching goals helps build confidence; promotes self-esteem; and, over the course of the season, enhances performance.

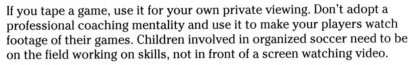

When setting goals, find the right balance by creating objectives that are neither too hard to achieve nor so easy that a player reaches them during the first week of the season. Also, don't limit a child to one goal, because if she fails to reach it and has nothing else to fall back on, she has a real sense of disappointment. Giving kids several goals to strive for opens the door for them to savor the feelings of accomplishment that fuel continued interest in the sport. In Chapter 8, we cover resetting goals at midseason.

Assigning Team Positions

Determining what positions your players are best suited for is sort of like putting together a giant jigsaw puzzle without a picture to go by. You have all these pieces right in front of you — the kids — and endless combinations to consider. Your challenge is to find a position for each child — a position that the child is capable of playing, that provides the most benefits for the team, and that the child embraces and derives plenty of enjoyment from playing.

Outlining age-group considerations

Selecting positions for your players is dictated primarily by their age and, to a lesser extent, their experience level.

At the beginning levels of soccer, small-sided games like 4-on-4 and 6-on-6 are most common. These games typically take on a kick-and-chase-the-ball mentality. The ball moves, and a pack of kids goes after it. That's great for introducing the kids to the sport and some of its most basic components. After all, soccer, in its most simplistic terms, is offense against defense. When your team has the ball, it's on the attack, and when it doesn't, it resorts to playing defense. During these early stages of development, positioning players takes a backseat to simply getting the kids on the field so they can run, kick, and swarm the ball. Assigning a 5-year-old kid the position of midfielder and trying to teach her all the responsibilities that accompany the position would produce the same bewildered look as attempting to teach your team the inner workings of the combustion engine. It's just not realistic and will leave them with a bad experience.

As children get older and progress in the sport, you want to expose them to all the positions on the field. Never confine them to one position for the entire season. In order to fully experience soccer and everything that's involved in playing it, they need — and deserve — the chance to play everything from goalie to midfielder. Rotating youngsters through all the positions during the course of a season gives them a wonderful sense of what soccer is all about and keeps their interest and enthusiasm high as they're introduced to new challenges and different aspects of the game. By taking this approach, you create all-around soccer players rather than just defenders or goalies.

Don't typecast a player based on his or her physical appearance. Children who are slightly overweight are often delegated to play goalie because goalies aren't required to run around much; they aren't even considered for a position like midfielder because they don't have the "look" of a player who can move with the ball and create scoring opportunities for the team. A child who gets typecast in one position early on may never get the chance to fully enjoy the entire soccer experience. You may have a wonderfully skilled player on your team just waiting to emerge, but if you don't give her the chance, she'll never know how successful she can be, and she may miss out on a wonderfully rewarding and truly enriching experience.

Lining 'em up according to their skills

As players gain experience and advance to higher and more competitive levels of play, they become involved in regulation 11-on-11 soccer matches, and you become more concerned with finding the right positions to match their talents and figuring out how you can best use their particular skills for the benefit of the team. Should your most talented and experienced players be up front to help generate more goal-scoring opportunities for the team, or should they be in defensive positions to help protect the net and limit the opposing team's chances to score? You make the call.

When positioning your players, take into account the positions you need to fill, the skills needed to successfully play those positions, the responsibilities that come with each position, and the types of kids who are best suited for handling these positions. Any child is certainly capable of playing, enjoying, and excelling at any position on the field, but keep some general characteristics in mind when determining who plays where when you start dealing with older, more experienced teams. (Turn to Chapter 3 if you want a brief introduction to each of these positions.)

When delegating positions, remind each player that you chose her for that position because of the special skills she has and the ability she demonstrates in practice. As the season progresses, you may recognize that a player you have on defense has really shown some quickness to the ball and may be better suited to play up front as a midfielder. (Making midseason adjustments for the betterment of the team is discussed in Chapter 8.)

Goalies

It takes a strong individual to play in front of the net, because a lot of pressure usually accompanies the goalie position. Even though defensive breakdowns and lapses in judgment lead to many goals, unfair blame is directed toward the goalie when he fails to make the stop. Ideally, you want your goalie to be technically sound, confident but not arrogant, and mentally strong so that he can concentrate on the game and bounce back after surrendering a goal. Athletic youngsters are naturals for the goalie position, which requires a lot of skill, including the following:

- A strong leg to boot the ball when executing a goal kick
- Excellent hand–eye coordination
- Great concentration skills

✔ Quickness

✔ Sound footwork

✔ The ability to go into heavy traffic to secure the ball without being afraid of contact

✔ The ability to sacrifice the body when diving for loose balls

A goalie must also be a good communicator. Because goalies have the best view of the play and usually the best angle to see what's unfolding, they can't be afraid to share what's going on with their teammates. They must be willing to shout instructions and provide plenty of vocal input to help derail the attack before the other team delivers a shot on goal.

Defenders

Quickness, the ability to read developing plays, and reacting to the opposition at the spur of the moment are benchmarks of good defenders. Good heading skills are helpful in defending corner kicks, and a strong leg is an asset to clear the ball out of the team's zone when under attack.

Defenders, made up of fullbacks and sweepers, also must be unafraid of contact, willing to aggressively go after attackers, and able to utilize tackles such as the hook tackle and sliding tackle (see Chapter 12) to extricate the ball from opposing players and regain possession for the team. Players who handle these positions must be true team players, because they don't experience the excitement of scoring goals. Instead, they derive their enjoyment from stopping other players from putting the ball in the net, which usually doesn't generate as much attention and applause from spectators.

Kids who are aggressive and possess a lot of determination are usually good fits for the fullback positions. You can count on these kids to chase down a loose ball in the penalty area with as much enthusiasm as they'd show hunting a $20 bill blowing down the sidewalk. Sweepers must be good listeners and able to quickly react to the goalie's instructions. Because the goalie has a better perspective on the developing play, she can communicate with the sweeper on where she needs him positioned, and the sweeper must be able to quickly adapt to the opposing team's attack and provide defensive support for the goalie any way he can.

Halfbacks

Because halfbacks, or midfielders, typically touch the ball a lot during the game, they need to be skilled in dribbling, passing, and receiving to take advantage of those touches and deliver the ball to their teammates.

On many soccer teams, the center halfback is the team's most talented player. Because he patrols the middle of the field, he gets a lot of touches of the ball. He should also be vocal, because he's basically the quarterback of the offense and can direct players and communicate as different plays unfold during the course of a game.

He also needs a good grasp of the basics and the ability to understand and anticipate when to join an attack and when to hang back and take a more defensive role. Because the center halfback is also in a position to receive a variety of passes from the fullbacks on the back row and intercept passes from the opposing team, he must be adept at receiving passes with his left and right foot, receiving balls with his chest and thigh, and using headers to advance the ball or clear it out of danger. When on the attack, this player often joins the action as a second striker, so having a strong leg to deliver shots on goal from long range is important, too.

Forwards

The forward positions, made up of strikers and wingers, require a steady amount of running, so players must have the stamina — and speed — to handle their responsibilities. Forwards must possess good footwork and be accurate with their kicks to take advantage of scoring opportunities.

Regardless of how many soccer teams you guide during your volunteer coaching career, you'll probably always have a youngster on each team who seems to have a knack for getting the ball in prime scoring position and putting it in the net with a high rate of success. Of course, all kids love to score goals, because that's the most attractive element of the game for them, especially when they're just starting out in the sport. But some kids desperately want to score a goal every single time they get the ball on their feet. These kids make a great center forward (striker) on your team.

Left and right wingers must be excellent sprinters who can outrun defenders to the corners, so conditioning plays an important role in how successful they are in this position. They must also possess quality passing skills.

Forwards are more effective in their roles when they develop other skills, particularly *feinting*, which is the ability to fake out an opponent in order to get by her with the ball. (If you want to find out more about this important skill, jump to Chapter 15 to see how it's done.) Players in these positions should also be proficient in receiving throw-ins, as well as in heading the ball on crosses from corner kicks.

Dealing with disappointment

Regardless of how carefully you choose positions for your players and the great effort and lengths you go to in order to ensure that each youngster is assigned a position that she enjoys playing, you're going to have kids who aren't content with their positions. With only one goalie on the field, you're sure to have a handful of kids who also want to play in the net. And out of all the kids for whom you've designated defensive roles, one or two are likely to have their hearts set on playing up front where they have a chance to score more goals. So what do you do?

With younger kids, you can simply remind them that everyone will have an opportunity to play each position at some point in the season. Use this situation as a learning opportunity to begin teaching them the essence of teamwork. Point out that in order for the team to work together as a cohesive unit and enjoy success, sacrifices have to be made, and that means not everyone can be a midfielder or a forward and score goals. Some players have to fulfill defensive positions that are extremely important.

One approach you can take to help older kids get over the disappointment of not being able to play positions they had hoped to man this season is to take a field trip to a professional, college, or high school soccer game. These games can be outstanding learning experiences for the entire team. While there, instruct your players to closely monitor the players who play their same positions. Having the youngsters on your team watch how players at the more elite levels of competition play the positions gives them a better sense of how important they are to the overall structure of the team. They may even pick up a few pointers along the way to enhance how they play the positions.

Every game and practice provides you an opportunity to share your feelings and sense of pride with your team. One of your primary responsibilities is to recognize and value every child's contribution to the team, no matter how big or small the impact on wins and losses. Every child provides something to the chemistry of the team, even if he doesn't score any goals or make any outstanding defensive plays. Measure each child's value to the team with more than statistics; make sure that no child's effort goes unrecognized or unappreciated. Check out Chapter 2 for more information on establishing a coaching philosophy that makes every kid count.

Understanding and Working with All the Kids

One of the truly challenging aspects of coaching youth soccer is that every child who straps on shin guards to play for you is amazingly different than his teammates in so many ways, but you must remember in your interactions with them that they're children and not miniature adults. The drills you choose for them, and the instructions you provide, must be appropriate for the age level you're coaching. Whether you're coaching a beginning team of 6-year-olds or an experienced team of 14-year-olds, you're embarking on a fascinating journey that challenges your creativity, tests your patience at times, and challenges your ability to interact with all types of personalities.

You're going to encounter youngsters whose soccer talents, physical development, and emotional characteristics cover an enormously broad spectrum. Some of your players may be charismatic and outgoing, and others may be shy and reclusive. You may have kids who are passionate and live for soccer, and others who would rather be just about anywhere other than on the soccer field with you. You'll have kids who are particularly talented, already have a special flair for the game, and are already excelling, and you'll have kids who are clumsy, uncoordinated, and have difficulty running without tripping over their own feet. How you handle all these different types of kids plays a large role in determining just how much fun they have playing for you and whether they want to return next season.

The shy child

Shyness is one of the most common characteristics you come across with youngsters on your team, particularly younger kids — and it can be one of the easiest to handle if you're extremely patient and gradually work to lure the children out of their protective shells. Shy children often go to extreme lengths to blend into the background and dodge attention. During practices, they avoid eye contact; they don't ask for help when working on skills; and they quietly move throughout the various drills while doing everything in their power not to draw attention to themselves.

During your practice sessions, rotate the kids who lead the calisthenics and stretching at the beginning. Select the shy child along with a couple of other players to lead the team. This selection is a small step toward helping the youngster become comfortable in front of the team. By having other players up there with him, he won't feel isolated or gripped with fear that all eyes are on him. Also, during team drills, give him a pat on the back after he does something well. The youngster may not enjoy a verbal acknowledgment from you that draws attention from other team members, but small acts that go unnoticed by everyone else can make a big impact on this child and help slowly draw him out.

While helping a child overcome his shyness, proceed slowly and carefully. Pushing too hard and too early in the season may scare him enough that he actually pulls back and further isolates himself from the team. The process is deliberate but truly rewarding when you succeed in coaxing the child out of the shadows he's suffered in and opening his eyes to all the wonderful opportunities and experiences that he's been missing out on up until now.

If a child's shyness isn't addressed during these critical formative years, it can handcuff his ability to interact in all sorts of social settings. Shyness compromises a child's abilities, paralyzes his chances of ever excelling in the sport, and drags him down with feelings of despair. Coaches are in a great position to help shy children step out of these protective cocoons, discover an inner courage they never knew they had, and derive enormous pleasure from participating — and interacting — in youth soccer.

The uncoordinated child

You're going to have kids on your team who aren't nearly as coordinated or skilled as many of their teammates. The other kids may unkindly refer to these kids as "klutzes." Uncoordinated kids struggle with the most basic soccer skills. They whiff as often as they make contact when trying to kick a ball; they stumble over their own feet; and they can't control passes coming at them or get the ball to an open teammate. Basically, not a whole lot goes smoothly for them, no matter how hard they try.

Some children just aren't athletically inclined, and it interferes with their self-esteem and how others perceive them. Regardless of these shortcomings, though, most of them are trying their very best. But some become enormously frustrated, and feelings of inadequacy settle in and further compromise their ability to perform basic soccer skills.

Helping a child improve her coordination takes practice. But you can pull her through this difficult time in her young life, and years from now, she may very well surprise you in how she blossoms into a solid, coordinated player who has a good handle on all the basics of the game. Here are a few tips:

✔ **Never allow frustration to show.** Even after repeated demonstrations of how to perform a skill, these kids often aren't going to pick up on it as quickly as you want them to. Be careful which words you choose, and never allow a frustrated tone to come over your voice or emerge in your body language. Never give them any reason to think that you're disappointed in their inabilities.

✔ **Encourage the kids to continue being active.** Although most children embrace the physical activity that accompanies a sport like soccer, kids who are wrestling with coordination problems cringe at the thought of playing in a game in which they're likely to struggle, fail, and ultimately disappoint their teammates, coaches, and parents. Children who see their friends performing at a level they believe they can never reach are likely to become disenchanted with the sport and adopt a more sedentary lifestyle that revolves around televisions and computer screens.

✔ **Encourage their parents to work with them at home.** Stress the importance of having fun kicking a soccer ball back and forth in the front yard, not on how well they perform the skill itself. Make sure the parents don't overdo the sessions. Have them keep the sessions short and the praise flowing.

The child with the short attention span

With kids, short attention spans are as common as runny noses. The younger the child, the shorter his attention span is likely to be — and the trickier your job is going to be in the process. When coaching an outdoor sport like soccer, distractions abound. Birds, airplanes, motorcycles, you name it — you have to compete with all sorts of things that are vying for the kids' attention.

As we discuss in Chapter 6, distractions put a greater responsibility on you to construct practices and devise drills that continually capture the kids' attention and keep their interest and excitement level high. The quickest route to losing a child's attention on the soccer field is to spend large amounts of time talking to him rather than keeping him on the move and actively involved in a wide variety of drills. (For information on coaching children with attention deficit hyperactivity disorder, a medical condition that results in extremely short attention spans, see the "Working with kids with ADHD" sidebar in this chapter.)

The athletically gifted child

Every team seems to have one child whose talent and ability level surpasses everyone else's by a substantial margin. This kid kicks the ball harder, scores more goals, passes more accurately, plays tougher defense, and wins more loose balls than everyone else. The game is remarkably easy for her. Thanks to her size, strength, speed, coordination, or natural talent — or a combination of the above — she gets the label of *team star*. The athletically gifted player stands out. Her teammates know she's the best player on the team. The parents of all the other kids recognize that she's the team's best player by far. You can certainly see how advanced she is compared with the rest of the team. So how do you handle coaching this child?

One of the greatest challenges that accompanies coaching a youngster who's far superior in skill development is providing her with drills that allow her to enhance her skills while not compromising the rest of the team in the process. Working on this skill development can be rather tricky, because you don't want to isolate the player from her teammates when working on drills, but you also don't want her to be bored and unchallenged performing a drill that she's already good at (but the rest of the team is just learning). Use your creativity to concoct clever ways to help those kids just learning a skill and the talented child excel at the same time.

If you're working with the team on delivering a shot on goal with a moving soccer ball, how can a youngster who's already highly skilled in this area of the game still derive benefits from this drill? For youngsters just learning to get their timing down, you roll the ball slowly and directly to them. You'll find a number of ways to increase the difficulty of the exercise for the athletically gifted player without drawing extra attention to her. You can roll the ball toward her with extra pace, which forces her to react quicker when delivering the shot. You can roll the ball a few feet wider than normal, which requires the player to move laterally before lining up the shot. Or you can send the ball to the side of her less-dominant foot, which gives her practice in using that foot in taking shots. As you can see, a little ingenuity on your part can go a long way.

Working with kids with ADHD

A child whose mind continually strays may have attention deficit hyperactivity disorder (ADHD), which usually appears before the age of 7. According to the National Attention Deficit Disorder Association, the most common characteristics of a child with ADHD are distractibility, which consists of poor sustained attention to tasks; impulsivity, which is impaired impulse control; and hyperactivity, which constitutes excessive activity and physical restlessness. Boys are three times more likely to have ADHD than girls.

Youngsters with ADHD certainly don't want to be inattentive any more than the child with bronchitis wants to struggle with coughing spells or the asthmatic child wants to gasp for breath. Some children may be on medication; others may not be on any type of medication; and others, when you get right down to it, may just be having a bad day. Finding out whether a child is on medication is important; see Chapter 4 for this and other topics you may want to discuss at your initial meeting with team parents. The best remedy for working with a child who has ADHD is to dispense plenty of praise for even the slightest improvement. ADHD youngsters are in constant need of praise and recognition, so when they follow your instructions or perform a skill in the appropriate fashion, pile on the praise and adulation.

It's easy to fall into the habit of piling the praise on the youngsters who continually put a smile on your face with their ability to pass, shoot, and defend so well. Keep yourself in check, and refrain from going overboard with the praise and adulation. Too many accolades can have adverse effects:

- ✔ Some kids may begin feeling unnecessary pressure, which can inhibit their performance and derail their enjoyment of soccer. These kids may suddenly feel that with all the attention being thrown in their direction, they have to shoulder more of the responsibility for the team's success and failure. If they don't score a certain number of goals, they may feel personally responsible for a loss.

- ✔ Going overboard with the praise can also alienate other members of the team, who may begin to feel as though the talented player is the coach's favorite. If you allow this alienation to happen, the team will harbor resentment toward you and the talented player, and that causes problems with the team spirit and chemistry you're trying to build.

Enjoying the work you do with the highly gifted youngsters on your team certainly isn't wrong. In fact, if these players possess good attitudes and aren't critical or condescending to their teammates, they have the potential to emerge as wonderful team leaders and positive role models. Just remember to maintain a proper perspective, and recognize that these talented players are just one piece of the team puzzle. The entire roster full of other kids needs your help, support, and guidance as well.

The child who doesn't want to be there

Children with chinks in their self-esteem armor often perceive sports participation as tests of personal worthiness. In their minds, avoiding the activity is better than risking failure, humiliation, and disappointment. These kids may have already written off soccer as a sport they can enjoy for of any number of reasons, including the following:

✔ They watched older siblings participate and felt the pressure to excel surrounding the activity. And even though they really don't want any part of soccer, their moms or dads signed them up anyway.

✔ They've played soccer for several years, have grown tired of it, and simply need a break.

✔ Something happened last season that affected their interest. Perhaps they had a problem with teammates or coaches, or perhaps they were hurt and are fearful now of suffering another injury.

✔ They simply don't like soccer and would rather be playing another sport. Sometimes kids are enrolled in sports that they discover they don't enjoy playing, and that's perfectly okay. The only way kids can learn whether or not they like a sport is by trying it. Problems arise when parents force their kids into playing a particular sport, especially when the youngsters' enthusiasm for participating doesn't match the parents'.

Talk to the child to find out the reason for his lack of interest. You can address many of these reasons, take care of and comfort the child, and restore his interest in playing again. Emotionally connecting with the child and helping him solve his dilemma can do wonders for reestablishing his enthusiasm for playing.

The disruptive child

If you have a dozen or so kids on your team, chances are you have a child who tests the boundaries of acceptable behavior. This kid has a need for attention, and misbehaving is his way of soliciting it, or he's simply being reared by parents who haven't bothered to instill any manners in him. At any rate, he tests your authority, challenges your team rules, and taxes your patience at times.

Coaches often find themselves walking a tightrope when dealing with disruptive players and fall too heavily on one side of the spectrum or the other, both of which have disastrous consequences:

✔ Some coaches are so overly concerned about being well liked by everyone that they sacrifice discipline and ignore team rules that are broken in the process.

✔ In an effort to keep the kids in line, some coaches are exceedingly harsh and throw around punishment far too often, quickly turning the season into a boot camp that makes everyone miserable.

You have to find an appropriate balance between the two behaviors. Keep in mind that children can enjoy playing for you, and like you, while respecting your authority and abiding by your team rules. You have to clearly outline to the players what type of behavior you expect from them during practices and games. When a player crosses a line, you have to address the situation immediately without embarrassing the player in the process.

Don't embarrass the misbehaving player at the first sign of trouble. Instead, speak to the child privately, and make it clear that you won't tolerate this type of behavior. Any time you speak to a player regarding a behavior or discipline issue, be sure to let the parents know about it right away as well. Keeping them in the dark only creates unwanted problems for you down the road.

If you allow the best player on the team to get away with inappropriate behavior, you send a disturbing message to the rest of the team that this player is more special than anyone else and is above the team rules. In fact, you elevate this player to a position more powerful than yours. Coaches who allow this type of insubordination to go on and avoid dealing with the problem usually do so because they operate under a win-at-all-costs mentality, and they turn their backs on confronting any type of problem that could impact the team's win–loss record.

You need to take control of the situation immediately before it leads to team dissension and, even worse, other players begin to copy some of the antics of this player. Quite simply, the only way that you can maintain the respect of your team and teach the merits of following the rules and respecting authority is to punish the offending player and let the team know that these types of behavior are unacceptable. Be sure to remind your players that those teammates who don't abide by the rules are making that choice themselves. Making different rules for different levels of ability sets a dangerous precedent. (We go into greater detail about disciplining children, including the disruptive sort, in Chapter 19.)

The child with special needs

All kids have a legal right to participate in sports like soccer, and that goes for those kids who have special needs, too. These special needs may result from conditions ranging from hearing loss and vision impairment to medical conditions such as diabetes or epilepsy. Youngsters who have physical conditions in which they don't have full use of their arms or legs also fall into this category. As a soccer coach, questioning your own qualifications about working with a special-needs child is natural. But think about it. You're a coach, and these kids are looking for your help and guidance. Just as you discover ways to successfully work with a child who has no coordination or is super-shy, you can work with a child who has special needs to safely include her without causing major disruptions to the team or the game.

Making accommodations for a special-needs player

In order for kids with special needs to participate in a sport like soccer, certain accommodations need to be made. These accommodations aren't designed to give the child or the team an unfair advantage or to put the team at a disadvantage; they're simply used to help eliminate some of the obstacles that may prevent the child from participating in the sport. Without those obstacles, she can benefit from the experience just like the other kids. You want to do everything you can to maintain the integrity of the game while also making it possible for this youngster to be part of the soccer experience.

If, for example, a child has a visual impairment and has great difficulty seeing a white ball, playing with a different-color soccer ball would make all the difference. Or, if a child has a physical problem that doesn't allow her to run up and down the field, maybe she can handle all the team's throw-ins, or perhaps she can be the team's designated corner kicker. These suggestions are just a couple of ways that you can include children, regardless of their disabilities, without compromising anyone's safety or enjoyment of the game. After these youngsters get an understanding of their roles and how they fit into the structure of the team, they'll have specific skills that they can work on and see improvement in during practices, just like their teammates.

Reviewing the situation with parents, players, and coaches

In Chapter 4, we discuss conducting your preseason parents meeting. We cover how important it is to find out from the parents whether any of their children have any conditions that you need to be aware of in order to meet their needs. If you happen to have a child with special needs, set aside some time before the first practice to talk to the family about their hopes and expectations for their child's participation. Open the lines of communication so that together you can come up with solutions that benefit everyone. Keep in mind that this season may be the parents' first foray into organized sports, and they may be nervous and apprehensive about having their child participate. They may turn to you for all the answers. Explore the endless possibilities that are out there, and figure out ways that this youngster can be included and be a valued and contributing member of the team.

Regardless of the age or skill level of your team, having a child with special needs on the squad can be enormously beneficial for your other players. Youngsters get a firsthand lesson in developing understanding, compassion, and patience for their teammates while also learning to accept everyone's differences. In Chapter 7, we discuss the importance of meeting with the opposing coach prior to the game. At this time, share any information regarding children on your team who have special needs, and find out whether any players on his team have special needs as well. Quite often, the league director goes over this type of information with all the coaches at a preseason meeting so that everyone is aware, well in advance, of any accommodations that need to be made. By working together and making the necessary accommodations, you can help ensure that these youngsters are an integral part of the team chemistry.

If you coach a team of older kids, you can ask them for their thoughts and ideas on how a special-needs player can be included. Your players can be great resources for you, and they may just surprise you with their creative suggestions on how to ensure that their teammate is a part of the action.

The bully

Most of us can probably recall those kids we went to school with who picked fights on the playground and pushed around the smaller and weaker kids. They tormented, teased, and were totally troublesome. Bullies aren't limited to playgrounds and school hallways — they can show up on the soccer fields, with intimidating scowls and overly aggressive play. Bullies thrive on attention and find pleasure in upsetting others. They also frequently feel weak and battle feelings of insecurity. The soccer field has no room for a bully and his intimidating tactics and physical play.

Kids who are picked on by a bully often don't complain, for fear of making the situation worse than it already is. That means you have to keep a close eye on the interaction of the kids — not only during practice, but also before and after practice, because bullies wreak the most havoc when adults are less likely to be around. That's another good reason to have a practice drill set up for the early-arriving kids, which we discuss in Chapter 6: It eliminates the chance for horseplay that can injure a child or cause emotional distress.

If you're having problems with a child bullying others, speak with the child away from the team and let her know that a change in her behavior is in order for the good of the team. Let her know that you admire her tenacity on the field but that her physical strength and motivation to overpower her opponent must be reined in and used strictly within the confines of the rules of soccer. Not following the rules negatively impacts her team and is counterproductive to what the entire team is striving to accomplish. Tell her that you value her as a player, but bullying isn't acceptable. If the child is simply picking on or making fun of her teammates, address the fact that she should be encouraging and supporting her teammates — these are the teammates she's going to be encouraging and counting on to get her the ball with a pass when she's open.

As a youth soccer coach, you have an obligation and a responsibility to do your best to bring out the best in your team members as both soccer players and individuals. If you don't address the bullying, others may believe that you condone the behavior. Be sure to point out that you know the bully is capable of being a better teammate. Work with her to be a more positive influence on the team. Make the conversation a productive one by being friendly yet firm. She may even pick up some pointers from you on how to be a better person by how you deal with her.

The inexperienced child

Sometimes, a child is a late arrival to the sport of soccer. For example, if you're coaching a 10-and-under team, one of your 10-year-olds may have never played organized soccer before, even though the rest of his teammates have been involved in the sport for several years. Getting the inexperienced child caught up to the skill level of his teammates in a relatively short amount of time simply isn't possible. You can't squeeze a few seasons' worth of practices, drills, and game experiences into a month or two, but you can help the youngster develop skills and be a contributing member of the team without compromising the practice time of the more experienced players.

You can create a passing drill for four players comprised of one talented athlete, two youngsters of average soccer ability, and one child who's inexperienced in the sport. The less experienced player will probably struggle a bit, but with the positive encouragement from the talented player who can take on the part of a teaching role, everyone learns from the situation, and the kids further cement the team bond.

The ball hog

Having a ball hog on your team — one of those players who hangs onto the ball as though he's guarding his most prized toy — can create real problems for the entire team because it directly impacts the other players' enjoyment of the game. Ball hogs typically aren't a problem at the younger age levels, because most kids haven't played long enough to develop their skills to a point that they can maintain control of the ball for extended periods of time. Ball hogs are generally found when kids begin to develop skills, their talent begins to shine through, and they realize they're getting pretty good.

A player can earn the ball-hog label for a number of reasons, all of which you can help him discard by taking the right approach. The player may be

- ✔ **Unaware:** Quite often, the child isn't aware that he's hanging onto the ball too long. Any drills that force kids to work with, and rely on, their teammates can be instrumental in keeping the ball-hog syndrome from infiltrating your team and creating dissension. Incorporating drills that stress passing (such as 2-on-1 and 3-on-1), practice drills like Keepaway, or scrimmages in which the team must complete a set number of passes in a row before taking a shot on goal (which we discuss in Chapter 6) into practices is great for eliminating ball-hog problems.

✔ **Receiving conflicting instructions:** One of the more challenging scenarios occurs when the child receives conflicting instructions from his dad or mom at home. The parents may tell the child that he needs to be more aggressive during games, or they may tell the child that he's the best player on the team and needs to exert more control and dominate the game. If you suspect that this is happening, have a quick meeting with all the parents following a practice. Remind them that you appreciate their help teaching the kids by reinforcing your lessons at home. If this gentle group reminder doesn't sink in with the targeted parents, arrange a private meeting. Share your concerns, and point out that their conflicting instructions disrupt the team environment you're trying to create.

✔ **New to the sport:** The child may be new to soccer, or maybe he's never been involved with a team before. He may need some extra time to get accustomed to the team setting. Help him to learn to utilize his teammates and to recognize the importance of passing the ball for the benefit of the entire team.

✔ **Misunderstanding his position:** Take a closer look at how you teach the responsibilities of the positions to your players, as well as the offensive and defensive philosophies you preach to the team. Do certain players tend to wander out of position, creating additional opportunities for them to handle the ball? Are your defenders creeping too far forward when the team is on the offensive and forgetting their defensive responsibilities in the process, giving themselves added touches? Spending a few minutes clarifying the responsibilities of each position and touching on the fact that the team can excel only if all players handle their positions may be all you need to quickly and easily remedy the problem.

✔ **Taking a cue from you:** Take the time to really examine your practices, because you may be fueling the problem. During exercises, are you allowing kids to unnecessarily hang onto the ball for extended periods of time while shunning their teammates? Are you enamored with the stellar play of certain individuals who mesmerize you with their dribbling skills as they negotiate their way down the field during practice? If so, the ball hogs are certainly going to carry this style of play over to games. Continually stressing the importance of teamwork during practice, and pointing out to players who show a tendency to hog the ball that they should've passed the ball to a teammate, helps eliminate this problem.

✔ **In need of altered practice drills:** Play games during practice where the purpose is to maintain possession of the ball, not to score goals. This approach isn't destructive to coaching soccer. By practicing possession, the entire team learns how to pass the ball, receive passes, and develop proper spacing to take advantage of the defense. You can even enforce a rule where each player on the team has to touch the ball before a player can touch it a second time on each change of possession. If a team breaks the rule, they lose possession of the ball to the other team. Or you can impose a limit on the number of touches a player is allowed during each possession. These types of drills ensure that everyone is involved in the game and forces players to find ways to get the ball to their teammates who haven't had a touch yet.

✔ **Ready for a conversation about his future goals:** Many times, a ball hog has aspirations of playing at a higher and more competitive level in the future. These thoughts may be fueled by what the player's parents are telling him at home or by a genuine interest of his own in excelling in the sport. Regardless of where the motivation comes from, talk to him. Let him know that when he begins playing at the more competitive levels of soccer, the players whom he goes up against will have the same skills — and perhaps better skills — as he does. That makes the ability to distribute the ball to teammates even more important, and if he doesn't hone those skills now, he may be a liability on his next team.

Also, stress to the player that the more he involves his teammates in the game, the more effective a player he will be as he advances in his soccer career and plays at more competitive levels. Talk to him about being a well-rounded player who not only can deftly handle the ball and score goals, but also thread nifty passes through a maze of defenders. Good soccer players have a penchant for playing all aspects of the game well.

Regardless of the reasons behind the emergence of a ball hog, dealing with the problem swiftly is imperative, because it affects everything from team morale to each child's overall enjoyment of the sport. Allowing the player to continue hogging the ball sends him a distorted message about how to play soccer, and it frustrates and alienates his teammates in the process.

Teaching players the essence of teamwork is essential to ensure that no single player monopolizes the ball at the expense of his teammates. When dealing with this lesson, don't make it a public display. The last thing you want to do is embarrass the player in front of his teammates and, in the process, make him suddenly afraid to take any shots or dribble the ball for any length of time for fear of being reprimanded again. A ball hog doesn't need to be disciplined; he simply needs coaching and guidance on how to work more effectively as a team. Don't detract from his aggressive play or drain his passion for playing the game; just make him aware that in order for the team to reach its potential, every child must play an instrumental role.

The average child

You're going to have all types of youngsters on your team — everything from ball hogs and bullies to behavioral challenges and klutzes. Some of these kids are self-motivated; others rely on you for motivation and inspiration. Some are involved to quench their competitive desires, to get a better grasp on some skills of the game, or merely for the social interaction and camaraderie of being part of a team. Some of these kids are going to be extremely coach-able and receptive to all your instructions and feedback; others may not be quite as receptive. Some of these kids are skinny, short, and not nearly as physically developed as their teammates, and some may be overweight and taller than others their age.

For the most part, the majority of your players are going to be your regular, everyday kids who enjoy playing soccer and being with their friends. They're not super talents destined for college soccer scholarships or disruptive influ-ences creating havoc with the team's chemistry and your blood pressure. They simply show up with smiles and shin guards to play for you, learn from you, and grow under your guidance. A lot of these kids may be involved just because their friends are playing, and they want to be involved with them. Some of these kids — through their involvement with you this season — will develop a real love of and passion for the game and continue playing it for years to come. Others will be content to try a new sport next season but will have a handle on the basics of the game if they ever choose to return to the sport in the future.

Chapter 6

Running a Great Practice

*N*othing wipes the smiles off the faces of young soccer players quicker than dull practices in which the same tiresome drills are used all season long. As the coach, your job is to keep the interest and excitement level high every time your youngsters step onto the field.

Creative practices that children eagerly look forward to attending week after week pay big dividends in their skill development, speed the learning process, enhance their overall enjoyment of the sport, and translate into plenty of that all-important fun in the process.

During your practices, youngsters must be constantly challenged, encouraged, and entertained. Be creative in your planning, enthusiastic in your instruction, and overflowing with your praise. Carefully craft your practices days beforehand rather than at the stoplight on the drive over to the field. Every drill must serve a specific purpose rather than just fill a chunk of practice time, and you must design every practice with the intention of helping youngsters progress in all areas of the game.

Each practice session you conduct is enormously important in each child's overall development. These outings, if they're well constructed and efficiently run, go beyond teaching and developing basic soccer skills. They also promote positive attitudes, efficient practice routines, team chemistry, healthy fitness habits, increased knowledge of the game, and reduced chances of injuries occurring when proper stretching is performed (which we dig into in greater detail in Chapter 18). Now that's a pretty impressive list!

Sure, game day is what all kids naturally look forward to the most. The trick is turning your practice sessions into equally fun-filled outings that generate the same type of interest. Sound practice planning that maximizes your time with the kids is the foundation of any successful youth soccer season.

Kicking Off the Season with a Great First Practice

Delivering an important presentation to the boss, meeting your future in-laws for the first time, getting a call from the Internal Revenue Service, and conducting your first soccer practice of the season — these situations can all be pretty nerve-wracking experiences, but they don't have to be. Well, at least running a soccer practice doesn't have to be.

If you've never coached a youth soccer team before, chances are it seems pretty daunting — and a lot more difficult than you expected — when you arrive at the field for the first time, and you have 15 sets of eyes suddenly staring up at you for guidance, instruction, and motivation. You may bring all the equipment the kids need, and you may have your clipboard at your side and a whistle dangling from your neck, but if you haven't come armed with a carefully crafted practice plan, you have big problems.

You have a lot at stake when you take the field for your practice session. The first practice of the season sets the tone and provides kids with an indication of what's in store.

Greeting the team for the first time

Just like in the preseason parents meeting that we discuss in Chapter 4, first impressions are oh-so-important for establishing the proper frame of mind for the first practice. A smile and a friendly pat on the back from you as your young players arrive help build a comfortable foundation and go a long way toward establishing those special coach–player bonds that can make a season so rewarding. When you show up to start a new job, you aren't left standing off to the side, wondering whether anyone is going to come up and talk to you or welcome you, so don't leave youngsters stranded or forced to linger on the side of the field when they show up.

Arrive at the field early so that as kids climb out of the car, usually with their parents, you're there with a friendly smile to welcome them.

Greet older players with a friendly handshake, and welcome them to the field. Talk with them about how long they've played soccer, which team and coach they played for last year, and how their season went. If they get a sense of your genuine enthusiasm — and that you're sincerely interested in them — the seeds of a relationship based on mutual respect will be planted and will grow stronger as the season moves along.

Until players get to know one another better, they're often reluctant to go up to one another and just stand around waiting for the start of practice. If you're coaching a team that has some experience playing soccer, you can help the kids start to become familiar and comfortable with one another by having players pair up as they arrive and loosen up by passing the ball back and forth. This warm-up gives you a nice head start on building some team chemistry. It also gives you a sneak peek at the experience and talent level of your team. By watching the players in these few minutes, you get a sense of how well they pass and receive the ball and how well they handle the ball in general. This method also works well with younger players, although the more inexperienced they are, the more explaining you have to do.

You may realize that the drills in your practice plan are either too easy or too difficult for this group and that some adjustments are in order. If so, don't panic. Some quick thinking can remedy the problem. If the drills are too easy, you can always bump up the difficulty by having more players take on defensive roles so that the dribbling, passing, or shooting drill is tougher to complete. For those drills that prove too challenging, you can always tone things down by removing the defensive element. Or when you're mapping out your practice, put together some drills that are both far more difficult and easier than what you originally planned, just in case you need to alter your practice and resort to the backup drills.

Making coach and player introductions

Just like a child's first day of school, his first soccer practice of the season can be a stressful time, particularly if he's never played the sport before. After all, he has new kids and coaches to meet, instructions to follow, and skills to learn. He's in unfamiliar surroundings, so anything you can do to alleviate stress and make him comfortable goes a long way toward getting things off to a smooth start.

The first step in that direction is to formally introduce yourself (and any assistant coaches, if you've already selected them) to the entire team. (In Chapter 4, we discuss the importance of proceeding cautiously before selecting parents to fill the important roles.) When meeting with your team, keep the following in mind:

> ✓ **Gather the team in an area of the field with the fewest distractions.** If you're standing with your back to another practice or game that's taking place, some of your players will be more interested in what's taking place behind you than in your introductions.

✔ **Be mindful of where the sun is when getting the team together.** You don't want a dozen youngsters squinting to see you because they're staring directly into the sun. Whenever possible, you should be the one facing the sun. Remember, paying close attention to the smallest details can make a giant difference in the impact you have with your team.

✔ **When speaking to the team, particularly children ages 8 and under, get down to their level so you can talk directly to them.** Standing up while the team is sitting isn't conducive for listening and learning, especially if the players have to strain to keep their heads up to focus on you. Your talk is more beneficial when you speak to them at eye level. If your squad is small, your best bet may be to sit cross-legged with your players gathered in front of you. If you have a dozen players or more, consider talking to them while bent down on a knee.

✔ **Let the kids know that they can call you "Coach" or "Coach Jim" or whatever moniker you're comfortable with.** Also, share a few quick tidbits about yourself, and if you have a son or daughter on the team, introduce him or her. That also serves as a good lead-in for the other members of the team to introduce themselves. If you don't have a child on the team, you can use creative introductions to put the kids at ease. Start by introducing yourself and share with them your favorite television show, for example, and then have them follow suit. Kids are more relaxed chatting about their favorite cartoon or sitcom and can learn interesting tidbits about their teammates in the process.

✔ **Many children are naturally shy, and some may even be afraid to say their names to the group, so make it a fun game by trying to guess the kids' names.** Throwing out crazy guesses gets the kids laughing and puts them at ease when sharing their names.

✔ **With older kids who are more experienced, share a little more detailed information about your coaching background.** Kids are naturally going to be interested in who they're playing for this season, and if they've been involved in the sport for years, they may want to know what type of experience you have being on the sidelines.

✔ **As with any team discussion, the shorter, the talk the better.** Short attention spans abound at the younger age groups, so the less time the players spend listening to you and the more time they spend running around on the field, the better for everyone involved.

To help you learn the kids' names more quickly, and to help the youngsters get to know their teammates, try the following:

✔ **Give everyone a nametag for the first few practices.** Put nametags on yourself as well as your assistants to help promote team unity.

✔ **Select a couple of kids to lead warm-ups at each practice.** Announce the names of the kids you choose so the rest of the team begins learning players' names. Rotate the players leading the calisthenics each practice.

A great way to get young kids to loosen up at the first practice and start getting comfortable with you is to introduce them to "Get the Coach." Give each of the kids a soccer ball. The idea is for them to touch you while maintaining control of their soccer balls while you do your best to dodge all the youngsters coming your way. The game gets the kids running around, laughing, and having fun right away, which is a great way to start the season on a high note. Plus, the kids build ball-control and ball-handling skills without even realizing it.

Focusing on basic skills first

Soccer practice can be an overwhelming environment for a young child whose only sports experience up until now consists of playing ball with a sibling or a neighborhood friend down the street. And soccer is truly unique because it requires a wide range of skills that utilize assorted body parts like the head, chest, thighs, shins, and all areas of the feet. These factors mean that you have to ease your players into practice and introduce them to the most basic skills during those first few weeks of the season to give them a sense of what's required to play this sport. With older kids embarking on a new season, providing them a refresher on the basics is an effective way to begin. In subsequent practices, you can jump to working on more advanced skills.

Working with younger kids

If you're coaching in a beginning-level soccer program, your job description is basically already filled out for you. With kids at this age who are unfamiliar with the sport (and some of them have never kicked a soccer ball in their lives), your initial focus is going to be on the rudimentary skills that every young player needs to acquire. The most important skill to begin teaching them is how to kick the ball in the general direction in which they're aiming. Clearly, this ability is essential for being able to derive any sense of enjoyment and accomplishment from the sport.

During early practices with younger children, you also introduce them to some of the other basics of the game: passing, receiving, dribbling, tackling, and goaltending. As they start to get a handle on those skills, you can begin to give them a feel for other areas of the game, such as trapping and heading. We provide you with pointers for correctly teaching these fundamental skills in Chapter 9.

Working with older kids

Most times, the older kids are probably going to have a decent handle on many of the basics of the game. Still, devote part of your first practice to going over these skills. A lot of kids probably haven't played soccer since last season, which could be a year ago, so a little refresher is helpful. From there, focusing on ball movement and retaining possession is usually a good starting point for a new season. Being able to efficiently work the ball down the field as a unit is vital at this juncture in the team's development.

Although skills such as throw-ins, corner kicks, penalty kicks, and direct and indirect kicks usually aren't utilized in leagues at the younger levels, your players need to become versed in these areas as they continue in their development this season. You may be tempted, in your enthusiasm to teach these aspects of the game, to overwhelm them the first time you get together. Refrain from throwing too much information at them at once. During that first practice, consider picking one new skill, such as throw-ins, and introduce the kids to that. In subsequent practices, you can slowly incorporate additional new skills into your sessions.

Coming to Practice Prepared

In Chapter 4, we discuss your preseason parents meeting and how you expect your players to arrive at practice properly prepared, with the right equipment and their water bottles. The same goes for you. Besides doing your homework and outlining the drills you want to use and the skills you want to focus on, your responsibilities extend to arriving at the field with not only your practice plan, but also all the equipment needed for a great practice. A part of that preparation includes an area of the game that a lot of coaches fail to give proper consideration to, and that's having a properly stocked first-aid kit.

Creating a practice plan

A well-constructed practice plan may take, dare we say it, a little practice on your part. But after putting together a couple of them, you'll get the hang of it. Putting together a quality practice plan — and then being able to execute it — is sort of like putting together a giant jigsaw puzzle. You have all these pieces in front of you in the form of the skills you want to teach, and you probably have at least a general idea of some of the drills and techniques you want to use to teach them. Now it's just a matter of finding the right spot to fit them all in and determining their most useful order during the allotted time you have with the team each week during the season.

Jotting down what skills you want to work on initially — and what you want to accomplish during those first couple of weeks of the season — helps jump-start your thought process and get you started along the way to mapping out useful practice plans (see the section "Focusing on basic skills first" earlier in the chapter). After you put those skills down on paper, go ahead and break your session down even further into how much time you want to devote to each area. If the league allows you to practice with your team twice a week for an hour at a time, you know you have two hours each week to work with the kids, and you can break down how much time you want to spend on different aspects.

Devise your practice plans well before your first practice, but don't outline every aspect of every practice all at once. That's counterproductive, because as your players develop skills and learn new ones, your practices constantly change to accommodate their improved level of play.

Also, some initial tweaking of your long-term plan is almost guaranteed after you gauge the skill level of your team (which we discuss in Chapter 5). When selecting drills, avoid using ones that turn out to be too easy for the kids because they won't learn much from them. You also want to steer clear of drills that are too difficult, because they limit the amount of learning taking place and frustrate youngsters when they're unable to enjoy any level of success.

We can't say it enough: Preparation is vital for a smooth-running and effective practice. Even though you feel prepared because you have your practice all mapped out, you'll have times when a drill or game that you designed simply falls flat. So now what? Have a couple of back-up drills listed on your practice plan that you can resort to if needed. You'll get a sense early in a new drill whether the kids like it and whether it accomplishes what you intended. If not, you have to be ready to make the switch and go with something else.

Bringing your balls and cones

What's a soccer coach's worst nightmare? Well, besides dealing with an overinvolved parent (which, by the way, we discuss in Chapter 19), a soccer coach most fears not having enough equipment for practice. In Chapter 4, we discuss the preseason parents meeting, and we note that your best bet is to let parents know right from the start that it would be extremely helpful if their children can bring soccer balls with them to practice. For the most part, children who are involved in a youth soccer program probably have balls to play with at home, so it's usually a reasonable request.

To make your practices the most effective, you always want to have at least one soccer ball per child.

Of course, you can pretty much guarantee that at least one child will forget her soccer ball at just about every practice. Ideally, the league provides you a few balls to work with for the season. If not, check with the league administrator to see whether he can loan you some used balls that may be sitting in storage. You don't need shiny new soccer balls to instruct kids. If it holds air and is the proper size and weight for the age group you're coaching, any ball will work just fine.

In the worst-case scenario, in which only a handful of players have soccer balls, you need to adjust your practice plan. Obviously, planning a bunch of 1-on-1 passing games isn't going to make the most of your practice time if you don't have enough balls to go around. You may have to make some minor adjustments, such as going to a 2-on-1 passing drill with a defensive player included. Although this change cuts down on the number of touches of the ball a child gets during the course of the session, the reduction isn't significant.

Small plastic cones or pylons are perfect for marking off areas of the field that you want to conduct a drill in. If the league doesn't provide this equipment, you can purchase a cheap set at your local sporting-goods retailer, or you can get creative. Old towels or t-shirts can work just as well to mark off the playing areas, and so can many other items. As long as whatever items you choose to mark off an area don't pose any injury risk to the children, using them is okay.

Packing your first-aid kit

Lugging a first-aid kit with you to practices and games all season long may seem like more trouble than it's worth, but the first time you have to deal with an injury, you'll see its enormous value and importance. Certainly, not opening the kit all season long would be great, but as we point out in Chapter 18, injuries are a part of soccer, and being prepared is better than simply hoping nothing ever happens to your players.

Inside your first-aid kit, you should tape your list of emergency contacts that the parents filled out and returned to you prior to the season. In Chapter 4, we talk about the importance of distributing these forms to parents at your preseason meeting so you know whom to notify in the event of an emergency.

Many leagues issue a first-aid kit to each coach. As we mention in Chapter 2, this point is one that you should find out about when you're learning about your league. If the league doesn't provide a first-aid kit, mention the importance of having one to the league administrator, who perhaps can correct the oversight. In the meantime, never conduct a practice or go to a game without your kit. You can use a toolbox or any other type of container, as long as it's waterproof, to protect your supplies.

The basic essentials that should be in every coach's first-aid kit include:

- **Antiseptic spray or wipes:** To clean out cuts and abrasions.
- **Assorted-size bandages:** To cover cuts or other wounds.
- **Bee-sting kit:** Pick these up at your local pharmacy to have on hand in case one of your players gets stung.

✔ **CPR mouth barrier:** In the event that you or another parent need to perform mouth-to-mouth resuscitation on a child.

✔ **Emergency tooth-preserving system:** For a tooth that gets knocked out. You can pick these kits up at a local pharmacy or check with your dentist on where to purchase one.

✔ **Freezer-type bags:** Great for holding ice packs.

✔ **Insect repellent:** For evening practices and games when those pesky mosquitoes make an unwanted appearance.

✔ **Latex gloves:** To wear while tending to a bloody cut.

✔ **Nail clippers:** Great for repairing torn nails that sometimes result from being hit by the ball.

✔ **Prescriptions:** As we address in Chapter 4, being aware of any medical conditions a child may have is extremely important. For example, if a youngster has asthma, keep a spare bronchodilator in your first-aid kit in case the child forgets his or his parents are late arriving to a practice or game and the situation calls for it.

✔ **Scissors:** To cut bandages and athletic tape.

✔ **Sterile eyewash and prepackaged sterile eye pads:** To use when debris or anything else becomes stuck in a child's eye.

✔ **Sunscreen:** Exposure to the sun is an often-overlooked health risk when it comes to youth soccer. The best defense to protect yourself and your players when outdoors is to use a sunscreen with an SPF of 30.

✔ **Tweezers:** To remove any debris that becomes lodged in a child's skin.

Here are a few other tips to keep in mind when it comes to your first-aid kit:

✔ **Be realistic:** Stock a reasonable amount of supplies in order to treat more than one youngster at a practice or game.

✔ **Keep tally:** If you have to use a few bandages during a game to treat some cuts, be sure to restock those supplies right away so that you aren't caught off guard at your next practice when the situation calls for one.

✔ **Keep supplies readily available:** Make sure your supplies are clearly marked and in some sensible order. If a situation arises where you're dealing with an injury, and you ask a parent to retrieve a supply from your kit, you don't want to waste any unnecessary time because the parent is unable to tell what's what. Freezer-type bags work great for keeping supplies in order.

Some youngsters on your team may be allergic to certain things — bee stings, for example. How quickly you respond with treatment can help minimize the severity of the reaction. You should know which kids have allergies from the information you gather on each player during your preseason parents meeting, which we discuss in Chapter 4. If you have a child on your team who's allergic to bee stings, make sure you have your bee-sting kit easily accessible. You don't want to waste valuable seconds digging for it when a child is in need.

Putting Smiles on Their Faces: Selecting Winning Drills

The quickest route to putting smiles on the children's faces and a spring in their steps is getting them involved in fun-filled drills that lead to not only learning, but also laughter. During your initial contact with the team, keep the drills simple, straightforward, and, of course, fun. The last thing you want to do is throw out complex drills that confuse and overwhelm the team and have the players questioning whether they want to come back for the next practice.

Use your imagination. Be resourceful. Don't limit your creativity to simply having players dribble a soccer ball through cones that you arranged in a straight line — boring! Children look forward to a drill like that about as much as they do a trip to the dentist. You're certainly capable of doing much better than that for your team.

In the sections that follow, we provide a primer for selecting fun and interesting practice drills that help build skills and keep the kids coming back for more. In Chapters 10, 14, and 17, we provide you a whole host of drills you can use for varying skill levels.

Evaluate your practice in the evening, while the day's events are still fresh in your mind, to determine which skills you should teach in a different manner, which drills the kids like, and which ones you should discard. You can even keep a practice notebook — sort of your own personal diary of the season — in order to best monitor progress and keep track of all sorts of important factors. Note what practice objectives you achieved and which ones you want to follow up on at the next practice. Did the kids have fun during the drills? If you noticed a drill for passing that the team really seemed to enjoy, highlight it in your notebook and use it again at some point during the season. Conversely, if a drill just didn't create a whole lot of enthusiasm among your troops or didn't produce the results you were looking for, you probably don't want to run that one again.

Rule #1: Idle time is boring

We're sure you cringe when you're stuck in a lengthy grocery-store checkout line when all you want to purchase is a simple loaf of bread and some milk. One of the last things you want to do is put your young players through that on the soccer field. To maximize your practice time with the team, your top priority should be to minimize standing-around time. Standing in line is acceptable at amusement parks and movie theaters — not on the soccer field.

Long lines drain the fun out of practice and are a real deterrent to learning and skill development, which are the basis of a productive practice. Also, lulls between your drills can bring the momentum of the activity to a screeching halt. You want the energy and enthusiasm of one drill to carry over into the next. This habit maximizes every second of your practice, and it doesn't allow the kids to become so bored that their attention drifts to what's happening on the field across from them.

When players and soccer balls are on the move, learning is taking place. When players look like statues, learning stops. Avoid long lines, mind-numbing laps, and long-winded lectures. You can decide whether children arrive at your practices with a bounce in their step or with their shoulders slumping.

Here are a few ways to ensure that every child gets lots of touches of the ball at practice:

- ✔ **Break drills down into the smallest number of players possible.** Utilize your assistant coaches, recruit parents . . . do whatever it takes to make sure that children never have to wait in line to participate in a drill.

- ✔ **Reduce the number of elimination-type drills that you use.** These drills tend to knock out the less-skilled players who actually benefit the most from additional repetitions. If you do conduct an elimination drill, set up a drill for players to participate in as soon as they're knocked out. You don't want youngsters to be eliminated from the drill and then stand around watching the team's most talented players participate.

- ✔ **Scale down your scrimmages.** Having a couple of smaller games going is always better than having one big game where children don't see the ball quite as often. Take a look at the "When are we going to scrimmage?" section, later in the chapter, for more suggestions on improving your scrimmages.

- ✔ **Don't waste a lot of practice time setting up cones for each drill.** You can also cut down on the time you spend moving cones by using different drills that can be done in the same area you have marked off.

- ✔ **Reexamine your drills.** Keep a close eye on not only the kids, but also your drills. See whether the kids are getting a lot of time with the ball. If not, you probably want to revise the drill or eliminate it from your future practice sessions.

> ✔ **Keep your explanations short.** If you can't explain the drill in 15 sec-
> onds or less, it's probably far too complicated for kids ages 8 and under.
> Give short demonstrations while introducing a new skill or going over a
> drill. The longer you spend talking, the less time the kids have to play.
> Variations on games like Monkey in the Middle, which we mention later
> in this chapter, don't require much explanation on your part because the
> majority of kids have all played these games and know what they're all
> about.

Rule #2: No one likes dribbling around cones

Instead of conducting that boring dribble-around-the-cones drill, consider
this approach. Take a look at your surroundings. Do you see trees and bushes
near the field? A light pole? You'll get a more enthusiastic response from the
kids when you point out that they have to dribble the ball around that big
tree over there and then negotiate that mound of dandelions to the right of
the tree, and so on, than you will if you line them up and have them go
through cones that took you 30 seconds to set up. If you don't see any trees
or anything else near the field that you can use, recruit parents and scatter
them at different spots around the field so that the youngsters have to weave
around all the adults with their soccer balls.

You can even use this drill with the older and more experienced kids by turning it into a fun little competition. Create a random obstacle course involving
trees and anything else in the area and see which kids can maneuver through
your course the fastest.

Another twist is to go through the course first while the team times you and
see how many players can outperform you. Issue a challenge to the team that
if half the players can beat your time, you will — as punishment for losing —
have to do something of their choosing . . . within reason, of course. This
punishment can be anything from having to wear your clothes inside out at
the next practice to singing a song of the kids' choice. Conversely, you get to
decide what the team has to do if they fail to come out on top. Although it
may be easy to opt for having the kids run a lap around the field, it's best to
stay away from that. (Find alternatives for the traditional running laps that
have been used through the years. Having players run laps as punishment
sends the message that conditioning drills are thought of as a negative, when
on the contrary, they're extremely important.) This drill also serves as a
great bonding exercise for the entire team, because the players will be
encouraging and supporting one another and cheering one another on as
they go around the course.

Looking at proven winners

You can take plenty of innovative approaches to turn your practices into lively and energetic sessions that promote learning and skill development. Visit the Internet or your local library to read up on the different types of drills that are out there. The key is to not restrict your thinking to what you read, though. Take any drill that you come across and look for ways that it can be tweaked for more learning and fun to take place. To get you started, we've found a few tried-and-true approaches that kids love.

Inserting parents into the mix

What better way to inject your practices with a whole new level of excitement than by getting mom and dad involved? Often, parents drop their child off at practice and then run a few errands, or they grab a seat on the sidelines and balance their checkbook, catch up on their reading, or strike up conversations with other parents. Why? Because no one asks them to get involved. You can liven up your practices, and boost the enthusiasm of the kids, by getting the parents out on the field with the team. It's fun and easy, and everyone benefits. Soccer just happens to be one of those truly special sports in which parent–child bonds can be forged by participating together. You can orchestrate the proceedings to make it happen.

Here are a few approaches you can incorporate into your practices to promote fun and build skills while helping parents and their youngsters connect on a whole new level:

- ✔ **Kids and Parents Scrimmage:** This scrimmage gives the youngsters on your team the chance to put what they've learned in practice to use in a game-like setting, and they'll enjoy doing it against their mom or dad or their friend's parent. This scrimmage works great for kids of all ages and abilities. It definitely gets the competitive juices flowing in the older kids as well. They embrace the chance to showcase a dribbling move to maneuver past their dad or to deliver a pass to a teammate that leaves a mom flatfooted and impressed by the accuracy of her child's kick.

  Let parents know about your plans ahead of time so that they show up in the proper attire and shoes. Otherwise, you're going to have a pretty tough time convincing a mom in her business suit and heels to join the action on the field. You can build the excitement level and get your team members eagerly looking forward to the next practice by letting them know during your post-practice chat that they'll be taking on the parents at the next practice. Don't be surprised when you see a lot of early arrivals at your next practice, because it figures to generate plenty of excitement.

✔ **Parent in the Nets:** Nothing livens up an ordinary shooting drill more than having the kids try to score on a parent who's manning the nets. You can turn it into a fun contest by having each child take five shots on the parent and see who ends up with the most goals. You can even switch the drill by reversing positions and seeing how the parents fare trying to score on their youngsters.

✔ **Kids and Parents 1-on-1:** Doing 1-on-1 drills between kids and their parents is a great way to boost the energy level during a practice that may be lacking intensity or enthusiasm. If you're doing a passing drill, have the child work with her parent and see how many successful passes each pair can make. If you're doing a drill working on offensive skills, have the child work on maneuvering the ball past her parent while maintaining control of it.

Taking an old-school approach

Are you looking for some other fun ways to entertain your young squad? Think back to your own childhood and the games you enjoyed playing at school or with neighborhood friends during the summer. Take those games and devise ways to work a soccer skill into them. It's not as difficult as you may think. To help you get those creative juices flowing, here are a few variations on some classic kids' games:

✔ **Monkey in the Middle:** Break the team into small groups of three. Each trio gets a ball, and the object is for the two designated passers to keep the ball away from the defender in the middle. This drill has it all. Players get practice on their passing, receiving, and ball handling, and the child in the middle gets to work on his defensive skills. Whenever the player in the middle is able to swipe possession of the ball, he becomes one of the passers, and the player he stole the ball from moves into the middle.

✔ **Stop and Go:** This twist on the ever-popular Red Light, Green Light game helps your players develop quick reactions and improves their balance. Give each player a soccer ball. Position yourself 50 yards away from the players, with your back to them. When you yell "Go!" the players begin dribbling toward you. When you yell "Stop!" you quickly turn around, and whichever players you catch still moving with their balls are sent back to the starting line. Continue the drill until you can see which players can successfully negotiate their way down the field without being stopped by you.

Being creative with the older and more experienced kids is just as important. The youngsters who have been playing the sport for a few years typically embrace any opportunity to showcase their skills against the other players on the team. The competitive juices start flowing at ages 12 and above, so any ways you can come up with to meet their thirst for challenging competitions will aid in their development and the team's overall progress.

With older kids, try a version of Keepaway from the Coach. Youngsters love chances to compete against — and beat — their coach, so here's a fun opportunity for them to try. Mark off a playing area with cones, and give each youngster a ball. The purpose of the drill is for each child to try to keep control of her ball while the coach and assistants try to knock the players' balls out of the playing area. It's ideal for learning ball control and shielding techniques, and it's a great confidence-booster when a player is able to fend off a coach's defensive moves. Another benefit is that youngsters gain insight into what defensive moves give them the most trouble or cause them to lose possession of the ball, which they can employ when they're playing defense in a game.

"When are we going to scrimmage?"

Scrimmages are great to give kids a taste of what playing in an actual game is like. But be careful not to overuse them at the expense of skill-development drills. Scrimmaging reduces the number of touches that a child gets with the ball, so it should never be the foundation of your practice. A few minutes of scrimmage time at the end of practice, just to get the kids accustomed to performing the skills they've been practicing in a game-like setting, is fine.

Rather than conduct a full-scale scrimmage, if your team is large enough, you can break the players into four smaller teams and run two scrimmages simultaneously on each half of the field. This trick increases the amount of touches of the ball a child gets. Also, with the smaller-scale game, each child is more likely to have to perform a variety of skills.

You can also get really creative and turn an ordinary scrimmage into an exciting one simply by adjusting the rules here and there to mix things up for the kids. Not only do you increase the fun, but you also enhance the skill development of your players and leave them begging for more at the next practice. Here are a few ways you can improvise on traditional scrimmages:

✔ **Passing Points:** Getting the message across to children that passing is an important part of the game can be difficult. After all, kids love kicking and scoring goals, so the skill of passing to a teammate often takes a backseat — but not in this scrimmage. Set this scrimmage up so that the team that successfully completes a designated number of passes in a row while maintaining possession of the ball receives a point, the same as if it had scored a goal. The younger and less-advanced the players are, the fewer passes they must complete. This way, passing, receiving, ball control, and possession — all important skills — become as important as scoring goals.

✔ **Lefty-Righty:** During games, players are forced to make and receive passes and even take occasional shots on goal with their less-dominant feet, as the situation dictates. Developing this skill can often be overlooked during the course of practices, when players are naturally going to use their dominant feet whenever possible to pass, kick, and receive balls. A good way to break them of that habit is to conduct a scrimmage in which all plays on the ball must be made with the youngster's less-dominant foot. Or you can conduct a regular scrimmage but award a bonus point for a goal scored by a player using her less-dominant foot or for a pass made by a less-dominant foot that results in a goal. Making these slight adjustments gradually helps the players become more comfortable and accustomed to making plays with both their feet and enhances their overall enjoyment of the game.

✔ **Soccer Ball Mania:** Getting kids a lot of touches with the ball is one of the biggest practice goals for all soccer coaches. Lots of touches lead to skill development. Holding a scrimmage in which two or three soccer balls are in play at the same time can be beneficial for several reasons. First, young kids love the action-packed game, with plenty of soccer balls bouncing around to keep their attention. Second, with the additional balls in play, your players get the chance to experience two and three times the action they see in a typical game. It also builds their timing, enhances their coordination, and improves their reaction skills. Bottom line, it's a scrimmage that provides endless benefits and leaves the kids smiling at the conclusion.

When designing your drills, try to make them game-like in nature. Doing so provides your team experience while reducing the amount of time you have to devote to scrimmages. For example, if all your shooting drills involve kicking a ball into an empty net and a player winds up to take a kick on game day and sees a goalie standing in his way, it's going to throw him off if he hasn't practiced that before.

Letting kids help select practice drills

As you negotiate your way through the season, make a note of the drills that the kids really seem to enjoy and that seem to be the most beneficial for them. For young kids, you can give each of the drills a fun name that gets their attention. For example, using the name Purple Bear carries a lot more meaning for them than simply calling it the 2-on-1 drill. As the season progresses, consider setting aside a segment of your practice each week for a different child to select his favorite drill for the team to do. This arrangement is a great way to include all the kids in the practice and really make them feel like a part of what's going on. It also gives you a good idea of what types of drills the kids like. Obviously, you may want to discard drills that no child picks or rethink ways to make those drills more entertaining, if you continue coaching this age group.

When you coach older and more advanced kids, you can ask them whether they fondly remember any other drills that they did with other coaches they played for over the years. Incorporating another coach's drill into your practice certainly isn't wrong. If it's fun for the kids and effective in working on a particular skill, you can make room for it in your practices.

Creating a Positive Atmosphere

You can be a great teacher of skills and have dozens of well-crafted drills on your clipboard, but that doesn't guarantee productive, fun-filled practices. You must be aware of, and attend to, a number of factors that impact how effectively you work with your players. The type of environment you create, through your words and actions — as well as how you go about providing feedback and assisting those kids who have difficulty learning skills — plays a large role in defining how successful your sessions are.

Setting the tone

The tone you set at the first practice of the season — and carry throughout — should be one built around praise, encouragement, and positive feedback rather than criticism, harsh instruction, and negativity.

You set the tone for your practices with your mood and demeanor. If you played soccer growing up — or any sport, for that matter — you can probably recall those days when you showed up for practice and the coach was in a foul mood. What did you do? You and your teammates grumbled to one another about what a miserable afternoon was in store for you. How much fun and learning do you think those sessions produced? Probably none at all. In order to have the most effective practices, you have to arrive in a positive mood every day. Regardless of what's going on outside your life as a soccer coach, you have to portray a positive attitude to your players. That means keeping your head up, walking with a spring in your step, and keeping a smile on your face. You won't even have to say a word. By using this approach, your players recognize from your body language that you're in a positive mood, and that translates into starting practice off on the right foot.

As the leader of the practice, you influence whether your athletes look forward to or dread coming to practice. Good attitudes are infectious. Do your best to spread yours around for everyone to soak up.

Keeping things consistent

Kids benefit the most from practices that are run in the same manner all season long. If they know what to expect, they arrive at the field prepared and ready to participate. If they're caught off guard because you deviate from how you've run practices in the past, you're probably not going to get their best effort.

Doing the same stretches and warm-ups at each practice provides kids a nice routine before they get into the heart of the practice. At your postpractice wrap-up chat, let kids know that when they arrive before the next practice, you want them to pair up and work on their passing and receiving skills, for example. Turn it into a fun contest to see which pair can complete the most number of passes in a row. You may be surprised by how many kids show up ahead of time, allowing you to start practice right on time with kids who are eager to get going. That's a great environment for some quality learning to take place.

You can also encourage the parents to take part in practice with their children. This involvement can help the parents, who may not be familiar with soccer, learn the proper techniques of a skill so that they can work with their child at home during the week. If the parents are interested, you may even want to give them some additional drills they can do at home with their child to work on various skills.

How long and how often

Sometimes coaches have a tough time curbing their enthusiasm. After all, when you see kids learning and improving — and hopefully having lots of fun in the process — you may want to spend more time practicing than they do. Normally, leagues have specific rules in place regarding how often and how long a team can practice. You need to be aware of this rule (an important league policy that we discuss in Chapter 2) before you begin creating practice plans for your team. If the league doesn't have any policies in place, exercise your best judgment when devising the team schedule. We recommend one practice a week, for an hour, for younger children who also generally have one game a week to play in. As kids get older, you can bump up the schedule to include a couple of practices a week with the single game. Only at the older and more advanced levels should your practices last longer than an hour.

Providing positive feedback

We all love to be recognized for a job well done. When the boss points out that we did something well — particularly in front of our peers — it means a lot. Vocal acknowledgment yelled out for the entire team to hear can really have an impact on a youngster. That type of praise is powerful in the mind of a developing child who is probably unsure of her skills and maybe questions her ability to play soccer.

Make sure you provide verbal accolades to every player during the course of your practice. Children know when their efforts haven't been appreciated. You never want a child to leave the practice field without hearing a single word of praise or recognition for his efforts. If you have to, have your team roster on your clipboard, and as you move throughout the practice, simply mark an X next to a child's name each time you give positive feedback. This way, you can easily monitor how your praise is being divvied up, and you won't commit the coaching sin of failing to recognize a child.

Establishing a positive learning environment is one step in creating a place where athletes like to be involved. You can be demanding while being positive. You can offer constructive criticism and still be encouraging. Good coaches find the balance between the two to help their athletes reach their full potential. Here are a few suggestions:

- **Children love and relate to contact.** A high-five is a great way to acknowledge a special play or an improvement of a skill. Be creative. Do low-fives, in which you and the player have your hand as low to the ground as possible. Kids really focus on performing a drill or skill the right way when they know you're waiting to slap hands with them.

- **Never shout negative comments when kids perform skills the wrong way.** Reserve that tone of voice for when it's really needed, such as when you have a discipline problem. (We discuss discipline problems in greater detail in Chapter 19.) A negative voice often makes the child afraid of making another mistake, which handcuffs her ability to play the game. Mistakes are a part of soccer, but if children feel they have no room for errors, they are less likely to make a play on the ball because they don't want to make a mistake.

- **Give specific, performance-based feedback to athletes rather than general comments lacking performance-related information.** Comments such as "Thatta boy" and "Way to go" probably aren't going to mean a whole lot to a child. Zero in on exactly what you're applauding the player for. Saying something along the lines of "That's the way to follow through on your shot" packs more of a punch and is more likely to stick in the child's head every time he winds up to take a shot.

> ✔ **Pointing out things that a child isn't doing well is certainly okay, but be sure to sandwich some positive feedback around the comment.** For example, you can say, "Sandy, that was excellent how you planted your foot, but I noticed you were looking down at the ball when you kicked it rather than scanning the field to see who was open. And I loved how you followed through on the kick. That's the way to put all your power behind it." This way, the child picks up a tip from the coach that she needs to be more aware of what's happening on the field around her, and her self-esteem gets a nice boost because the coach recognized how well she kicked the ball.

You want to praise kids who already have basic knowledge when they perform skills the proper way, but you don't want to go overboard and begin to lose credibility with the team. You don't want to overlook errors just for the sake of avoiding bringing it up to a player. After all, part of your job is to spot errors and, rather than dwell on them, work to help the child correct them and become more efficient in that area of his game. Children who are showered with excessive praise for performances that they know border on mediocre or aren't their best will begin to tune you out. Also, their respect for you and your knowledge of the sport will drop a level or two, and that's tough to get back during the remainder of the season.

Helping players who need it

Even if a child is struggling to pick up a certain skill after repeated tries, be sure to acknowledge his effort. Eventually, he'll make improvements in this area of his game. In the meantime, the fact that he never gives up and is constantly working, even when things aren't going well, are great attributes that are going to benefit him not only during his soccer career, but also into his everyday adult life. Reward effort as much as outcome. Repeated effort, especially in the face of failure and adversity, is one of the most important ingredients for future success.

If a youngster just can't quite get a handle on a skill, show her how she can correct it instead of telling her what she's doing wrong. Demonstrate to her, and then let her copy your move. When you spot a player doing something wrong, you may be tempted to tell her to watch Jimmy do the drill. This instruction immediately sends the message that Jimmy is better than she is, so rather than helping the player learn this particular skill, you may have damaged her self-esteem. Take the time to show the player exactly what you mean, and acknowledge even the slightest improvement the next time she performs the drill to keep her headed on the right track.

Do your best to avoid the ol' paralysis by analysis that you have probably heard of before. Basically, you want to avoid giving a child so much instruction and information that his brain goes on overload and he isn't able to perform even the most basic skills. Instead of helping him improve, you actually push him further back in his development.

Taking time to look beyond sports

As a youth soccer coach, the practices you devise have a direct impact on each child's development and enjoyment of the sport. Although you may not have given this fact much thought, while you're at practice, you're in a unique position to impact more than just each youngster's ability to kick a soccer ball or deliver an accurate pass. By becoming the coach, you step into a special and important position of role model, teacher, and friend. The players on your team look up to you for leadership, guidance, and perhaps even advice in areas that don't encompass the actual sport of soccer itself. By taking the time to observe, listen, and talk to your players about other areas of life, you can make a positive difference for them.

With children who are a little bit older, you can use events in the news as teaching points. Perhaps a well-known athlete the kids are familiar with has been suspended for using performance-enhancing drugs. You can ask the kids what they think about this situation. Ask them whether they think this player is cheating and whether they're disappointed that he was using illegal substances to gain a competitive advantage. Get the kids to talk to you about the issue instead of always instructing them. It can be a great way to get some good dialogue going. And during the appropriate time in the conversation, you can share your views on the issue and use them to reinforce the importance of staying away from harmful substances.

Some topics that you may want to discuss with older kids that impact their performance on the field, as well as their overall health, include the following:

- **Performance-enhancing drugs and supplements:** Many youngsters may be interested in taking these substances because of their desire to become bigger, stronger, and better at soccer without really understanding the health consequences of their actions. Talk to your team about the dangers of using performance-enhancing drugs and supplements, and stress that players can receive the same benefits through hard work and dedicated practice, which is also a much safer route.

- **Tobacco:** The dangers of using tobacco are well documented, but those messages may not be getting through to youngsters. Studies indicate that an increasing number of high school and middle school students use some form of tobacco. Talk to your players about the dangers of using any form of tobacco and how it not only affects their health, but also hinders performance. A warning is sure to carry a little more weight when a child begins to think that he won't be able to run down the field as fast as another player, for example.

Ending Practice on a Positive Note

Ending your practices on a positive note will send the kids home happy and, just as important, will have them eagerly looking forward to the next practice. How do you do that? Saving your best drill or fun scrimmage idea for the final minutes of practice is one of the most effective coaching tricks around for concluding on a high note. Although you certainly want all your drills to be fun, using drills that generate the most excitement and enthusiasm at the end of the session ensures that everyone goes home happy.

Before you turn the kids loose to their parents, have a quick team talk. Because the kids have just had a really good time and their spirits are up, this moment is a great opportunity for you to give their confidence another boost.

Talk to the players about how proud you are of them for working so hard and doing their best. Point out that you're seeing steady improvement in their play, and tell them how impressed you are with how quickly they're picking up new skills. Speak in general terms about the entire team at this point. If you recognize just a few players for their outstanding practice, you run the risk of alienating children who may have turned in their best efforts of the season but head home somewhat disappointed that you didn't acknowledge them. At times, it may be appropriate to single out a player or two. Perhaps a youngster who has been struggling with his passing skills did really well in the passing drill today. Pointing out what a great job that player did while you're praising the entire team is a great way to boost the spirits of a player who isn't enjoying as much success as most of his teammates.

The post-practice chat isn't the time to critique an area of the game that a lot of players may be struggling with or to rehash a drill that didn't go well because some of the kids weren't focused or were having problems executing. You never want to send kids home feeling that they disappointed you or failed to perform up to expectations. Even in those practices where nothing seems to go right — and you will have days like that during the course of a season — you have to find some nugget to praise and build on for the following practice. Even complimenting them on their hustle after loose balls is good, because you'd love to have that quality ingrained in every player.

Finally, spend just a few seconds going over the schedule for the week. Double-check that everyone will be at the upcoming game, and update any schedule changes that may have developed due to rainouts or other factors. Thank your team for listening to your instruction and working hard; conclude with a team cheer, if you have one; and call it a day.

Chapter 7

Getting Your Game On

. . . .

In This Chapter

▶ Covering the pre-game, halftime, and post-game chats

▶ Going through your pre-game routine

▶ Coaching during the game

▶ Winning and losing with poise

. . . .

You've spent the week practicing, working on skills, and providing instruction to your players. Now game day has arrived, and it's time for the players to put everything they've been learning from you to use. You have opposing coaches and referees to meet, a playing field to look over, and a starting line-up to create. You have warm-ups to oversee, a pre-game motivational talk to deliver, and halftime adjustments to make. You also have substitutions to monitor, instructions to communicate, and a post-game talk to give to wrap up the day.

Being on the sidelines for a youth soccer game requires you to be not only a coach, but also a cheerleader, tactician, master motivator, and constant model of good sportsmanship. Yes, coaching is a big responsibility, but certainly one that you're equipped to handle. You've spent large chunks of time preparing your team to take the field. After reading this chapter, you'll be fully prepared to handle game day and all that comes with it.

Taking Care of Pre-Game Responsibilities

You may be somewhat surprised to learn that your game-day tasks extend beyond calling out plays, substituting players, and providing enthusiastic support from the sidelines. Before your team hits the field, you have a few tasks to fulfill. The following sections make up a helpful checklist to guide you through your pre-game responsibilities.

Arrive early, and inspect the playing field

Before you allow your youngsters to take the field, you and your assistant coaches should carefully inspect the entire playing area. Keep an eye out for hazards such as broken glass, loose rocks, a raised sprinkler head, a loose piece of sod, or anything else that can injure a child during the course of play. Don't rely on the opposing coach or a member of the league's grounds crew to do this inspection. Remember, every player participating in the game is your responsibility, and every step you can take to ensure the safety and well-being of those players benefits them.

Often, games are played one after another at a local facility, but don't skirt the pre-game field check just because another game was played there. You don't know whether anyone else has done a check of the field throughout the day, and taking another look never hurts. Plus, the field is getting plenty of use, so a chunk of grass is more likely to be torn up, and a young player may trip up if it isn't properly replaced before your game begins.

Greet opposing coach and the officials

Before the game starts, head over to shake the hand of the opposing coach. This trip to the other side of the field displays good sportsmanship and sets a good example for the players and spectators.

During this chat, let the coach know whether any of your kids has any special needs, and find out whether any of his do as well; then make the necessary accommodations or come up with suggestions that are fair for everyone involved. If one of his kids has a vision problem that makes it hard to see the ball coming right at him, for example, perhaps you can suggest that if the ball hits the child in the hands and the team doesn't gain an unfair advantage from it, the official should just let play continue. Let the coach decide, but by demonstrating that you're willing to ensure that each child on both teams has a fun and rewarding experience, you set the tone for a great day of soccer and further reduce the chances of problems arising during the game.

Sometimes when kids with special needs are participating, the league director relays that information to all the coaches at a preseason coaches meeting. If your league doesn't have a coaches meeting, you may want to contact the league director yourself to make him aware that a child on your team requires special accommodations so that the director can let the other coaches know in advance of your games. We discuss kids who have special needs in greater detail in Chapter 5.

Meeting with the referees who are officiating your game is another example of good sportsmanship. When you introduce yourself to the officials, let them know that you want to be informed if any of your players says or does anything unsportsmanlike. The same goes for any comments from parents or other spectators. Remember, you want to do everything you can to work with the officials — not against them. Just because they wear striped shirts doesn't mean that they aren't doing their best for the kids, just like you are.

During your meeting with the referee, alert her if any of the children on your team has any special needs. If the official knows this information beforehand, she can make the proper adjustments. For example, if a child has a hearing problem and may not hear the official's whistle, the official can make a hand signal to the child to let him know the whistle has been blown and play has been stopped. Being considerate of all children and meeting their needs is a big part of being a top-quality soccer coach.

Pre-Game Team Meeting

Conducting a pre-game team meeting is an important piece of the game-day experience for youngsters. Letting kids know what's going to be taking place right up until gametime is enormously beneficial to them. Here are some tips to keep in mind when holding this meeting:

- ✔ **Meet with the team away from the parents.** Choose a spot to gather the team that eliminates potential distractions. Children, especially younger ones, have extremely short attention spans. If they can see their parents or any other family members who have shown up to watch the game, they won't listen to what you say. That dramatically limits the effectiveness of your chat. Also, avoid being near the other team. Kids naturally want to see who's on the other team, watch them warm up, and compare their abilities with their own, which is another distraction that you don't need to contend with.

- ✔ **Keep it brief.** Keep your talk with younger kids to five minutes or less. You don't want to defuse the players' energy and enthusiasm for the game by delivering a lengthy state-of-the-team address. Kids have short attention spans, particularly young ones just starting out in the sport, so you don't have to bog them down with instructions and strategies. Tell them to have fun, and send them out on the field with a smile. With older and more experienced kids, you should set aside more time for your pre-game talk because you have a lot more ground to cover; game strategy takes on a more prominent role at higher levels.

- ✔ **Relax, and have fun.** Speak to the team in a calm and relaxed manner. If you appear nervous or uptight, your players are more likely to develop those same feelings, which infringes on their performance. If you're laughing and joking, the team feeds off that and approaches the game in a much more relaxed manner.

  Stress that the most important thing is for each player to do her best and to have fun. If the kids genuinely believe that, it frees them to play more loosely. They also aren't fearful of making a mistake or losing a game.

✔ **Good sportsmanship matters.** Remind your players to display good sportsmanship at all times; to show respect toward officials, regardless of what calls are made; and to shake the hands of the opposing team at the end of the game, regardless of who wins. We see far too many examples of bad sportsmanship in all youth sports. You have an opportunity to make your team a model of good sportsmanship in your league and one that others will strive to emulate.

✔ **End with a team cheer.** Conclude the talk with a team cheer, or have the players put their hands together with a chant of "1-2-3 . . . team!" or "1-2-3 . . . together!" Besides being symbolic, a chant is a final helpful gesture that reminds all the players that soccer is a team sport and that everyone must work together.

During your meeting with the team, make sure that everyone has all the necessary equipment — typically, shin guards and mouth guards at the younger levels. In more advanced levels of play, make sure each child brings the right pair of cleats that meets the league regulations. As we discuss in Chapter 4, children should never be allowed on the field without all the proper safety equipment. Also, check to make sure that everyone has a water bottle. A good team rule to enforce is that every child must bring a water bottle to all practices and games.

Providing some inspiration

A big part of coaching comes down to motivation. To get the best out of your players, you have to inspire them to want to get the most out of their abilities every time they step on the field. This endeavor can be challenging. A motivational talk can be a great tool to get all the kids fired up and excited about performing their best in the game — if it's structured the right way.

You already know that the kids on your team are vastly different in their emotional make-ups, and that's magnified on game day. Some possess that inner drive and arrive at the field eager to get under way and compete against their peers. Others are excited simply because they have the chance to wear cool uniforms and see their friends. And some youngsters are petrified that they're going to have to kick a soccer ball while all sorts of unfamiliar faces in the stands watch their every move.

So how do you approach this motivational talk? Get everyone to focus as a team and work together. If you can accomplish that, the focus and positive energy will spill over onto the playing field. Here are some tips to help ensure that your words pack a punch:

✔ **Be positive:** Touch on areas of the game that the team has shown progress in during the week, and let the players know that you're looking forward to seeing them put those skills into action today. Positive reinforcement of their skills gives them that extra boost of confidence to perform up to their capabilities.

✔ **Avoid pressure phrases:** Stay away from saying things such as "Let's score five goals today" or "Let's hold them to two goals." Keep in mind that children can only give you their best effort; they can't control the outcome of games.

✔ **Focus on your team:** Talk about your team, your players, and how confident you are in their abilities. Discussing the strengths and weaknesses of the other team (a team they may know very little about) doesn't do your team much good.

✔ **Avoid clichés:** Overused sports clichés such as "no pain, no gain" are laughable, not motivational. You don't need to resort to these types of sayings to get the most out of your players. Speaking from the heart with genuine passion serves you and your team far better in the long run.

Think back to your playing days in youth sports. Whether you played soccer or some other sport, you probably remember some of the speeches that you heard prior to games. Some were no doubt good, and others were beyond awful. Learn from your playing experiences; steal from the good speeches, and stay away from the bad ones. If you didn't participate in sports, that certainly doesn't mean you aren't qualified to give a motivational talk. Speak from the heart. Put yourself in those small soccer cleats. Think about what you would want to hear from an adult. What would get you pumped up to play your best? If you incorporate those ideas into your talk, you'll be fine.

Assigning positions

Before you even get to the field, have your starting line-up mapped out and your substitution rotation firmly in place. This organization ensures that all players get an equal amount of playing time. If you don't develop a plan, you'll discover that after the game starts, keeping track of how much time a child plays and which position each child has played is virtually impossible. Every child on the team signed up to play, not to sit on the bench and watch.

You can delegate to an assistant coach the responsibility of monitoring playing time to ensure that it's equally distributed throughout the game.

Go over the line-up with your players. By announcing who's playing where ahead of time, you make sure the players aren't caught off guard or surprised when game time rolls around. Letting them know well in advance also gives them time to mentally prepare for their responsibilities. For more on the importance of playing time and how to assign positions, flip to Chapter 5.

Covering field conditions

During your pre-game check of the field (see the "Arrive early, and inspect the playing field" section earlier in the chapter), you may notice some uneven spots or a part of the field that has some rough patches that can make passing more difficult. Make sure you inform your players of these areas, because they can impact the game or a player's ability to dribble the ball. Even if the field is in great shape, pay attention to the length of the grass. A closely trimmed field plays faster than a field with longer grass. If the grass is long, make sure your players are aware that they have to put a little more force behind their passes to get them to teammates. The pre-game warm-up, which we discuss later in this chapter, also helps them get accustomed to conditions that they may not have any experience playing in.

In the more advanced levels of soccer, the conditions of the field can have a larger impact on the game. Wet or rainy conditions translate into a faster-paced game, because the ball travels across the grass much quicker than usual. A wet ball is also more slippery and a little more difficult to handle. Wet conditions can create problems with timing on passes to teammates and make trapping and tackling a little trickier. Taking a few seconds to relay that information to your team helps them get into the proper mindset as they take the field for their pre-game warm-up session. You can even involve the kids by asking them questions about the playing conditions and how they think those conditions will affect their play. Getting your players in the habit of paying close attention to the field is another step toward making them well-rounded players who understand all aspects of the game.

Keeping instructions simple

Children have a lot on their young minds when they arrive at the field. They wonder whether they know any of the kids on the other team, whether Grandma brought enough film for the camera, and what kind of snacks they're getting after the game. If you coach a team of older and more advanced kids, they're looking to turn in an impressive performance to help the team win the game. Simplify everything when giving instructions. The less technical, the better.

The following are a few pointers for keeping instructions simple:

- ✔ **Don't overwhelm:** Don't overload the team with a lot of discussion about game strategies or fancy plays. The pre-game chat simply isn't the time or place to pile on the instruction. Also, never introduce anything that hasn't already been covered several times during practice.

✔ **Avoid confusing phrases:** Soccer has a unique language all its own, but stay away from using phrases and terms that kids are unfamiliar with. If you haven't spent any time during your practice sessions discussing *marking up,* for example, expecting a youngster to comprehend that term two minutes before game time is hardly realistic.

✔ **Be specific:** Children relate best to specific instructions that are easily understood and implemented. Using general terms like "Get back on defense" is often confusing and unproductive. A specific remark, such as "Jimmy, cover number eight going down the sideline," is much more beneficial.

✔ **Sidestep repetitiveness:** You don't want to sound like a broken record. If you do, your players begin tuning you out. Vary your comments. Avoid giving the same instructions. If you find yourself repeating the same instructions, take a close look at spending more time on that skill in your upcoming practices, because that may be a sign that the team needs additional work in that area.

Warming Up

A good pre-game warm-up is comprised of activities that get kids' bodies loosened up, gradually elevate their heart rates, and prepare them for competition. Youngsters who take the field with muscles that are stretched and bodies that are loose have a reduced chance of suffering an injury, are more mobile and quicker to the ball, and are more likely to perform at a higher level. The older the child, the more susceptible he is to muscle pulls and strains.

During the warm-up, create a positive environment that has players confidently performing skills and enthusiastically looking forward to the game. Send positive messages through your words, facial expressions, and body language. An upbeat, positive attitude creates a positive and upbeat tempo that's conducive to a great warm-up.

You may see the kids only once a week for an hour of practice between games, so game day may be four or five days after your last practice, and many of the kids probably haven't even touched a soccer ball since you saw them last. A good pre-game warm-up helps reintroduce some of the skills that you worked on at your last practice and gets the players reacquainted with the feeling of running and kicking a soccer ball. We cover the essential exercises for pre-game warm-ups in Chapter 18 (along with pre-practice warm-ups and a host of other issues to keep your kids healthy and safe).

The Whistle Blows!

The players have (hopefully) listened to your pre-game talk. They've gone through the warm-ups. They've taken their positions on the field for the start of the game. The ball is in play. Now what? While your players' skills are being put to the test on the field, your game-management skills are also being tested. Suddenly, you have to motivate your players, communicate with them, and rotate them in and out to ensure equal playing time.

Motivating during the game

Motivating kids is a never-ending job when you're a successful youth soccer coach. Even if you deliver the world's best pre-game motivational speech, it may be rendered meaningless if you don't keep positively motivating the players during the game.

During games, kids may get frustrated when skills that they had no problem performing at practice just a couple days ago aren't nearly as easy now. You have to convince your players that they're doing great and instill in them the confidence to keep plugging away out there. The following sections outline a few tips to keep in mind when you're motivating players during the game.

Don't suffocate the players

Allow kids plenty of room to make some of their own decisions during the game. If you're constantly shouting instructions and telling them what to do every step of the way, you hinder their growth and development in the sport. Sure, they're going to make mistakes, but that's all part of playing soccer and learning the sport. Giving children the freedom to play and to make some of their own decisions fuels their growth and enhances their learning.

Ease up on the yelling

Your team is excited on game day, and you are as well. Keep your emotions in check. Don't spend the entire game shouting instructions to every player who makes a move on the ball. Hearing their coach's voice booming every time they're involved in the action can be disconcerting to players. Sure, you'll have instances in the game where you want to get a teaching point across, and the only way to deliver it is to shout it out to your players. Just be sure to convey the instruction in a positive manner. Instructions that are delivered in a negative fashion or frustrated tone aren't readily accepted by the players and likely are a detriment to their productivity.

Stand still

A coach who runs up and down the sidelines all game long — whether shouting instructions or simply being a cheerleader — is a distraction to the players trying to focus on the game. If you find yourself covering as much ground during the game as your players (and getting the same aerobic workout), chill out a bit.

Correct errors

Children often react differently when they receive instruction and feedback in practice than they do in a game. After all, being singled out during a game may be traumatic for some youngsters, who would prefer not to have all that attention heaped on them in front of family, spectators, and the opposing team. Choose your words carefully.

If a player isn't following through on his shots like he typically does in practice, offer some instruction in a positive manner. For example, you can say, "Billy, remember to follow through with your kick at your target just like you did so well all during practice this week." By taking this approach, you provide the player some important feedback that enhances his play during the game while giving him a boost of confidence by pointing out how well he performed the skill in the past.

Encourage hustling

You never want your players to be outhustled, because that's one area of the game that isn't controlled by talent or athleticism. The least talented player on the field can make the biggest difference by outhustling a player to a loose ball. Always encourage your players to give it their all when running after a ball, and reward their hustle with applause and praise. Whether they got to the ball first or not doesn't matter. Getting that kind of effort from your players all game long is a real feather in your coaching cap.

Encouraging communication on the field

Soccer is a truly unique sport for a lot of reasons. One of the most notable is that play is nearly continuous, with very few stoppages, so communicating on the run is crucial for success.

Encourage your players to talk to one another and communicate what's taking place on the field at all times. Their voices can be just as effective a tool as their feet and heads, whether they're on offense or defense. Basic comments — such as "I'm on your right," "I've got number five," or "You've got a defender right behind you" — can be extremely effective. Monitor the communication techniques of your team, and give them feedback, the same as you would when teaching your players any aspect of the game.

You may have players who constantly yell that they're open when they're not, which is counterproductive for the team. Conversely, when players are open and shouting for the ball, are their teammates able to get the ball to them, or are they unaware of the communication and miss out on the opportunity? Let the players know whether their type of communication is beneficial and appropriate for the game situation. Also, be on the lookout to see whether good advice is communicated and used by teammates effectively. Communication among teammates is a skill that many coaches overlook. By encouraging communication among players, it's as though you have a few extra coaches on the playing field. If you work on it at practice, you'll see your team operating smoothly and as a cohesive unit during the game.

The timeout

Although regulation soccer doesn't have timeouts, some beginner programs allow coaches to call them to help organize players and offer instruction. If your league has them, use them to offer positive encouragement and reinforce some key points you've been working on in practice.

With older or more advanced teams, run plays that the team has become very good at executing in practice. Give each of the plays you devise a creative name (or let the kids name the plays), and during the game, encourage your players to shout out the name of the play they want to run when the right opportunity presents itself. When kids are comfortable with a play and can run it successfully during the game, it can swing the momentum, get them feeling good about themselves again, and provide them renewed confidence.

Substituting players

Most youth soccer leagues typically allow coaches to make unlimited substitutions during stoppages in play throughout the game. Many beginner leagues may even allow you to change players during the actual course of the game, much like a line change in hockey. This change helps ensure that the kids receive an equal amount of playing time and doesn't leave anyone stranded on the bench for an uncomfortable amount of time.

League policy dictates your substitution patterns and impacts kids' playing times, so get familiar with these rules. Generally speaking, most leagues allow player substitutions after a goal has been scored, when your team is setting up for a throw-in, during an injury timeout, and after a goal kick has been called for either team. Usually, you aren't allowed to substitute on corner kicks or free kicks. In more advanced leagues, in which the rules of soccer are adhered to more closely, your opportunities to substitute players are greatly limited.

In most cases, substitutions can be made only when the referee gives the okay for the player to take the field while the player he's replacing exits. Again, in beginning soccer, the rules regarding substitutions are extremely flexible, so players may be able to go back and forth on the field like an assembly line. In more competitive leagues, players stepping onto the field or leaving the field must do so at the halfway line, which we cover in Chapter 3. A player must step off the field before his substitute can take the field, though this rule often isn't strictly enforced in youth soccer leagues.

When you're substituting a player, bring him out after he's done something well rather than when he's made a mistake. If a youngster makes a bad pass and is suddenly taken out of the game, he's going to be afraid of making a mistake in the future and losing playing time. Also, when you bring a player to the sidelines after he's done something well, you have the chance to give him a pat on the back or a high-five and recognize the nice play he just made.

The Halftime Speech

The first half is over. You've probably seen goals scored, as well as pretty passes; successful tackles; great saves; and (because you're coaching youth soccer, and the players are still learning and developing) a fair share of poorly executed passes, missed tackles, and other assorted miscues. If you're coaching beginning soccer, you've probably even witnessed a player staring in the sky at an airplane while the ball rolled by him or an opposing player scooting right by your defender who was waving to Grandma. Now you probably have only 10 minutes — tops — before the second half begins.

What you say during your halftime chat should be clear, concise, and uplifting. You don't have to verbally replay the entire half of the game for the team. After all, your players were out on the field, and they know what happened — well, except for the little guys who were watching the plane and waving to Grandma. But you do want this time with your team to be productive, enlightening, and beneficial.

Improvising is key. Every halftime is drastically different all season long. You have to adjust your message to fit the mood of the team and how they performed in the first half. And you can't cram everything you saw into the few minutes you have with the team. You have to be selective and choose one or two points that you want to stress or adjustments that you want to make.

Addressing kids of any age

The following are a few tips to keep in mind when gathering your troops at halftime.

Stress rest and rehydration

The players have been running up and down the field. Let them sit down and drink some fluids before you begin talking to them. Giving them a chance to catch their breath makes them more receptive to your comments. A shaded area off to the side of the field provides an ideal area for your players to sit and get refreshed. Sometimes, even getting away from the field for a few minutes does wonders for re-energizing your squad for the second half.

Keep your composure

Avoid rambling. Wanting to share all sorts of information with your team at halftime is natural. Instead of rambling on about a dozen different things, stick to just a handful of points that you want to get across before the team returns to the field. Limit how much information you throw at the team, and what you do say is more likely to sink in and be used by your players in the second half. Don't send your troops back out on the field scratching their heads, wondering what you were talking about.

And never let the team know that you're frustrated or upset. Kids feed off your emotions and your body language. Being overly emotional detracts from your ability to coach and to effectively interact with your players. Whether your team is up by five goals or trailing by five goals, maintain a positive attitude and demeanor. Avoid slumping shoulders, a bowed head, and a slow walk. Approach halftime with the same positive energy you brought to your pre-game talk, and your team will respond accordingly.

Highlight the positives

Stress great play by the entire team, not just a select few individuals. Point out the way the defenders worked together when they were pressured in their own end, for example, or how the midfielders connected on passes to create good scoring opportunities. Hearing praise for the hard work they put forth during the first half makes the players more enthusiastic to build on those efforts and duplicate those plays in the second half. Although constructive criticism is critical to getting the most out of your players, be sure to balance it with plenty of positive reinforcement to infuse them with added confidence.

Make adjustments

One of the most challenging aspects of coaching soccer is that no two games are ever alike. Everything from the playing conditions to your opponent's skill level and ability is constantly different. On top of that, your team will have games when everything you've worked on in practice comes together perfectly and other times when they can't seem to do anything right. Recognizing what adjustments need to be made and being able to share them with your team during this brief time period are the cornerstones of good coaching.

If you need to solve a problem, comments such as "We can't allow them to keep beating us down the field" aren't very productive. You need to offer solutions that the kids can grasp and put to use. A more appropriate approach is to specifically tell the defenders to play back five yards from where they've been playing, which youngsters can clearly understand. Also, solicit feedback from your players. They're in the heat of the action, so they can be great resources for ideas on overcoming problems.

Focus on what you've worked on

Sometimes, coaches get so caught up in what the other team is doing that they lose sight of their own team's strengths and what they've worked on in practice during the week. When your team has the ball, what skills have worked well for them in practice or in previous games? Don't deviate and suddenly expect players to perform at a higher or different level. Pay close attention to how they performed, and reinforce that they play their own game.

Yes, it's a cliché, but it may make a difference in how the kids perform: Play to your team's strengths. For example, if you're a great passing team, focus on ball control and connecting with teammates, and don't worry so much about what the opposing team is doing. Reminding your team to play its own game generates a certain comfort level while promoting confidence and a renewed sense of teamwork.

Working with more experienced teams

When coaching older or more experienced teams, you can use the halftime break for a number of things. Because you're under time constraints, you don't have a lot of time to get into in-depth strategies, but if your instructions are clear and to the point, you can impart some great advice that can impact your team's second-half performance. The following sections include some of the areas that you may want to touch on — depending, of course, on what transpired during the first half.

Get feedback from your players

During the game, you have your vantage point on the sideline where you're taking in all the action. But with all your responsibilities, you can't monitor every single thing that's taking place on the field. Utilize the different perspectives that your players possess for some great advice. By asking your players whether they have any suggestions to employ in the second half, you're reinforcing your respect for them and their knowledge of the game, and you may gain some valuable feedback that can benefit the team.

Your goaltender is in a great position to survey the whole field, and maybe she's picked up on how the opposing team has been able to maneuver the ball down the field. Or perhaps one of your midfielders noticed that the other team's defenders have a tendency to move up in certain areas of the field and that can be exploited with a long cross-field pass.

Another benefit of this approach is that when players know that you'll be seeking their advice, they focus that much harder during the game and are much more aware of different situations taking place on the field.

Address changing weather conditions

Mother Nature can cause all sorts of disruptions and, in the process, wreak havoc with your strategy. If the weather changes during the course of your game, be ready to make the necessary adjustments in your team's style of play. For example, in windy conditions, take a more aggressive approach when the wind is at your team's back, because the opposing team is going to have greater difficulty moving the ball out of its end.

Keep moving

Are your players constantly on the move, or are they turning into spectators when the action moves away from them? Are they providing support for their teammates by sliding into open spaces when they don't have possession of the ball? Are they pushing forward when the team is on the attack, like how you stressed in practice? Are they moving back when their help is needed to defend? Remind players who don't have possession of the ball to keep moving to ensure that they're always in the right position when they're called upon to make a play.

Make offensive adjustments

Often, your team may turn in a great half of play only to come off the field a little frustrated because the players don't have any goals to show for all their hard work. At this point, your observation skills come into play. Making a minor tweak to the team's approach can actually make a major difference in its play. Perhaps your team has played a great first half in its ability to move the ball all over the field, control the pace of the game, and generate plenty of scoring opportunities, yet the players are showing signs of dejection because they haven't been able to notch any goals. Maybe through you observe that all your team's shots have been low on the ground. Mention to your players that they should try getting some shots on the goalie in the air to test the goalie's skills in that area of the game.

Stress the fundamentals

A lot of times, throwing out even the most basic reminders can make a big difference for your squad. Maybe the team is having trouble moving the ball downfield — not because of anything the opponent is doing, but because your players aren't looking up and scanning the field while they're dribbling. A quick, simple reminder not to look down at the ball the entire time they're dribbling can get your offense back on track. With their heads up, they'll be able to make the right choices when delivering passes to teammates or taking shots. Remember, you can never steer your team wrong by resorting to the fundamentals of the game.

Adjust to the striped shirts

Some referees call games extremely tight and whip out red and yellow cards with the speed of Las Vegas blackjack dealers. Other referees may seem like they've forgotten they have whistles dangling around their necks and allow lots of contact between players. Make note of how referees are calling the game, and make any necessary adjustments in your team's approach. For example, if the referee is allowing a little more contact than your team is accustomed to, you may want to have your players take a slightly more aggressive approach when attempting to steal the ball.

Remind them to use the entire field

With the pressure of the game and the added distractions around the field, players may suddenly become one-dimensional in their thinking. They may develop tunnel vision and disregard a lot of the field except what's directly in front of them. Moving the ball downfield with that type of limited view is tough. Utilizing the entire field is critical to the team's success. If your players are constantly trying to forge down the center of the field, that approach is going to be easily defended by the opposing team. Stress sending some passes out wide along the sideline to stretch out the defense and use the entire field. This technique may be pretty helpful in creating some open space to generate some more scoring chances for the kids. Perhaps all they've used are short passes, so you can suggest attempting some longer passes to different areas of the field to catch the other team off guard.

Winning and Losing Gracefully

No one enjoys losing, but in youth soccer, for every winner, there has to be a loser.

In the bigger picture, the ability to win and lose with grace and dignity transcends the soccer field. Years from now, when a youngster is vying for a job promotion, he can reflect on what he learned from you about how to handle himself in his wins and losses. He can be proud of his accomplishments without gloating while praising his opponents for doing their best. Or he can hold his head up high and congratulate an opponent on winning and a job well done.

Talk to your team about playing fairly, abiding by the rules, and winning and losing with grace. Just as you devote time teaching your players the proper way to deliver a header, talk to them about the appropriate way to congratulate a winning team and the right way to conduct themselves when they're celebrating a victory. Ask them how they feel when they win and lose, how they want to be treated when they lose, and how they should treat their opponents when they win. Opening the door to these types of discussions lays the foundation for some great behavior that will make you proud.

How to win gracefully

You've probably heard the saying "It's not whether you win or lose, but how you play the game." Those words are certainly appropriate in youth soccer. The game doesn't have room for showboating, rubbing goals in the other team's face, or extravagant victory celebrations. Teaching children how to win gracefully may be one of the most difficult chores you have as coach, especially considering all the poor examples of professional athletes that children constantly see on television.

First of all, players need to know that celebrating goals is okay. After all, the object of the game is to score more than the opponents, and high-fiving teammates when something works well is certainly acceptable. You just want to instill in your players that they refrain from excessive celebrations or exhibiting any kind of behavior that could be perceived by the other team as crossing the line.

In youth soccer, mismatches are simply unavoidable with such a wide range of kids' abilities. If your team is dominating an opponent that simply doesn't have the talent or skills to compete with you, do everything you can not to run up the score. Running up the score reflects terribly on you and your team and serves no purpose in the development of your players. If you find yourself in a lopsided game, consider some of the following approaches, which will keep your team's interest level high, allow players to work on a broad range of skills, and not humiliate the opposing team in the process:

- ✔ **Put the emphasis on passing.** Make your team complete a set number of passes in a row before taking a shot on net. This way, your players can work on another aspect of their game without piling on the goals.

- ✔ **Shift players around.** Move defenders up to midfielders, and vice versa, to challenge them on playing a different position. This shift helps develop all-around players, allows them to work on different aspects of their game, and keeps them fresh by providing new challenges for them.

- ✔ **Limit shots.** Allow your team to take shots only from outside the penalty-box area, which increases the difficulty of scoring chances. You can also make other subtle changes — for example, say that any time a player takes a shot on goal, it must be with his less-dominant foot, or limit the team's shots on goal to headers.

How to lose gracefully

Losing isn't the worst thing to happen — behaving like it's the worst thing to happen is far worse. Crying, throwing equipment, sulking, blaming the officials, swearing, and refusing to shake hands with the opposing team are all examples of behavior that simply can't be tolerated under any circumstance. (Jump to Chapter 19 to discover more about dealing with some of these types of behaviors that may arise throughout the season.)

Regardless of the outcome of the game, you must have your players line up and shake hands with the opposing team. Sure, this display of sportsmanship can be difficult for players who have just given their best effort and come up short. Teach your team respect for other players and for the game of soccer itself. Teach your players to acknowledge a well-played game by the other team and to keep things in perspective. Soccer is just a game, and next time they could be on the winning end. No matter how cocky the opposing team may be, your team can rise above that, offer a handshake or high-five, and congratulate the other players by saying "Good game." Be sincere. Sincerity in the face of adversity or a loss is a great attribute. You also want to instill in your players the habit of shaking the referee's hand after the game.

The Post-Game Talk

What you say to your team members — and how you say it — following a game has a tremendous impact on their enjoyment of the sport. A pat on the back, an encouraging word, and a genuine smile goes a long way. Don't allow the scoreboard to determine your demeanor during your post-game chat or to determine whether or not you're proud of your team. Kids want to know that you appreciate them for the effort they gave, not for the outcome of the game.

Accentuate the positive

Keep the focus on fun. The most obvious way to ensure that the focus is on fun is to ask the kids whether they had fun playing the game. Hopefully, you get a chorus of yeses. If so, poll the team to see what they enjoyed most about the game. If you have some kids who don't answer quite as enthusiastically as you hoped, find out immediately why they didn't have fun, and make whatever adjustments are necessary to ensure that they have smiles on their faces following next week's game. The reason can be something as simple as wanting to play defense rather than midfield so they don't do all the extra running. Or maybe a player got kicked in the shin or hit by the ball. Talk to your squad. Solicit feedback. Gauge feelings. Probe the players for answers. Find out anything you can do to make sure that their experience continues to be fun or returns to being fun the next game.

Allowing what the scoreboard says at the end of the game to dictate what you say to your team afterward is an easy trap to fall into. But that shouldn't be the case. Wins and losses don't define your team's effort, the improvements players make in certain areas of the game, or whether they had fun playing. A defensive lapse that resulted in giving up the game-winning goal stands out like a sore thumb, and it's an easy target to dwell on when discussing the game with your team. Youngsters who've been around the game a few years know when they make a mistake or misplay a ball; they don't need to be reminded of it afterward or feel responsible for the loss.

Your job, whether the team played its best game of the season or got clobbered, is to point out some of the good things that happened. Perhaps a child made a nice play to block a shot in the first half to save a goal or deny a good scoring opportunity. Maybe your midfielders' great communication produced a great scoring chance. Maybe the players made great improvements in the corner kicks they practiced all week. By keeping the comments positive, your body language buoyant, and your tone of voice upbeat, you send them home feeling good about themselves and eager to return to practice in the coming days to continue working on their game.

Recognizing good sportsmanship

Recognizing great shots, nifty passes, and stellar defensive plays is pretty easy, because those plays clearly stand out in your mind at the conclusion of the game. What's often a little trickier, but equally important, is recognizing displays of good sportsmanship that took place during the game. Pointing out these instances, and genuinely showing your admiration for them, reinforces to your team the importance of displaying good sportsmanship at all times.

Be on the lookout for good sportsmanship, and make mental notes when it occurs during the course of play. You may notice the way Jenny tells an opponent "Nice shot" after she scores a goal or how Bobby congratulates an opposing player for a nice defensive play he made. Even if you see a player on an opposing team demonstrate good sportsmanship, bring it up to your team. A comment like "That was a nice move on number five's part to help up Steve after he got called for tripping in the first half" sends a message to your squad that good sportsmanship is just as important as heading, trapping, and shooting. The more good sportsmanship is stressed, the more likely the entire team is to adopt this wonderful quality and become a model team. Remember, how your team behaves on the field is a reflection of your coaching, so don't neglect touching on this area of the game in your post-game chat.

Dealing with a tough loss

Participating in youth soccer teaches the players on your team many valuable life skills, but it can be a painful process. As the coach, you should understand that you'll have games when the team fails to perform up to your expectations. In some games, the team may turn in a splendid performance but fail to come away with the victory because the other team simply plays better. In other games, the ball may take a lucky bounce that results in the opposing team's notching the game-winning goal. That's soccer.

No coach is immune to seeing her squad commit mistakes following a flawless week of practice or failing to convert scoring chances that were easy goals earlier in the season. Remember, rarely do teams go through seasons undefeated, so setbacks are going to occur. In fact, losses and how the players deal with them are great character-builders for that game called life, so don't let the sting of a disappointing loss linger too long. Remember, what you say to your team — and how you say it — has a huge impact on the players' self-esteem and confidence and on how they handle winning and losing during the remainder of the season.

If you're coaching older or more advanced kids, losing a league championship game or getting knocked out of a tournament is a disappointing event in these kids' lives. Here are some tips to help them bounce back:

✔ **Allow them to be disappointed.** Kids pour their hearts and souls into sports, so it's only natural that they take losing hard, especially in a playoff or championship game. Don't tell them that winning and losing aren't important or that it was just a game. Those words are hollow and carry no weight with older children who have a love of soccer and a passion for competing and doing their best. Give them time to digest the setback and then help them move on.

✔ **Hand out the post-game snacks.** Don't fall into the trap of rewarding your team only when things go well. Sticking to the same routine, win or lose, helps reinforce what you've hopefully been preaching all along — that doing their best and being good sports are what playing sports is really all about.

✔ **Help them learn from the experience.** Every game can be used as a tool to help your team learn and grow in the sport. Take the time to discuss the game with the players at the next practice, when they'll be most receptive to feedback. Ask them what they thought they did well and what areas they struggled with, and work on those troublesome areas in practice to help them become more confident and comfortable.

Losses that occur in the league-championship game or season-ending tournament leave a big void because the team has no more games left to play and no more practices to attend. Sending the kids into the offseason on a positive note is important. Explain how proud you are of the effort they gave all season and how they improved in so many areas of the game. Share with them that if they continue to work hard and enthusiastically embrace the sport, good things will happen, and they're likely to return next season with renewed interest and excitement.

Offering words of encouragement to your child

Most volunteer youth soccer coaches have children on the team. The following are some conversation catalysts that will enhance the game-day experience for your child. Be sure to share these ideas with the other parents from your team.

✔ **Let's have fun out there today.** Yes, this phrase is pretty basic and tossed around all the time in youth sports, but it represents the true essence of youth soccer. Children who don't have fun every time they step on the soccer field are being robbed of wonderful opportunities. Every chance you get to instill the importance of having fun — and back it up with the way you coach and interact with your child and his teammates — goes a long way toward establishing children's love of soccer and participating in healthy physical activities in general.

✔ **I'm really enjoying coaching you this season.** This handful of words packs a powerful punch on a youngster's psyche. Positive reinforcement — thrown out in a general conversation — is a great confidence-booster and self-esteem-builder for a child. It also strengthens the bond you two share and opens the door for more fruitful conversations all season long.

✔ **Follow the rules.** The playing style of your team reflects on you and your coaching ability. Every time your team steps on the field, you want your child to abide by the rules. Teams that play by the rules will be known and respected throughout the league.

✔ **Support your teammates.** Reminding your child to offer encouraging words and support to his teammates helps strengthen team bonds. This reminder can be even more useful if a child on the team is really struggling with his confidence. With older kids, you can confide in your child that you want to see him offer some encouragement to the child who had a bad week of practice.

✔ **I really liked how you and the team . . .** Throwing out accolades for how the child and her teammates practiced and excelled in a specific area of the game aids in development. Saying something along the lines of "You guys really worked hard on defense this week and did a great job shutting down those 3-on-2 advantages," for example, fuels her confidence to perform well if that situation arises during today's game.

Chapter 8

Refining Your Approach at Midseason

In This Chapter

▶ Reviewing progress at midseason

▶ Going over individual and team goals

▶ Making adjustments at practice

---

*T*he soccer team that you welcomed to your first practice of the season is dramatically different from the one that you're working with as you reach the halfway point of your season. Your team has improved in different aspects of the game. Some players may be more proficient at passing; others emerge as pretty decent defenders; and some of the kids who didn't appear to have much in the way of basic coordination at the beginning of the season are demonstrating that they can now run and kick the ball without losing their balance or stumbling, which is worth applauding.

You have a pretty good sense of which players are catching on to skills and which players are struggling or lagging in certain areas of the game. You're more aware of who the quick learners are and who requires extra individual attention when introducing a new skill or concept.

How you adjust to the ever-changing dynamics of your team, from the drills you choose to run to the practices you orchestrate, makes a major difference in whether the fun, learning, and skill development continue or grind to a halt. Revising coaching strategies, adjusting practice plans, setting goals, and reviewing each player's progress with his or her parents are all essential mid-season responsibilities. In this chapter, we take a look at how you can accommodate the ever-changing needs of your players to help ensure that the season continues to be a rewarding and memorable one.

Conducting the Midseason Review

Reviewing the progress of the team at the midpoint of the season serves a number of valuable purposes. It can keep a season that's moving along smoothly on track, as well as rescue one that's showing signs of drifting off course. Think of the midseason review as the road map that helps you eliminate any wrong turns on the way to your desired destination.

Like adults, kids appreciate feedback — especially when they're performing something really well. Think about starting a job and receiving a review from your boss after a few months. She gives you feedback on areas that you're excelling in, sheds light on areas that you may not have been aware of, and offers suggestions on those areas in which you can make some additional strides. Sharing similar information with your players keeps them up to speed as the season moves along.

Recognizing improvement

Recognizing every youngster's improvements, no matter how big or small they may be, is essential in the skill-building process. What may seem minor and insignificant to you often looms large and impressive in your players' young eyes. Making a big deal out of the smallest things, particularly at the youngest age levels, can help forge a lifetime love of soccer and keep kids actively involved in the sport for years to come.

Closely monitor the progress of the children so that when they do reach new levels, you're there to deliver a high-five, a pat on the back, or enthusiastic praise for what you've just seen. It may be something as subtle as using their nondominant foot to deliver a pass during a 3-on-2 drill, or it may be something as obvious as heading the ball into the goal during a scrimmage. Your ability to recognize these improvements can be the difference in the season. You can fuel their desire to continue learning and striving to add new skills to their repertoire or disappoint them by sending the message that their efforts weren't worthy of your attention. Don't leave them wondering what's really in it for them to continue showing up at the field.

Don't rely on the scoreboard as your gauge for whether your team is improving. Wins and losses aren't a good barometer for measuring the development of your team. For example, even if your team surrenders a bunch of goals during a game, taking a closer look may actually reveal that the team turned in one of its better defensive outings of the season. Some unlikely bounces may have led to a couple of goals, or perhaps your goaltender let a couple of shots get by that he typically stops. If you take a closer look at the defensive area of the game that you worked on in practice during the week — such as getting back on defense quicker after a turnover is committed — and the players excelled in that area, you have to recognize that afterward. Think about it. These kids listened to your instructions during the week, responded to your wishes, and hustled back on defense, which is a great improvement. If you use the scoreboard as the determining factor in how well they played, the kids don't get the recognition they deserve.

Chatting with the parents

A preseason parents meeting (which we discuss the importance of in Chapter 4) opens the lines of communication before the first soccer ball is ever kicked. After you've laid that foundation, don't lose contact with the parents. Setting aside some time to talk to them about how their children are enjoying the season demonstrates how much you truly care. It's comforting to parents, many of whom may be involved with their children in an organized sport for the first time. Most important, communicating with parents gives you some valuable insight into what their children are thinking and feeling about playing soccer for you.

As your season approaches the halfway point, let parents know that you want to set aside a few moments in the upcoming week to speak to them regarding their children and their thoughts on how the season has gone so far. A good time to make this announcement is following a game, when most parents are likely to be on hand. Find out a good time to call them during the week for a brief conversation, or, if it's convenient, set aside some time after practice to chat in person.

Is Junior having fun?

One of the best ways to gauge whether the youngsters are enjoying the season is to solicit feedback from their parents. After all, parents can share with you whether their son is excited about games and is wearing his uniform around the house two hours before the game or whether he basically has to be coaxed to the car when it's time to leave for the field.

Use your time with the parents to get them actively involved in setting goals for their child's skill development (see the "Setting Goals for Your Players" section later in the chapter). Doing so helps steer the child down a successful path. Encourage the parents to be creative in working with their child. Goal setting should be a fun activity that allows a parent and child the chance to bond. For example, they can make colorful charts to put on the refrigerator or hang in their child's bedroom so they can monitor the child's progress in working toward whatever objectives you create for him.

What else can we do?

Sometimes, what you hear from the parents isn't encouraging, and as a coach, you have to be prepared to deal with that. If something isn't working as well as you had hoped with a youngster, and she's rapidly losing interest in playing soccer, you have to explore all the options at your disposal.

It's never too late to rescue a child's season. After speaking with the parents and uncovering a problem, don't allow it to linger. Act quickly, and determine the best course of action that addresses the situation and meets the child's needs. Her parents may be able to provide a solution for you, or meeting with the child may be all it takes to determine what needs to be done. All problems are correctable, so don't let a youngster's season be sabotaged without doing everything possible to help her.

The following are relatively common situations that arise, particularly with younger children, and a few suggestions that can help:

- ✔ **Lack of time at a desired position.** The solution may be something as simple as penciling in the youngster at a different position. Ideally, you've been rotating all the kids around so that they get the chance to play a variety of positions. Maybe at the halfway point of the season, a couple of kids haven't gotten the opportunity to play a position they've had their eyes on all season. That's easily correctable.

- ✔ **Embarrassment about something that happened during practice or a game.** Some memories tend to sting and reside in a child's consciousness long enough that they actually impact the youngster's enjoyment of the game. If a kicked ball struck a child in the face, or she tripped over the ball while racing in on a breakaway, she may still be upset. Any time you recognize that a child may have been embarrassed by something that happened on the field, exercise your best judgment and decide whether speaking with the child is warranted or would help ease any feelings of humiliation.

Sometimes for the child's sake, you're better off not saying anything about an embarrassing situation. The less attention you direct toward the event, the less likely the child may be to worry about it. If you do feel the need to soothe the child's bruised feelings, try sharing something humiliating that happened to you during the course of your youth-sports career. When children get a sense that everyone endures humorous moments and that these moments are part of participating in sports such as soccer, they're free to put the moment in the past and move forward.

- ✔ **Struggle with making friends.** Maybe the youngster was hoping she'd be placed on a team with some of her friends, but she doesn't know any of the other kids and has struggled to forge friendships. If that's the case, you may consider incorporating more team-bonding drills into your practices to allow the kids to get to know one another better. That helps the child in question and gives the players on your team the chance to form tighter bonds, which pays bigger dividends in the quality of their play.

✔ **Too much contact.** Youngsters often enroll in a sport like soccer without realizing that so much contact is involved. After a few games of getting kicked in the shins or taking the occasional tumble when they're tripped by an opposing player, the game suddenly isn't quite as much fun as they thought it would be. Unfortunately, if that's the primary culprit for their antisoccer feelings, you can't do a whole lot to help. No positions on the field reduce a child's chances of being in contact with opposing players.

Although you never want to encourage a child to quit a sport, in cases like this one, speak with the parents; share your concern that you don't want to make the child any more miserable than she already is; and perhaps suggest some other sports that you think would best suit the child if you feel comfortable making those types of recommendations.

Setting Goals for Your Players

Goal setting is as popular a coaching tool as motivational halftime talks — and it can be one of the most effective means for getting the most out of your players when employed correctly. As we explain in Chapter 5, choosing goals for each of your players to strive for builds confidence; promotes self-esteem; and, over the course of a season, enhances performance. Goals also help keep kids focused and interested and provide a real sense of accomplishment when they're able to reach those goals.

Establish personal-improvement goals for each player that tie into trying to win the game but that aren't strictly dependent on achieving wins. Individual goals that each child can realistically reach allow the players to have much more control over their success. Winning games doesn't always correlate with which team played the best. Teaching your young athletes the ability to compare their current performances with their performances from earlier in the season — instead of evaluating their performances based on which team won the game — gives them a true sense of their progress.

For goal setting to be at its most effective, you need a good handle on the skills and abilities of your players. After half a season of practices and games, you should be ready to sit down with each of the players and map out a plan for the remainder of the season.

If you're coaching a team of 6-year-olds in a beginning soccer program, simply selecting basic goals for each youngster to work on that benefit the entire team, such as making accurate passes to teammates, is sufficient. But with older and more advanced players, you want to choose specific goals for them to strive for that are vastly different from their teammates'.

To make your goal setting successful, keep these points in mind:

- ✔ **Encourage practice:** Encourage players to practice skills at home with their parents. Just a few minutes in the backyard a couple of times a week can pay big dividends in a child's development. Don't force it or make practicing seem like dreaded homework; gently encourage five minutes of passing the ball back and forth with a parent, for example.

- ✔ **Stay balanced:** Come up with goals that are neither too difficult for the youngster to achieve nor so easy that the child meets them right away and has no further challenges.

- ✔ **Be realistic:** Set goals that work within the framework of the team setting. A goal of scoring 10 goals during the season is unrealistic for several reasons: The outcome is largely out of the child's control, and the youngster may become so consumed by reaching the 10-goal plateau that she begins taking shots that aren't beneficial to the team and stops passing the ball to her teammates.

- ✔ **Use short-term goals:** The younger the child, the shorter the attention span, so working with a series of short-term goals leads to greater improvements and increased confidence in a quicker period of time.

- ✔ **Create backup goals:** Create several goal levels so that if the player doesn't reach the top goal but manages to reach the second out of the list of five, she still gains a sense of accomplishment. Having just one goal to strive for turns it into an all-or-nothing proposition that risks leaving the youngster disappointed in her performance.

- ✔ **Get player feedback:** The process is more effective if you have a short discussion with each of your players to gain some insight into which areas of the game each wants to improve on. For example, a youngster may have her heart set on learning how to deliver a header, but if you choose trapping the ball with her chest as the goal, you're probably not getting quite as enthusiastic an effort from her. Helping players select realistic goals that they have an interest in achieving helps drive their development.

- ✔ **Applaud progress and effort:** Regardless of the outcome of the game, take the time to applaud and acknowledge players who are reaching their individual goals. For example, if one of the goals for a youngster on your team is to become comfortable taking shots on goal with his less-dominant foot, and during the course of the game a situation called for him to use that foot, and he got off a quality shot, recognize him for that. Failing to acknowledge that type of progress, which can be easy to overlook if your team happens to get beat 8-0 that day, sends the message that goal setting and working to achieve and improve performances really aren't that important to you after all. And even if the child fails to reach the primary goal you set, pile on the praise for his effort and hard work.

✔ **Factor in injury:** If a youngster is returning from an injury, take that into account before setting goals for that individual. Even if the youngster is quite talented, you may have to lower the goals until she has a few practices and games under her belt and is back up to normal speed. At that time, you can revisit and adjust the goals to coincide with the health of the player.

Setting team goals may seem like a good idea, but these goals can lead to all sorts of problems. For example, if one of your team goals is to win four of your last five games of the season, and the team drops two games in a row, suddenly the goal is unreachable with three games left to play. Chances are the team played two of its best games of the season, yet your players are disappointed in their performance because they lost. Team goals represent the proverbial double-edged sword. When the team is winning and meeting goals, confidence is soaring and everyone is pleased with the outcome. But when games don't end in victories, the team becomes blanketed in disappointment and self-doubt.

Revising Your Practice Plan

As a youth soccer coach, nothing brings a smile to your face quicker than seeing your players learning, developing, and progressing. After all, that means the drills you choose are making a difference in the skill development of your players, the practice plans you put together are producing the desired results, and the instruction and feedback you dispense are really sinking in with the youngsters. Yet, you can't be satisfied with these improvements. You have to push the players to excel and get even better during the remaining time you have them under your care.

Conversely, because coaching soccer can be such tricky business, the team may not be performing as well as you had hoped or may be struggling to master a particular skill. To ensure that feelings of frustration don't wash over the team and sink the season in disappointment, you want to make alterations in your practice plan to fend off these problems. Begin by taking a close look at your drills. Perhaps they're too difficult or aren't really tailored to the skill you want to focus on. Second, watch the players' faces. Are they smiling and energetic? If not, they probably aren't learning a whole lot. Figure out ways to inject more fun into the drills, and increase the tempo of your practices, which can spark more enthusiasm and lead to more excitement and learning.

For youngsters to gain the most from their participation with you, you have to continually challenge yourself to devise drills that bring out the best in your players and challenge them to continue their development in the sport. You can't simply rely on using the same core drills all season long, because that brings learning and development to a halt and buries fun in the process. The need to alter your approach to practices and games is one of the best problems that you can have as a youth soccer coach!

Making changes to your practice plans as you maneuver through the season isn't as difficult as you may think. Although incorporating several new drills into your practices is always a good idea, you can also rely on tweaking basic drills that you've been using the first few weeks of the season. Simply make some minor adjustments to increase the difficulty level and meet the needs of your developing players. For example, even the most basic drill that many coaches run, like the 2-on-1 drill, can be easily revamped to incorporate a new challenge for your players. For instance:

✔ Have the kids use only their nondominant feet during the drill to help challenge them and promote that area of their game.

✔ For kids who are more fully developed, require that the shots on goal be headers. This requirement forces the passer to deliver a chip pass into the air that allows her partner to make contact with his head.

Part III
Beginning and Intermediate Soccer

The 5th Wave   By Rich Tennant

For those of you coming directly from ballet class, I'd like you to practice dribbling the ball _without_ a jeté this time.

In this part . . .

A coach who doesn't have the ability to teach fundamental techniques and provide good drills to share with his team is about as effective as a repairman who owns no tools. In the following chapters, we serve up an array of offensive and defensive techniques, skills, and drills that promote learning and leave the kids begging for more.

Chapter 9

Teaching the Fundamentals

*O*ne of the most important characteristics of being a good soccer coach is being able to teach. Even if you're knowledgeable in the sport, played it growing up, or enjoyed a high level of success playing competitively in high school or college, you can't help your players unless you can pass along information that helps them learn and develop skills.

Being a top-quality soccer coach means presenting information correctly and clearly while providing useful and positive feedback. It means acknowledging and applauding skills performed properly and recognizing when players use improper mechanics, as well as being able to correct them. It also means employing a coaching style that promotes learning, rewards effort, stresses safety, and focuses on fun.

In this chapter, we start from square one, with the basic soccer skills that every player needs to acquire and work on. These skills can start out very simply and progress to more advanced stages. Here, we go over the first steps of teaching elementary soccer skills, including shooting, ball handling, passing, receiving, heading, goaltending, and defending. We discuss these skills largely in the context of teaching the youngest of budding soccer stars, but the fundamentals are applicable to players of any age.

Focusing on the First-Timers

When children are learning how to read, you don't throw *The Grapes of Wrath* or *Moby Dick* at them. You don't even mention nouns, verbs, and adjectives. You start them out with basic sounds and words, slowly work up to simple sentences, and build from there. If you think about it, you should apply the same approach to coaching soccer.

Soccer is a complex sport that requires a broad range of skills, and your job is helping your players develop them. But that doesn't mean you have to churn out an army of miniature supertalents who are destined to earn college soccer scholarships. When children have never played the sport before, you need to stick to the basics, regardless of their age. This season may be their introduction to soccer, and overwhelming them with long-winded instructions, complex drills, and intricate plays isn't the route to helping them foster an interest in or love of the sport.

Be realistic: You're going to be with your team only a couple of hours a week. Typically, with younger children, you have one practice and one game each week. So if you can provide them a strong foundation on a few basic skills — and put a smile on their faces while doing so — you deserve a pat on the back for a job well done. And when you see the kids returning to play in the league next season or, better, when they request to play on your team again, you'll know you truly made a difference in their lives.

Soccer has a language all its own, and using lingo and terminology that confuses the kids is just silly. Even seemingly simple terms like *shooting* and *ball handling* can be perplexing to a child who hasn't learned yet that he can't touch the ball with his hands. (For more on soccer basics, see Chapter 3.)

Use only phrases or terms that you've taken the time to clearly explain and that you confidently can say all the kids on the team have a firm grasp of. Clear instructions in terms everyone understands make your practices more effective and enjoyable.

Shooting: Teaching the Instep Kick

Children who are beginning in the sport need to be introduced to the basic element of correctly kicking a soccer ball at a target. Doing so allows them to achieve success and, in the process, build confidence. And you won't find a better target than an empty net.

Start the team off with no goalies, no defenders, and no pressure: Just line the players up, and have them kick the stationary ball into the empty net. As children learn and gain confidence in performing this skill, make slight alterations to increase the difficulty and provide challenges to enhance their development. The next logical step is adding motion to the drill. You can accomplish this motion in a few ways:

- Roll the ball to players, and have them kick it toward the goal to help them get used to dealing with a moving ball
- Have the players run toward a stationary ball and kick it.

After youngsters gain proficiency in these areas of the game, you can bump up the challenge even further by adding a defender or goalie to the drill (for more information on adding these wrinkles, see Chapter 14).

Children have a natural tendency to kick the soccer ball with their toes, but that isn't the most effective area of the foot to use. Teaching youngsters to use their *instep* (the area on top of the foot where the shoelaces are located) is much more beneficial. Kicking the ball more accurately and longer distances is easier with that area of the foot than it is with the toes. (They can also use the instep — and the inside of the foot — for delivering passes, which we discuss later in this chapter.) Check out Figure 9-1 for correct and incorrect contact points when performing the instep kick.

Before teaching children the art of the instep kick, let them know where their instep is located. Most youngsters can quickly point out where their sole and inside and outside of the foot are, but the instep may be new to them.

Figure 9-1: Show your players the right way to kick a soccer ball.

Right   Wrong

To teach the instep kick (which you can see in Figure 9-2), have the player:

1. **Pick out a target.**

   Children need to look up from the ball to pick out their target. The target should be something large, such as the goal. Or it can be a teammate stationed a short distance away.

2. **Look back at the ball.**

   It's the ol' Keep Your Eye on the Ball rule. After locating their target, beginners need to look back at the ball when they're ready to deliver the kick. If they're not looking at the ball, they're probably not going to be able to make an accurate kick.

3. **Plant the nonkicking foot alongside the ball, pointed toward the target.**

Figure 9-2:
A child lines
up, takes
his shot,
and follows
through on
his instep
kick.

One of the most important factors in determining the success of a kick is the placement of the supportive, or nonkicking, foot. Youngsters generate greater ball velocity when they approach kicking the ball at an angle (as you can see in Figure 9-2a) because of the increased hip rotation. In other words, the ball goes faster and harder when you plant your foot alongside the ball (see Figure 9-2b) and kick. Kids who plant their foot directly behind the ball are more likely to kick with their toes.

4. **Make contact with the instep — not the toes.**

   Kicking the ball with the toes reduces the shot's accuracy. When kids approach the ball at an angle and kick with their instep (see Figures 9-1 and 9-2), their shots have just as much speed and go where they aimed.

5. **Kick the middle of the ball.**

   Kicks that miss the center of the ball either rise or roll along the ground. As children progress, you can teach them how to work the ball in various ways, but mastering the ability to connect with the center of the ball (see Figure 9-2c) is vital before venturing on to other kicking skills.

6. **Follow through toward the target.**

   Many youngsters have a habit of stopping their foot as soon as it makes contact with the ball, which results in a big loss of power. Teach them to kick through the ball, finishing with their leg pointing at the target, to achieve maximum force on each shot (see Figure 9-2d).

Youngsters, in their excitement to score a goal, understandably forget some of the basic kicking fundamentals from time to time. When that happens, they often don't make direct contact with the ball. If their plant foot is too far away from the ball when they go through the kicking motion, they're going to contact only the top half of the ball, which results in a shot that dribbles along the ground. Adjust their spacing so that their plant foot is nearer the ball, and they may see a big difference in both the power and accuracy of their shots.

Ball Handling

Ball control, ball control, ball control. It's the key to success in soccer. The more often your team has possession of the ball, the greater the likelihood that good things are going to happen. Maintaining possession of the ball means fewer scoring opportunities for the opposing team and additional offensive chances for your team, and that's the name of the game.

Dribbling do's and don'ts

Ball handling, often referred to as *dribbling,* consists of moving and maintaining possession of the ball. It's needed to move the ball down the field to create scoring opportunities, as well as to keep the ball away from the opposing team while you're backed up in the shadows of your own goal.

Dribbling is one of those skills that can be a little tricky to teach children, who typically are more interested in kicking the ball as hard as they can. To get them started, have them walk while bumping the ball forward with their instep, keeping it on the ground roughly a foot ahead of them as they go. After they're comfortable with this skill, introduce other surfaces of the foot, like the inside and outside of the foot, that can be used for dribbling too.

When they're comfortable doing this drill, encourage them to walk as quickly as they can while controlling the ball. Eventually, they progress to jogging and then running at full speed with the ball. Ultimately, your goal is to have your players become comfortable enough that they can move with the ball without having to constantly look down to see where it is (see Figure 9-3).

Some coaching pointers to keep in mind:

- ✔ The player's head should be up at all times to scan the field for open teammates and protect the ball from approaching defenders.

- ✔ To help maintain possession of the ball, the closer an opposing player is, the closer the offensive player should keep the ball to her body.

- ✔ Players should never run faster than the ball can be controlled.

Figure 9-3:
Dribble with the head up, scanning the field, not looking down at the ball.

Right   Wrong

Deciphering dribbling problems

You may have players who are great during practice at dribbling the ball, but when game time arrives, they turn into different players. The nervousness of playing in front of family and friends or having unfamiliar kids charging at them trying to swipe the ball are common culprits behind this change.

The most common dribbling problem that kids have is a tendency to stare down at the ball. During practice, have the kids work on controlling the ball without glancing down at it. They can walk alongside you and carry on a conversation without looking at the ball. Or get parents involved in the practice, and have them walk next to their children to see whether the kids can look at them the entire time they're working their way down the field.

Passing

Passing the ball is often about as much fun as homework and early bedtimes. After all, the attention — and cheers — are usually piled on the players who score rather than the ones who deliver the pass that results in the goal. So getting kids to understand that assists are just as important as goals takes a concentrated effort on your part. The effort, however, is worthwhile when you see your team working as a cohesive unit.

Delivering two types of passes

The inside-of-the-foot *push pass* is the most commonly used technique for delivering a ball to a teammate, particularly for beginning soccer players. It's termed a push pass because players use a long follow-through as they push the ball along the ground toward their target (see Figure 9-4).

In order to deliver a push pass:

1. **The ball should be directly between the player and her intended target.**

2. **The player's nonkicking, or plant, foot (a right-hander's plant foot is her left foot) should be approximately 3–6 inches from the ball and pointing toward the target.**

   The planted leg should be slightly bent.

3. **The kicking leg should be slightly bent, and the player should make a short backswing.**

4. **The child makes contact with the center of the ball below her ankle.**

   The player's ankle should be locked and her toe pointed up as she makes contact in the middle of the ball with the inside of the foot at the arch. While making contact with the ball, the youngster raises her knee. This technique helps deliver topspin on the ball, which gives it added pace and moves it along.

5. **The player follows through, with her leg toward the target.**

   The inside of the foot ends up facing the intended target of the pass.

As players progress, they can use their instep to make longer passes that travel greater distances through the air. These longer passes are lofted in the air so that defenders between the player with the ball and the intended recipient of the pass are unable to make a play on the ball.

Figure 9-4:
A short push pass using the inside of the foot.

A successful long pass requires the following steps:

1. **The child plants the nonkicking foot slightly behind and to the side of the ball (see Figure 9-5).**

2. **The kicking foot contacts the bottom half of the ball — kicking underneath the ball lifts it off the ground.**

   The toes of the kicking foot are pointed down, and contact with the ball is made with the shoelaces.

Figure 9-5:
For longer passes, the youngster kicks the ball with her instep.

Diagnosing what went wrong

Becoming an accurate passer takes time and lots of practice. Early in children's development, they experience their share of frustration when their passes don't hit the intended targets. Here are some common problems:

- ✔ **The ball misses to the left or right of the target:** Youngsters often stop their kicks as soon as they make contact with the ball, which cripples the accuracy of their passes. Have the children concentrate on following through at their targets, and their passes will start finding their marks with much more regularity. A useful explanation that children relate to is telling them their belly button should be pointing toward their target.

- ✔ **The kids have trouble keeping the ball on the ground with push passes:** If a player's plant foot is too close to the ball, the ball pops up in the air. Have the players move their plant feet back a few inches, which provides greater control and accuracy.

Receiving

Naturally, goal scorers must be good at kicking. They also must be exceptional at receiving passes. Otherwise, their goal-scoring opportunities are greatly diminished. Not only is pass receiving integral for producing offensive opportunities, but it's also vital to escaping defensive pressure when your team is backed up in front of its own net.

Just about every part of the body can be used when receiving — everything, in fact, except the hands. The essence of receiving is gaining control of the ball — whether it's bouncing, rolling, or airborne — and keeping it near the body by using the feet, the thighs, or the chest.

Cushioning at impact

The art of receiving involves cushioning the soccer ball as it makes contact with the player's body. An effective approach for introducing children to this concept is to have them visualize a water balloon or egg coming at them that they must keep from breaking.

Foot
When using the foot to trap an incoming ball, a player must

1. **Position himself in front of the incoming ball.**

2. **Extend his leg and foot out before the ball arrives.**

The pass receiver's foot should be about 4 inches off the ground, or about halfway up the ball, when it gets to him (see Figure 9-6).

3. **Pull his leg back as the ball makes contact with his foot to help soften or cushion the ball to keep it in his possession.**

The pass should be controlled with the side of the foot, toward the ankle (see Figure 9-6). If the ball takes an unexpected hop, the leg helps control the pass, because the ball is being played closer to the ankle.

The foot should be relaxed, which helps control the pass, particularly when it comes at the player quickly.

Figure 9-6: Receiving a pass with your foot is an important step in the game of soccer.

Although you can use all parts of the foot for receiving, keep the focus on the inside of the foot for younger players, because it's the easiest to learn.

Thigh

The thigh is an extremely effective area of the body to use for receiving because of the large size of the contact area. A player using his thigh must

1. **Be positioned in front of the incoming ball.**

2. **Stand on one foot.**

Raise the other knee and thigh to meet the ball (see Figure 9-7).

3. **Cushion the impact as the ball makes contact with the thigh by lowering his knee until the ball drops down to his feet.**

If the child's thigh isn't parallel to the ground, or the ball isn't received halfway between the knee and the hip, the ball will probably bounce out of control.

Figure 9-7:
Here, we show the right and wrong way to receive a ball with the thigh.

Right   Wrong

Chest

The chest is typically the most difficult area of the body to teach youngsters to receive with, because it brings their hands into the picture, which often results in illegal touching. To successfully trap the ball with their chest, players must

1. **Be in front of, and square to, the approaching ball.**

2. **Puff out their chests when meeting the ball.**

3. **Quickly pull the ball back as it contacts the chest to cushion the impact and allow the ball to fall to their feet.**

   Arching the back too much usually causes the ball to bounce over a shoulder and is difficult to control. See Figure 9-8 for the right and wrong ways to receive a ball with the chest.

Troubleshooting receiving

Your players may have the following problems when receiving the ball:

✔ **The ball bounces off the player's body and can't be controlled:** In this case, the foot, leg, or thigh is too firm on contact. The ball caroming out of control is the most common problem associated with receiving for a youngster. When using her foot to trap, the ball ricochets off her legs if she holds them out stiffly. The leg should be bent and relaxed, and pulled back toward the body as soon as the player makes contact. The same goes for the thigh. The longer a player can keep the ball in contact with her thigh, the more control she's going to have.

Figure 9-8:
Receiving
the ball with
the chest is
tricky,
because
kids may be
tempted to
use their
hands.

Right   Wrong

✔ **The player loses balance when trapping with the chest:** The biggest
problem associated with receiving with the chest is that a youngster can
easily become off balance; thus, the ball strikes his chest and bounces
out of his control. Make sure he holds his arms out to the side, which
improves his balance and enables him to suck in his chest at contact to
ensure greater control.

✔ **The ball bounces over the player's foot:** Check the height of the player's
receiving foot. If it's not a few inches off the ground, the ball tends to
bounce right over the youngster's foot. Also, if she's receiving the ball
with the front of her foot instead of in the center of the foot with the arch,
that contributes to control problems as well.

✔ **The player isn't getting to the pass:** The player isn't reacting to the ball
quickly enough. As soon as a player delivers a pass, the youngster must
begin running in order to beat out the defender.

Heading

On the list of skills you're teaching your team this season, heading ranks at
the bottom as far as importance goes. That's simply because children at the
youngest age levels aren't able to get the ball airborne, so the opportunity to
head a ball doesn't come into play. Introduce them to the skill so they're
aware that the head can be used, and as they gain experience and advance
with the sport, it gradually becomes a part of the game for them.

Using your noggin

Use your head when introducing this aspect of the game to your players, because following proper technique at all times is extremely important when teaching this skill. As we talk about in Chapter 2, the safety of your players should always be a top priority. Be aware of the type of ball you use in your league. If the league you're coaching in requires the kids to play with a regulation soccer ball rather than one whose size and weight is modified for younger children, you don't want to use that when introducing children to this skill. A heavy ball can injure a child's still-developing head and neck.

The best way to introduce children to heading is to use a beach ball. It's fun for the kids, but more important, they get the proper technique down before they attempt heading with a real soccer ball. In order to execute a header:

1. **The player must keep his eye on the incoming ball at all times and his mouth closed.**

2. **His feet should be shoulder width apart, and his knees flexed.**

3. **As the ball makes contact with his head, he stiffens his neck and chest muscles while driving the ball toward the target.**

When introducing this skill with a soccer ball, start by holding the ball in the palm of your hand, and have players step forward and strike the ball with their heads. This helps curb some of their fears. Check out Figure 9-9 for the proper part of the head with which the child should make contact.

Figure 9-9:
Heading a ball can be scary; make sure your players do it the right way.

Right

Wrong

Correcting heading errors

It's common for youngsters to struggle when learning the proper heading techniques, which can be tricky to master:

- ✔ **The child's head isn't making solid contact with the ball:** Younger and inexperienced children often have a habit of closing their eyes right before contact with the ball. Work with them on keeping their eyes glued to the ball.

- ✔ **The ball isn't going toward its intended target:** If the child's neck muscles aren't tight at impact, the ball is simply going to bounce off her head. Tightening neck muscles, and following through by pointing the head at the target, will get those headers going in the right direction.

Goalkeeping

Goalies are the only players who are allowed to use their hands to touch the ball in the field of play (as we discuss in Chapter 3). Thus, their position requires a wide range of skills that are different from anything else you're teaching the rest of the team. They must be able to jump in the air and make difficult saves with their arms outstretched, and dive on the ground for balls while opposing players swarm around them, trying to put the ball in the net.

Making stops

First and foremost, when making a play on the ball, a goalie must learn to tightly secure the ball and pull it closely into her body (as shown in Figure 9-10). After a shot has been stopped, your team doesn't want to give up another scoring opportunity simply because the goalie failed to protect the ball that was in her grasp.

Figure 9-10:
Securing a
loose ball on
the ground.

Young goalies have small hands, and although the ball the league is using hopefully is the appropriate size for the age range you're coaching (see Chapter 4), it can still be awkward for youngsters to gain total control over. This fact is particularly true when opposing players are bearing down on them, and they have a huge net that their team is counting on them to protect.

For youngsters getting their first taste of this complex position, learning the fundamentals is imperative for gaining any type of enjoyment from playing the position, as well as having some success along the way. First, they must assume the ready position (see Figure 9-11a) when facing any type of shot. Being in proper position requires the following:

- ✔ The goalie's shoulders should be square to the ball, with his feet shoulder width apart.

- ✔ His head and upper body should be erect, while his knees should be slightly flexed.

- ✔ His hands should be above waist level, with his palms forward and his fingers pointing upward; and his eyes should be focused on the ball.

When goalies are making saves on shots that are chest high or above their heads, their hands should be in a diamond position (see Figure 9-11b), with their fingers spread and their thumbs almost touching.

Figure 9-11:
The ready position and proper hand position for handling shots.

a   b

When dealing with a loose ball, teach children to cuddle the ball the same way they would protect a puppy in a rainstorm. By surrounding the ball with his body, it's safely secured, and the child also reduces the risk of suffering injuries to his fingers or hands by spike-wearing opponents looking to notch a goal. (See Figure 9-12 for the right and wrong ways to gather the ball.)

Right

Figure 9-12: A goalkeeper should bend his arms and gather the ball gently, while keeping his knees together.

Right   Wrong

When making a play on a shot in the air, above her head, she extends her arms, keeping her elbows slightly flexed, and catches the ball with her fingertips. She withdraws her arms to cushion the impact of the ball and secures it to her chest. (Check out Figure 9-13 to see how a goalie should play a shot in the air.) Also, encourage the goalie to jump up with one knee pulled up in front of her. This move not only protects the goalie from opponents charging toward the net, but also discourages them from even trying to do so.

Correcting goaltending errors

When a midfielder makes a mistake during a game, it usually results in her team losing possession of the ball. When a goalie makes a miscue, the result is a lot more obvious: a goal for the opposing team. Although goaltending is simply one facet of the game, a lot of pressure accompanies the position. Teaching sound fundamentals can go a long way toward reducing the burden on your young goalie.

Right

Figure 9-13: These goalies demonstrate the right and wrong ways to play a ball in the air.

Right   Wrong

The following are some things you may want to remind your goalie of:

- **Keeping their eye on the ball:** You'll notice a lot of traffic in front of the net, and goaltenders can easily get caught up in the excitement of watching all the commotion going on. Work with your goalie to focus on following the path of the ball at all times and being in the proper position to make a play on the shot.

- **Staying focused:** Staying focused on the game can be extremely difficult for a youngster, particularly if his team is dominating offensively and is spending the majority of the game at the other end of the field. Consequently, when he's finally called upon to make a save, his concentration isn't at its peak. Lack of concentration is the perpetrator of many goaltending miscues.

Work with your goalies to follow the ball all game long. Encourage them to watch the ball closely when the action is at the other end of the field, and focus on how they would position themselves to make stops based on where their own team is attacking with the ball. Even though they aren't being called upon to make saves at that particular moment, they can still improve their own play by visualizing proper positioning based upon where the shots are coming from. You can also keep them actively involved in the game by having them constantly communicate with their teammates about what's happening on the field.

Defending

For children, learning how to play defense certainly isn't as appealing as shooting or some of the other skills that we cover in this chapter. Nonetheless, it's a significant aspect of the game, especially considering that your team is required to play defense in roughly half of every game.

Pursuit: Preventing bad things from happening

One of the basic tenets of good defensive play revolves around pursuit. If defenders don't pursue the player with the ball, bad things are generally the result, specifically in the form of offensive pressure, good scoring chances, and a scoreboard full of goals. Often in youth soccer, a player dribbling the ball is treated like he has chicken pox — everyone stays away from him. This distance allows the player an obstacle-free run down the field and leaves you wondering what happened to all the good defensive work that your team put in during practice the past week.

Your defense begins to take shape when your team grabs onto the concept that every time the opponent takes possession of the ball, the nearest player aggressively goes over to mark that youngster. Disrupting the opponent from the outset not only makes beginning its attack that much more difficult for the team, but also forces the team to handle the ball under intense pressure and make an additional pass or two to get started. As you know by now, the more times you force a team to execute a pass or dribble with a defender in its face, the more likely a turnover is to occur, giving your squad the chance to gain possession of the ball and start an attack of its own.

Making a steal

Playing defense is all about reading and reacting. Because the youngsters on your squad have little, if any, playing experience, that means introducing them to an entirely new concept. Initially, start a child off playing 1-on-1 against another youngster who has a ball, much like a basketball coach would do, with one player dribbling a basketball and the other trying to swipe it.

In soccer, in order for the defensive player to be successful, she must keep herself between the opponent and the goal. When she sees an opening and makes a play on the ball, that's called tackling. As we discuss in Chapter 3, it's a term that doesn't have the same meaning as it does in football. Tackling involves the defender stealing the ball from the player without committing a penalty. Effective tackling relies on timing.

Defenders should step in when the attacker provides an opening and go for the ball rather than the opponent. When tackling, players shouldn't lunge at the ball, because good dribblers will easily maneuver around the player and create an advantage for his team. Proper tackling requires planting the non-kicking leg near the ball and using the other leg to knock the ball away. When using the *poke tackle,* which works best when approaching an opponent from the side or slightly behind, the player reaches in with his leg, extends his foot, and pokes the ball away with his toes.

Correcting defensive miscues

Stopping or slowing an opposing player's dribble can pose several challenges for defenders:

- ✔ **Players are running by them with the ball:** This miscue is usually the result of a defensive player not keeping his eye on the ball. Offensive players who use head and body fakes can get a defender leaning in the wrong direction and then scoot past him with the ball. Defensive players who focus on the ball and not the player are more likely to be in proper position to steal the ball or force the player to attempt a pass.

✔ **They lack focus:** A child's mind tends to wander when her team loses control of the ball, and she finds herself suddenly stuck in defensive mode. Simple reminders and encouraging words that she needs to steal the ball back in order to generate some shots on goal may help refocus her attention and enthusiasm for playing defense.

Helping Kids Who Just Don't Get It

You may well be the best coach in your league. Your practices are more fun for the kids than a trip to the local toy store. Your players are learning and progressing — well, except for a couple of youngsters who just aren't quite getting it. They haven't grasped the fundamentals of kicking a soccer ball yet. For weeks, their timing on their passes has been off. They keep repeating the same basic mistakes that the rest of the team hasn't made since the start of the season. So now what?

Now the real challenge of coaching soccer comes in. All kids don't progress at the same rate. Some pick up what you say in minutes and follow your instructions perfectly. Others require a couple of practice sessions before everything sinks in and they perform skills exactly like you intended. And some kids struggle mightily every step of the way.

Making a difference

Take a closer look at how you coach these kids who are struggling, and see what adjustments you can make in your methods to steer them back on the right track. Are you spending too much time talking? Nearly all children have short attention spans of varying degrees. If what you say during the course of your practice sessions, or how you say it, doesn't interest them, the simple fact is that their minds wander. Distractions abound in an outdoor sport like soccer. A cricket in the grass, a noisy truck down the street, or a big weed in the field are just some of the things that may lure a child's attention away from what you're trying to teach her.

Keep your instructions simple, and give the players lots of repetitions. Children learn and improve by performing the skill, not by listening to you talk about the skill. Increase the number of repetitions these kids are getting during practice, and see whether that generates significant improvement.

Are the kids who struggle happy with the positions they're playing? Maybe the child had his heart set on being the goalie, and when you told him he was going to be a midfielder, his interest in learning and playing quickly fizzled. Give all the kids a chance to play all the positions. Yes, it can be difficult to pull off, considering that you may have more than a dozen youngsters on your team. Giving them this complete introduction to the sport keeps their interest and energy levels high. So talk with the child who's struggling. Maybe the chance to wear the cool goalie gloves and protect his team's net will jump-start his enthusiasm.

Don't make a spectacle out of a child who's struggling. Children, especially as they get older, know how their skills match up to those of the rest of the team. The last thing they need is for the coach to make their deficiencies stand out even more during practice by being singled out for extra work on the side-lines. If a child just hasn't been able to master delivering passes, you may be tempted to work 1-on-1 with her on that skill while the rest of the team per-forms another drill at the other end of the field. Although initially, you think you're helping by giving the child extra attention and practice, the attention is really going to embarrass her and make her feel even worse about her lack of development in this area of the game.

Help a struggling child by devising a drill in which a designated passer gets a 2-on-1 started. When you take this approach, the youngster who's having some difficulty passing is getting a high number of repetitions in an area of the game that he needs help on, he's working with his team rather than being isolated from it, and your practice time isn't being compromised by one player's struggles because everyone is actively involved in the drill.

Whatever the situation, never allow the tone of your voice to reveal frustra-tion or disappointment. The same goes for your body language. Be calm, patient, and understanding as you work with these youngsters. Don't neglect them or give up on them just because they haven't been able to contribute as much during games as most of your other players. Stick by these kids, encourage them, and applaud their efforts every step of the way. They need you. Who knows? Years from now, when they're still actively involved in the sport, they may look back and realize that you're the reason they still strap on shin guards every summer.

Is the child simply mismatched for soccer? Could another sport be more suit-able for his interests and abilities? Some children simply aren't attracted to contact sports like soccer. Maybe they're tired of being kicked in the shins or aren't getting any enjoyment out of all the running that's required during the course of a game. If the child's parents seek your advice about whether he should continue with soccer, be honest and helpful. Suggest specific sports that have the potential to provide their child the opportunity to enjoy a fun and rewarding athletic experience.

Recognizing physical problems

A child's development can be hampered because of issues that are out of your control. Yet if you spot some of the warning signs, you may be able to make a difference. Be on the lookout for the following:

- ✔ **Attention deficit hyperactivity disorder:** A child's lack of focus may be the result of attention deficit hyperactivity disorder. According to the National Attention Deficit Disorder Association, the most common characteristics of a child with ADHD are distractibility and poor sustained attention to tasks, impaired impulse control and delay of gratification, and excessive activity and physical restlessness. If you think someone on your team may be displaying signs of ADHD, talk to the player's parents about your concerns.

- ✔ **Vision problem:** A child's struggles with kicking a soccer ball properly or his inability to deliver an accurate pass to a teammate may be due to a vision problem that can be easily corrected. If you sense this problem, mention it to the child's parents. Perhaps a trip to the eye doctor is all this child needs to pull everything in focus and turn his season around.

As we cover in Chapter 4, one of the most important reasons to hold a preseason parents meeting is so you can learn about any children on your team who have special needs that you need to be aware of. If a child has a hearing problem, and you don't know it, you can imagine the difficulty the child is having trying to keep up with what you're saying. Or if a child has a physical limitation or past injury that hampers how she performs a certain skill, you need to be conscious of that as well. The same goes for everything from asthma to diabetes, all of which can impact a child's performance.

Chapter 10

Fundamental Drills

· ·

In This Chapter

▶ Having fun with the offense

▶ Practicing defensive skills

· ·

*H*elping youngsters learn and develop the many skills needed to play soccer is going to take place during your practices. The players don't learn on game days, when, right in the middle of the action, they may be more interested in waving at Dad over at the sidelines with his camcorder or Grandma in the stands snapping pictures than they are in kicking the ball rolling toward them. With all the hoopla and excitement that surround game day — the colorful uniforms, the spectators, the cheering — a young child simply has too many distractions to completely focus on the game and what you're saying.

The best instruction and the most skill development take place during your midweek practices. At these sessions, you can share your knowledge of the game, pass along pointers, and enhance your team's abilities in all aspects of the game through the fun-filled exercises you choose. Giving clear directions and closely monitoring the well-organized exercises ensure progress and are the springboard to long-term enjoyment of the sport.

The talent level of your players dictates which drills you use during your practices. If you have a group of exceptional players who have been playing soccer for several years and are pretty efficient in most areas of the game, you may want to jump to Chapters 14 and 17, which provide a series of inter-mediate and advanced exercises you can use. Or you can choose among the drills that we present in this chapter.

You can take some of the drills that we walk you through in this chapter that seem too basic for your squad and make adjustments in their difficulty level to best match the needs of your players.

Working at a Beginner's Pace

Learning all the basic techniques of the game, as well as becoming comfortable putting them to use, can be overwhelming for beginning players. As you introduce drills, keep in mind that the simpler, the better. No matter how creative your practices are, don't lose sight that you want your players to develop those solid fundamentals that we tackle in Chapter 9, and that's going to happen only if you provide them quality instruction.

As you go through the season, focus on one or two skills during each practice so your players aren't bombarded with all sorts of instructions that can leave them frustrated and confused. For example, focus on shooting and passing in one practice, which we provide a sample practice for later in this chapter, and slowly introduce other skills at later practices.

Before you begin conducting your practice drills, spend a few minutes getting your players warmed up so they're prepared for the drills to follow. It's never too early to establish good warm-up and cool-down habits, especially in a sport like soccer, in which the players use so many different muscles. Check out Chapter 18 for all your warm-up and cool-down needs.

Offensive Drills

The long-range goal of your practices is to get the players comfortable and confident in their execution during small-scale games and drills so that they can transfer those skills to the playing field on game day.

The beauty of your practice sessions is that you can select any drill and fine-tune it to meet your team's needs. For example, if your players are struggling on offense, you can conduct a 2-on-1 drill that not only helps them develop their skills, but also builds their confidence level as they enjoy success moving the ball downfield.

Shooting: Hit the Coach

Kids love getting hits in baseball and scoring touchdowns in football, so with soccer, their primary interest is going to be — you guessed it — shooting on goal. For a young soccer player, nothing matches the thrill of kicking a ball into the net — well, except for those youngsters who get more pleasure from chasing butterflies in the middle of games.

When introducing beginners to the sport, Hit the Coach serves as a great way to kick off practice, loosen the kids up, and get them comfortable with you.

How it works: Give each of the kids a soccer ball, and have them form a circle as you stand in the middle. The idea is for them to kick the ball at you while you do your best to avoid being touched by any of the balls headed your way. It gets the kids running around, laughing, and having fun right away, which starts your practice on a high note. Plus it doubles as a team ice-breaker and a skill-building drill, because the kids are kicking the ball at a target.

Coaching pointers: Refrain from instruction, and just let the kids have fun. During this drill, you want the kids at the youngest age levels to begin getting comfortable being around one another and getting a feel for kicking a ball at a target.

Passing

Impress upon your squad the importance of passing to the team's overall success — be sure to continually acknowledge good passes during practices and games — and your players will begin to embrace this aspect of the game.

Passing Frenzy

Passing Frenzy can help youngsters learn to make accurate touch passes to a nearby teammate, using the inside of their foot.

What you need: 10- x 10-yard grid. 4 players. 2 balls.

How it works: Use the following steps for this exercise:

1. **Position three players in a line, as shown in Figure 10-1, with about 5 yards between each of them.**

2. **Give the player in the middle a soccer ball.**

3. **Position another player opposite the threesome, about 10 yards away, with a soccer ball.**

4. **On your whistle, the players begin passing the balls back and forth among themselves.**

   The single player is forced to make quick and accurate passes, because the balls come at him rapidly.

5. **Perform for a minute and then rotate so that each child in the group gets a few turns being the single player.**

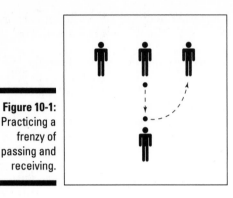

Figure 10-1:
Practicing a
frenzy of
passing and
receiving.

Coaching pointers: Keep a close eye on the accuracy of the single player's passes. If balls are missing their mark, make the necessary corrections in the player's technique to get her passes back on track. The child may be using her toes rather than the inside of her foot to kick the ball, which drastically decreases accuracy.

If the drill proves too difficult initially, use one ball until the kids get comfortable passing that one back and forth. Then work in the extra ball when you sense that they're ready for the additional challenge.

Passing Fancy

Players learn to make accurate passes with a moving ball, because Passing Fancy doesn't allow them time to gain control of a ball by stopping it before kicking it. With the emphasis on speed and accuracy, players have to be quick on their feet and constantly make plays on a moving ball.

What you need: 15- x 15-yard grid. 6 players. 6 balls. 7 cones.

How it works: Play quick, one- or two-minute games of this exercise:

1. **Set up a 15- x 15-yard section of the field, as shown in Figure 10-2.**

   Mark off the area with cones around the perimeter. Place an additional three cones in the center to serve as obstacles.

2. **Put a team of three on each side of the center row of cones, and give each player a soccer ball.**

3. **On your command, the players begin kicking the ball to the other side of the playing area.**

   The object is for each team to try to get all six balls onto the other half of the field at the same time.

With the cones placed at different points along the center line (use fewer cones for inexperienced or less-skilled players), players are forced to make not only quick passes, but also accurate ones.

With inexperienced players, reduce the number of balls involved and as they get more comfortable performing this exercise, add balls to keep it challenging and interesting.

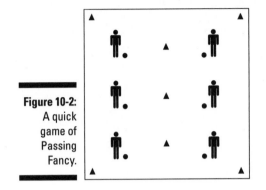

Figure 10-2:
A quick game of Passing Fancy.

Coaching pointers: Because this drill forces children to rush their passes, which they're called upon to do many times during games, they may get a little sloppy on the techniques you're working on. Keep a close eye on the positioning of their feet and how they deliver the passes. Encourage push passes in this drill (see Chapter 9 for the blow-by-blow on performing a push pass), and make sure the kids make contact in the middle of the ball with the inside of their foot at the arch as they follow through toward the target.

Ball handling

The ability to handle the ball in a variety of situations is an important skill for every young player to have. Here are some drills that you can use to help them build those skills.

Elimination

Elimination helps youngsters learn to dribble the ball with their head up, to protect the ball from oncoming players, and to steal the ball from another player.

What you need: 10- x 10-yard grid. 4 players. 4 balls. 8 cones.

How it works: Mark off the playing area with cones, and position a group of four players in the area, each with a ball (see Figure 10-3). The object is for the players to maintain control of their ball while attempting to knock other players' balls out of the playing area. When a player's ball is knocked out of the area, he's eliminated from the game.

As we mention in Chapter 6, we don't highly recommend knockout games because the lesser-skilled players are eliminated first and are left standing on the sideline, losing out on valuable practice time. But you can set up a side drill, so that as soon as a player is knocked out of this one, she moves over to the next drill. Try a passing drill with an assistant coach until other players can join in or whatever else you want the kids to work on. Don't let them stand around watching the Elimination drill.

Figure 10-3:
These four players try to knock each other's balls out of the playing grid.

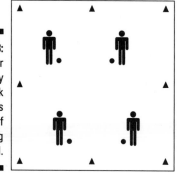

Coaching pointers: A lot goes on during this drill, but make sure players are using legal techniques when attempting to knock another player's ball away.

Keepaway

Keepaway has a little bit of everything. It's an ideal way for players to work on their touch passes, receiving, maneuvering the ball with both feet, shielding, tackling, and pressuring.

What you need: 15- x 15-yard grid. 6 players. 2 balls. 8 cones.

How it works: Have enough of these games going on simultaneously so no one is left standing around watching.

1. **Select four offensive and two defensive players.**

2. **Mark off a playing area with cones.**

3. **Begin the exercise by giving soccer balls to two of the offensive players (see Figure 10-4).**

   The object is for the offensive players to keep possession of the balls.

4. **Award the offensive players a point every time they successfully make three passes in a row, and give the defensive players a point every time they steal the ball.**

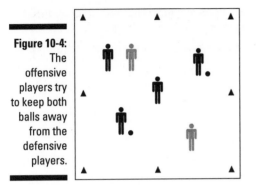

Figure 10-4: The offensive players try to keep both balls away from the defensive players.

Coaching pointers: Stress proper form on the passing and receiving, and make sure that the defenders aren't committing penalties during their efforts to steal the balls. Remind players that the closer a defender is to them, the closer they must keep the ball to them in order to maintain possession.

Heading

If you're coaching a soccer team comprised of youngsters ages 10 and under, you can hold off conducting heading drills until you've worked with them on all the other basic skills of the game. As we discuss in Chapter 9, you want to introduce the heading concept to the kids so that they're familiar with it, and as they get older, you can direct more focus toward helping them learn this skill.

Quick Reaction Headers

With younger children, one of the best ways to introduce them to the art of heading is to use a beach ball. Quick Reaction Headers gets them used to directing the ball where they aim.

What you need: 5- x 5-yard grid. 3 players. 1 ball.

How it works:

1. **Break the team into groups of three.**

   Each threesome stands in a line. The two end players, each with a ball, face each other (see Figure 10-5). The youngster in the middle stands an equal distance between the two end players, facing the player on the right to begin with.

2. **One of the players on the end tosses the ball to the player in the middle, who heads it back to her and then quickly turns to receive another lob from the player on her other side, which she heads back to that player.**

Continue for several repetitions so the player in the middle gets used to spinning around and making a play on the ball.

3. **Switch positions so that each player gets a number of repetitions in the middle.**

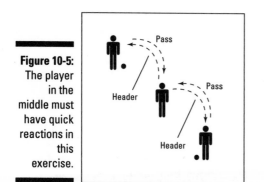

Figure 10-5: The player in the middle must have quick reactions in this exercise.

Coaching pointers: Heading is often one of the most difficult skills to teach children, and they really have to be accurate with their technique when performing this one. Remind your players to keep their eyes open throughout the drill, because youngsters just learning this skill have a habit of closing their eyes right before contact, which dramatically reduces the chances of delivering a successful header. Spend several practice sessions working with a beach ball with your team (a cool idea we introduce in Chapter 9 to help take the fear out of learning this skill), and make sure your players have the proper form down before introducing regulation soccer balls into the mix.

Circle Headers

Circle Headers gives youngsters a feel for using headers to deliver passes and take shots on goal.

What you need: Area of field with goal. Entire team. 1 ball.

How it works: The goalie (GK) stands in front of the net. A teammate stands a few yards in front of one of the goal posts, holding a ball (see Figure 10-6). The designated header (♦) for this particular exercise begins about 15 yards away from the goal. You (or an assistant coach) stand about 8 yards away from the header with a ball in your hand. Begin the exercise:

1. **Lob a ball to the header, who heads it back to you.**

2. **The header sprints toward the net.**

3. **She receives another lob pass from the teammate stationed there.**

4. **She attempts to head the lobbed pass past the goaltender.**

For inexperienced players, you may want to skip step 1 of this drill and simply keep the focus on heading the ball into the net. For more experienced players, the lobs can be chip passes delivered by players.

Coaching pointers: If players aren't able to head the ball back accurately or get much force behind their shots on goal, give them a quick refresher on their form. More than likely, the youngster's neck muscles aren't tight at impact, and he probably isn't following through with his header. Reinforce that his head should be pointing at his intended target.

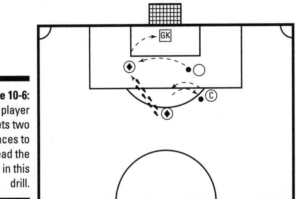

Figure 10-6: The player gets two chances to head the ball in this drill.

Putting it all together: Give and Go

Give and Go is a simple drill that touches on passing, receiving, shooting, and goaltending. Rotate the players throughout the drill.

What you need: Area of field with goal. Entire team. 1 ball.

How it works: Check out where the players are located in Figure 10-7. The goaltender (GK) takes his position in front of the net. The designated shooter (♦) for the drill stands in the middle of the field, about 20 yards out from the goalie. One offensive player stands about 10 yards to the right of the shooter, and another stands between the goalie and the shooter. On your whistle:

1. **The offensive player to the side of the designated shooter delivers a pass to him.**

2. **The shooter gains control of the ball and delivers a pass to the other offensive player in front of him.**

3. **The shooter cuts at roughly a 45-degree angle.**

4. **The offensive player passes the ball back to the shooter.**

5. **The shooter takes a shot on goal.**

The difficulty of the drill can be increased for older kids by adding a defensive player to the mix who tries to stop the pass from the shooter to Player B, for example. Or you can make the initial pass to the designated shooter purposely more difficult by bouncing it so he has to use his chest or thighs to receive the ball, or by sending the pass out of range so that he really has to work at chasing it down and gaining control of it.

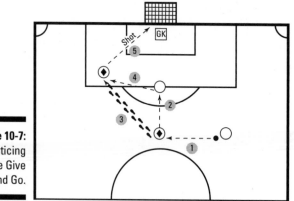

Figure 10-7: Practicing the Give and Go.

Coaching pointers: The shooter is eager to deliver a shot on goal, so make sure he's using the right techniques to corral the pass, send the return pass, and take a quality shot. If he doesn't have much force behind his shot on net, he probably didn't follow through when he kicked the ball. Or if the shot dribbled along the ground, he may have positioned his plant foot improperly, which usually results in making contact with only the top half of the ball. For more on proper positioning of the plant foot when shooting, see Chapter 9.

Defensive Drills

Children are naturally more attracted to learning offensive, rather than defensive, skills. Learning how to deliver a kick that results in a goal is more interesting to a developing player than how to successfully defend a 2-on-1. But one of your many responsibilities as coach is to teach youngsters all the basic elements of soccer, and that includes tackling, defending, and goaltending.

Playing defense may not seem as glamorous to youngsters just learning the game, but if they are to be well-rounded players, half your practices and drills should cover this aspect of the game. If your defensive drills are creative and challenging, you may have some kids begging to play defensive positions on game day to help their team protect the net.

Although several offensive drills we mention earlier in this chapter have defensive benefits as well, the following drills really emphasize the defensive side of the ball. You can use them, make your own modifications, or let them inspire a whole new drill.

Defending

Disrupting an opposing team's attack requires a broad range of skills. Here are some exercises to help your players improve those all important defensive techniques.

Ball Touch

Ball Touch helps youngsters learn to compete for a loose ball and make the switch from offensive to defensive mode.

What you need: 15- x 15-yard grid. 2 players. 1 ball.

How it works: Begin with a player on either side of you (see Figure 10-8). Roll a ball out, and on your command, the two players race to see who can gain control of it. When a player has the ball in her possession, she must see how long she can protect it before the other player steals it. Continue the exercise for 30 seconds to a minute while players continue to take an offensive or defensive mindset based on whether they have possession of the ball.

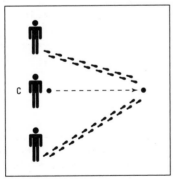

Figure 10-8:
Ball Touch helps players switch from offense to defense and back again.

Coaching pointers: Players going for the loose ball are likely to make contact with each other, particularly older and more experienced players, who may be more competitive. Keep a close watch to ensure that penalties aren't being committed as players vie for the ball.

1-on-1

Being able to stop a player from advancing the ball down the field is one of the benchmarks of great defensive play. The 1-on-1 focuses on defensive footwork and incorporates offensive skills as well.

What you need: 30- x 30-yard grid. 2 players. 1 ball. 2 cones.

How it works: Set up 2 pylons 25 yards apart (see Figure 10-9). Start the drill with one offensive player at the pylon with a ball and one defensive player about 5 yards away. The object is for the defensive player to stop the offensive player from working the ball down the field to the other pylon. If the defensive player knocks the ball loose, you can work the exercise a couple of different ways:

- ✔ When possession of the ball changes, you can have the players switch roles. The player who stole the ball then tries to move it downfield toward the opposite pylon.

- ✔ When the defensive player pokes the ball away, the offensive player retrieves it and continues to work toward reaching the pylon with the ball.

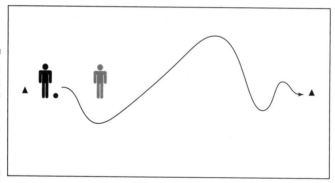

Figure 10-9:
A child gets a lot of practice with the 1-on-1 exercise.

Coaching pointers: Monitor the defender's footwork, and make sure that she doesn't get herself out of position by going for any body fakes by the other player. Also, watch the defensive player's movements to ensure that penalties aren't being committed in her efforts to swipe the ball.

2-on-1

This drill teaches defenders how to control a 2-on-1 and provides offensive players the chance to work on their passing, dribbling, and attacking skills.

What you need: 10- x 10-yard grid. 3 players. 1 ball. 2 cones.

How it works: Place two cones a couple of yards apart, as you see in Figure 10-10. Designate two players for offense and one player for defense. The offensive players must dribble the ball through the cones without losing possession of the ball. The 2-on-1 isn't a shooting drill, so emphasize that players must maintain control of the ball while attempting to get through the cones. Allow players to maneuver with the ball past the cone, but they can go through the cone in only one direction.

Coaching pointers: This drill tests your defensive player's footwork and reactions, because she's required to cover a lot of ground all by herself. Remind her not to go for the offensive player's head and shoulder fakes, but to keep her eye on the player's chest to help reduce the chances of being caught leaning to one side and creating an opening that the offensive players can use to their advantage.

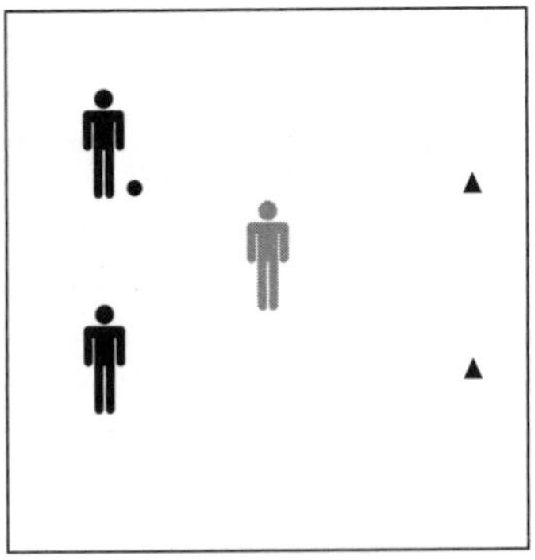

Figure 10-10: The defensive player has his work cut out for him in the 2-on-1.

Goaltending

Proper footwork, good hand–eye coordination, and quick reflexes are all valuable assets for any young goaltender learning to play the position. Many beginning soccer programs don't utilize goalies, so a youngster can be involved in the sport for a couple of years before he gets the chance to guard the nets. The following drills are designed to help make that move to the front of the net a smooth one when the time comes.

Read and React

This drill works on several aspects of goaltending, including:

- Helping youngsters learn to read an opposing player's body language and figure out whether they're setting up to unload a shot or deliver a pass to a teammate.

- Testing players' footwork. The drill requires quick movements from side to side in order to stop the back-to-back shots coming the goalie's way.

Read and React also provides benefits to the offensive players, who work on their passing, receiving, and shooting skills.

What you need: Area of field with goal. 5 players. 1 ball.

How it works: The goaltender (GK) assumes his regular position in front of the net. Put two offensive players about 5 yards away from each goal post, and give them each a soccer ball (see Figure 10-11). Position two more offensive players out in front of the net about 15 yards from the goal and about 10 yards away from each other. Move younger or less experienced players in a little closer. On your whistle:

1. **The players with the balls deliver passes to the players out in front.**

2. **After receiving the passes and controlling the ball, one player delivers a shot on goal.**

3. **The other youngster returns a pass to the player who just sent him a pass.**

4. **The player receiving the second ball fires a short-range shot on goal.**

The first few times through the drill, let the goalie know which player is initially delivering the shot and which one is making a pass. For more experienced players or those players who are comfortable with the drill after a few times through it, you can pick which player you want to shoot and which one you want to pass without letting the goalie know.

Figure 10-11:
Several shots on goal in a row test the goalie's ability in Read and React.

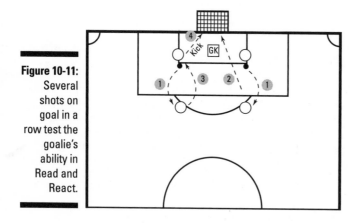

Coaching pointers: This drill is for goalies to work on reading plays, reacting, and moving from post to post, but don't neglect the techniques the offensive players use. You want accurate passes, proper form receiving passes, and a correct follow-through when delivering a shot on net.

Goalie's Delight

Goalie's Delight helps goalies become proficient at stopping a flurry of shots when facing lots of offensive pressure during games. It also helps develop the shooting skills of offensive players.

What you need: Area of field with goal. 3 players. 10 balls.

How it works: The goalie takes his normal spot in front of the net. Position two players about 15 yards away, and give each player 5 balls lined up in a row (see Figure 10-12). The drill begins with one player taking a shot on goal. As soon as the kick is delivered, the second player sends a shot on net, and the players keep alternating shots as quickly as they can. This quickness forces the goalie to make several difficult saves in succession from a variety of angles.

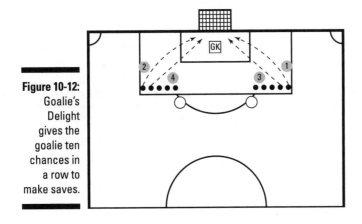

Figure 10-12: Goalie's Delight gives the goalie ten chances in a row to make saves.

Coaching pointers: Watch the goalie's hands to ensure that they're properly positioned on his saves and that his hands are in a relaxed position as an extension of the arm.

Breakaway

Breakaway helps goaltenders learn to move side to side and get in position to stop shots. Offensive players gain practice on both their passing and shooting skills.

What you need: Area of field with goal. 3 players. 1 ball.

How it works: The goaltender takes his position in the net. Two players start about 20 yards away from the net. The players move in on net, passing the ball back and forth until someone decides to take a shot. To increase the difficulty, add a defensive player to the mix. Or make players deliver shots with their less-dominant foot.

Coaching pointers: In order to effectively defend Breakaway, goalies must be able to move side to side quickly. Footwork is crucial to success and should be monitored closely during this drill. Also, make sure that the goalie protects the ball with her entire body when she stops a low shot on the ground. This protection prevents opponents from getting their feet on the ball for a follow-up shot and reduces the chances of the goalie's hands or fingers being injured if an opponent tries kicking at the ball.

Putting It All Together: A Sample Practice Session

Okay, so your kids are ready to go. You have some drills that you want to use. It's time to put it all together. A sample one-hour practice for a team of beginning players could look something like Table 10-1. As we discuss earlier in the chapter, limit the concepts you cover during each practice to one or two. In the example in Table 10-1, we focus on passing and shooting.

Table 10-1	Beginner "Passing and Shooting" Practice Plan	
Duration	*Activity*	*Comments*
5 min.	Warm-up	Get the kids in the habit of warming up every time they're participating in strenuous activities with some basic stretching and movement (see Chapter 18).
10 min.	Hit the Coach	A quick game of Hit the Coach (which we cover earlier in the chapter) to get the kids used to kicking at a target.
10 min.	Shots on Goal	Line all the kids up about 5 yards in front of the goal with a ball, and have them kick the ball into the net to begin reinforcing that the name of the game is to get the ball into the opponent's goal.

Duration	Activity	Comments
10 min.	Partner Passing	Pair team members up, and spread out on the field. Start with the partners 5 yards apart, and have them work on passing the ball back and forth. If the team is doing pretty well, you may want to have all the players take a step or two backward to increase the length of the passes and make it more challenging for the players.
15 min.	Passing Fancy	Conduct the Passing Fancy drill (covered earlier in this chapter). If you have enough kids on the team, you can run a little mini tournament in a couple of different playing areas. Have the winners square off and the losing groups play each other so that you always have all the kids actively involved. Or if you have enough kids to make four groups, play a round-robin tournament in which all the groups get the chance to play one another.
10 min.	Scrimmage	Always end practice on a high note so that the kids leave the field with smiles on their faces. There's no better way to do that than to have a fun scrimmage pitting the coaches and parents against the kids. Besides being a lot of fun for the kids, it help them work on the basic skills of both passing and kicking the ball at the goal that you've focused on during this practice session.

Of course, you can be flexible with your schedule and adjust it according to how the practice is progressing. For example, if you see a number of kids struggling with a certain drill, you may want to run it for a few additional minutes and just reduce the amount of time you spend scrimmaging at the end of practice. Your practice plan doesn't have to be carved in stone, but it's your guide to helping your team members learn and progress during their time with you.

Chapter 11

Coaching Offense 101

*W*hat do kids love most about playing soccer? Sure, some may go for the colorful uniforms and the cool shin guards, and others may simply enjoy chasing the ball up and down the field. But most kids love the chance to score goals and feel the exhilaration that accompanies booting the ball into the net. Kids typically hunger to learn the offensive part of the game, and teaching them the techniques is like waving bags of candy in front of their faces. The eyes widen; the ears perk up; and smiles form.

As a soccer coach, this is where your job becomes more fascinating — and also more fun. When your players have a couple of years of soccer experience behind them and have a pretty good understanding of the basics of the game, you get the chance to open the offensive playbook and challenge them to reach new heights in their play. You can teach a variety of offenses and introduce an array of new passes that enable the team to create additional scoring opportunities. But even if your team is relatively inexperienced, we have some pointers here that you can put to use too. We think your team will be eager to learn these new offensive skills.

Building a Beginner Offense

Regardless of what age or level of soccer you're coaching, adhering to some key offensive principles lays the foundation for your team to enjoy plenty of success when it's on the attack. The following are basic offensive tips to keep in mind this season.

Keep the players moving

An attacking team whose players are constantly on the move — whether they have the ball or not — is much more difficult to defend than a team that stands around watching the player with the ball while she dribbles around, looking to create something. Continually encouraging your players to keep moving and working to get to an open area of the field where they can receive passes makes a big difference in the effectiveness of the attack. And for the youngest of players, it can help loosen up the swarm of players that you typically find around the ball.

If no one is open, the dribbler's responsibility is to either send a square pass (see the "Square pass" section, later in the chapter) back to a teammate to reset the offense and begin the attack again, or dribble to a different area of the field and create space, where she can deliver a pass downfield. An offense that's constantly moving puts enormous pressure on a defense. The more you force the defense to move and react, the greater their chances of making a coverage mistake that results in an advantage for your team (and possibly a great scoring opportunity as well).

Spread out

The more space that exists between your players, the greater the chances of producing a successful attack. Players who are able to keep plenty of space between themselves and their teammates — and avoid the dreaded bunching-up syndrome that's especially common at the younger ages of soccer — have more dribbling room to operate and more opportunities for executing passes that efficiently move the ball down the field. Teammates who bunch up bring more defenders into the picture, thus providing them more chances — and easier chances — to steal the ball.

Keep the ball moving

When your team is on the attack, you want your players doing everything they can to make things as difficult as possible for the defense. That means keeping the ball moving. One of the biggest mistakes beginning soccer players make is stopping to gather themselves and get the ball under control when receiving a pass. A stationary target is easy pickings for defensive players — and they're going to pounce all over it.

Work with your team on receiving passes and trapping balls that keep moving. If you let the opponents simply run right at your player, they're going to steal a lot of balls and ruin a lot of your team's attacks in the process. Check out Chapter 10 for drills that help kids in this area.

Involve everyone

The best way to develop soccer players who will want to strap on shin guards for years to come is to focus on a more possession-oriented attack that keeps all players actively involved. Relying on just a handful of players to knock the ball down the field and hopefully connect occasionally on the long passes isn't going to be fun for the rest of the players involved, and it hinders their development and drains some of their enthusiasm for playing the game.

Continually stress that when your team has the ball, everyone is on offense, and that when they don't have possession, everyone is on defense.

Understanding Field Position

As players gain more experience, they start to recognize in what areas of the field they can be more aggressive with their passes and what areas pose more danger. Certain areas of the field dictate that players rein in their aggressiveness so it doesn't hurt the team. Even with the youngest players, talk about what areas of the field require certain types of plays to give them a sense of what they should and shouldn't be doing. If your team is relatively inexperienced, approach such instruction by simply dividing the field into offensive and defensive halves.

Dividing the field in half is a little too simplistic with players who have some experience, but breaking the playing area into thirds gives youngsters a pretty good gauge of how their play should be handled. Your kids are likely to find themselves in all three areas of the field at various junctures throughout the game. How they respond while there makes a difference in how your team fares in moving the ball and creating scoring opportunities, as well as how successful it is in limiting the opposing team's attack.

Offensive third of the field

The offensive third of the field is the area at your opponent's end of the field where your team can be at its most aggressive on the attack. Down here in the shadows of your opponent's goal, turnovers aren't nearly as costly as they are elsewhere on the field, and mistakes aren't as magnified. An errant pass or turnover down here doesn't result in a scoring opportunity for the other team. Although you hate to give up possession of the ball at any time, you prefer to do so here, where the opponent still has the entire length of the field to negotiate rather than in front of your own goal or even at midfield, where the opponent is one pass away from generating a great scoring opportunity.

Middle of the field

With games involving kids who have a couple of years of soccer already behind them, the play in this area of the field is often the difference-maker, deciding which team generates more scoring opportunities. Basically, the team that best controls this area of the field wins the majority of the time.

If you have players who have a good grasp of their responsibilities, you can take a more aggressive approach when your team is in control of the ball in this area of the field. As long as everyone is aware that they need to be alert and on their toes, you can encourage aggressive passing. If your players happen to turn the ball over, they have to be able to react quickly and cover for one another, especially if the opponent is a counterattacking team (see the "Counterattacking" section, later in this chapter, for more on this subject).

Defensive third of the field

This is that area of the field where your players have you biting your nails and reaching for the antacids — especially if what you've been teaching them about field positioning hasn't sunk in quite yet. Here, your team finds itself under the most pressure. A poorly executed pass or an ill-timed maneuver can create immediate problems for the team, particularly your goalie, who is suddenly staring at a booming shot by the opponent from close range.

You want your team to be fully aware that at this end of the field, players should send clearing passes toward the sidelines, not down the middle of the field. An opposing player who picks off a pass in the middle of the field is in great position to get off a shot on goal or create a pass to a teammate for a scoring opportunity. Clearing passes that are kept to the outside pose far less risk. If the other team happens to steal these passes, it puts far less pressure on your team, because the sidelines serve as an additional defender. Defenders who are pinned in along the sideline are more limited in which direction they can proceed. Dribbling 1-on-1 against a defender should also be more limited in this area, because the defender has nothing to lose by being ultra-aggressive down here. Sticking to safe passes that move the ball out of danger is the best plan.

Moving the Ball Downfield

As a coach, you'll gain immense satisfaction when your team takes possession of the ball and moves it downfield. Being able to do so requires the ability to execute a number of passes, which we take a look at in this section. Check out Figure 11-1 to see these options.

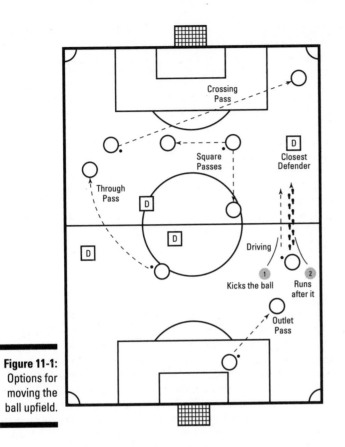

Figure 11-1:
Options for
moving the
ball upfield.

Outlet pass

An *outlet pass* is any pass that gets the offense started from deep in its own end. When your team is backed up and playing defense, and you create a turnover in the vicinity of your own goal, a defender's pass up the sideline or through the middle is an outlet pass that pushes the play in the other direction. Goalies also deliver outlet passes when they have possession of the ball and deliver a pass to a teammate who gets the attack going (see Chapter 12 to provide your goalies with the proper skills to initiate the attack).

Through pass

Any time your player has the ball, you want his head to be up and his eyes scanning the field for an open teammate or a crack in the defense that can be exploited by either dribbling or passing. If an available teammate is open downfield, you want him to execute the play — often referred to as a penetration or *through pass,* because it penetrates the defense and moves your attack forward. It can be done anywhere on the field where the offense has taken advantage of an opening left by the defensive team.

Driving

A player uses this method when she has lots of open space, is running at full speed, and doesn't want the ball to slow her down. It's executed in the middle and attacking thirds of the field. *Driving* is sort of like making a pass to yourself, because the player pushes the ball several yards ahead of herself, and then when running toward the ball, she's able to make decisions about what to do next with it. How far she pushes the ball ahead depends on how much space she has to work with and how close the nearest defender is.

Square pass

A *square pass* is a pass that's played to a teammate who is beside or behind the player with the ball, as opposed to moving the ball up the field. This pass is also referred to as a *possession pass.* Although making square passes isn't as glamorous to kids as threading a diagonal pass through a maze of defenders (see the following "Crossing pass" section), they can be instrumental in how successful your team's attack is. Players who have the discipline to refrain from making a risky pass, and who are willing to send a square pass to a teammate, are assets to the team. Getting your players to understand that a teammate behind the play may actually be in a more advantageous spot and have a better angle to keep the attack progressing takes lots of practice. The square pass is one of those skills that should be introduced to players who have been around the sport for a couple of seasons.

Using drills where the offensive team is outnumbered can help your kids learn the value of a square pass. Coaches often devote a large amount of time to practicing 3-on-2 and 2-on-1, but sprinkling your practices with drills such as 2-on-3 and 3-on-4 is just as important, because it forces the offenses to utilize possession passes until they open up an opportunity to strike and can take a shot on goal. Although your team will have advantages in numbers throughout the game, you're just as likely to encounter situations where you're a man short. Practice both of these scenarios to prepare your team for all situations.

Crossing pass

A *crossing pass,* also known as a *diagonal pass,* is used to generate scoring opportunities. It's a pass that's usually played in the offensive third of the field. As its name suggests, it's a ball that's played forward from right to left or left to right. Crossing passes that are executed properly can quickly put a defensive team at a disadvantage. Because the ball is suddenly delivered to the other side of the field, defenders are forced to make adjustments in coverage to respond to a crossing pass.

Different Styles of Offense You Can Run

When your team gains that coveted possession of the soccer ball, your players are ready to proceed with the attack. But what type of offensive approach is best suited for your squad? Well, that depends on a number of factors, including the experience and ability levels of your players. You have several styles of attack to choose from — take a look.

Counterattacking

The *counterattacking* style of offense attempts to capitalize on an opponent who isn't properly prepared to defend when possession changes hands to your team. This aggressive offense features the following:

- Players pushing the ball quickly through the midfield by dribbling
- Players moving the ball with long diagonal or through passes (see the "Crossing pass" and "Through pass" sections, earlier in the chapter)

A counterattack can be successful because long passes can chew up big chunks of the field and quickly get the team into prime scoring position, but it's also a risky style of play. One long pass can be intercepted by the opposition, so as quickly as your team gained possession of the ball, it can turn the ball over and find itself right back on defense again.

Frontal attack

The *frontal attack* unfolds much more slowly than a counterattack. This style of play also brings more players into the picture, because the essence of this approach is encouraging safe, short passes that the players use to maneuver the ball down the field. It's a reliable ball-control approach that can be great for young players, because it keeps everyone actively involved in the game. The biggest disadvantage is that by making so many passes (even relatively safe ones), you have a greater chance of turning the ball over.

Overlapping

Overlapping is one of the more advanced offensive approaches in youth soccer, and it puts a real premium on accurate passing and receiving. It's the type of offense that should be used only with experienced players who can handle the requirements of this style of play. Still, even with younger or less-experienced players, you can introduce the concept to them so they're at least somewhat familiar with it as they continue their soccer careers.

When *overlapping,* the player handling the ball gets help from a teammate who rushes up at the sides at top speed and receives the pass, which immediately creates new attacking possibilities for the team. The team can continue executing the overlap as it works its way downfield, or it can use the technique sparingly to catch the opponent off guard at different points during the game. Typically, overlapping is used to scoot by the opponents on the sidelines. The overlapping player can come from the player's right and run down the sideline (see Figure 11-2a), or he can come from the player's left and loop around (see Figure 11-2b). If the defenders commit to covering the overlapping player, the player with the ball can exploit that by dribbling into the open territory. Here are a few other tips to keep in mind:

✔ **Make the defender commit:** In these situations, the defender has a real dilemma, because he doesn't know whether the ball handler will distribute the ball to an onrushing teammate or keep it and look to create a play dribbling. If the defender chooses to rush the attacker, that opens the door for the overlap.

✔ **Play the ball ahead of the player:** Because the overlapping player is running at full speed, the pass must be played well out in front of him. Passes that require him to slow down throw off the effects of the overlap and make it ineffective.

Figure 11-2:
Overlapping
pass
options.

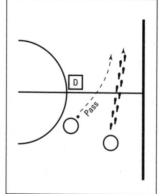

a

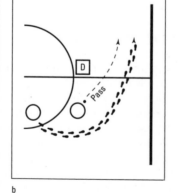

b

Because overlapping requires efficient passing skills, this offensive technique should be introduced after the team has a pretty good handle on the basics of passing. Teaching youngsters to pass a ball to a spot, instead of directly to a player, takes lots of practice to get down as kids learn to adjust their ball placement to the speed of their teammates. The Passing Fancy drill in Chapter 10 is ideal for helping youngsters begin learning to play the ball into space.

Kicking the Offensive Skills up a Notch

Before you can introduce any attacking philosophies, your players must have at least a sense of some of the other skills that are applicable for their age, experience, and level of ability. Having the knowledge to perform different types of passes that make running your offense more efficient is one of the keys to generating successful attacks. Players who have the basics of dribbling, passing, shooting, and receiving down are ready to progress to the next level — and you can help them get there.

Shielding

To be effective dribblers, players must be able to efficiently shield the ball. The *shielding* technique in soccer involves the attacking player keeping his body between the defender and the ball. Players who learn this art of controlling the ball are effective attackers because they have a lesser chance of surrendering possession of the ball and are better suited to operating in tight quarters. Shielding is a big asset to the team, because the players can distribute the ball to an open teammate and help their team generate good scoring opportunities that may not materialize without the ability to shield. Some points to keep in mind when teaching shielding:

✔ **Stay sideways:** The proper position for shielding is for the player to turn sideways (see Figure 11-3). This technique puts more space between the ball and the defender. It also opens up the attacking player's field of vision and enables him to make a play.

✔ **Don't turn back:** Although younger and more inexperienced players naturally want to turn their backs on a defender to protect the ball, it simply gives the defensive player unnecessary advantages: The defender can more easily poke the ball away, and the offensive player can't see her teammates downfield, which brings the attack to a standstill. It also handcuffs her ability to beat the defender 1-on-1.

This Guard the Treasure drill is great to help young players become familiar with the concept of shielding. The entire team can participate in the drill at one time on one half of the field, which makes it easy for you to monitor everyone. The players gradually learn that by keeping their bodies sideways, they make it difficult for the defender to gain possession of the ball.

What you need: Half of the field. Entire team. One ball for every two players.

How it works: Pair players up, and give each twosome a ball. The object of the drill is for the designated offensive player to keep the defensive player from touching the ball — while not touching it himself. Because the offensive player isn't allowed to touch the ball, he learns how his body can be used to protect it.

Figure 11-3:
Shielding involves keeping your body between the ball and the opponent.

Chip pass

A *chip pass* is a lofted pass with backspin. It can be used throughout the field to get the ball over a defender. Here are the steps to follow in teaching it:

1. **The player approaches the ball from the side and turns to strike the ball with the inside of his foot (see Figure 11-4a).**

2. **He snaps his knee while coming forward at the ball.**

3. **He keeps his ankle in a locked (firm) position at contact, which helps ensure that backspin is delivered on the ball.**

4. **The player makes contact with the side of his shoelaces below the center of the ball (see Figure 11-4b).**

   If he is directly behind the ball, he makes contact with the top of his shoelaces, using a downward jabbing motion with little follow-through (see Figure 11-4c).

Figure 11-4:
This player
uses a chip
pass to get
the ball over
a defender.

a   b   c

Outside-of-foot pass

Often, throughout a game, when going against a defender, the only opportunity to advance the ball to a teammate is by using an outside-of-foot pass. It can be a little tricky to teach simply because delivering one doesn't come naturally for kids and requires an awkward motion to complete. Here are the steps to help your youngsters use the outside-of-foot pass effectively:

1. **The child's passing foot (see Figure 11-5) should be pointed down and slightly inward.**

2. **Her nonpassing foot should be turned slightly away from the ball.**

   This gives the youngster ample room to make the pass.

3. **The player's ankle must be locked when she's delivering a pass with the outside of the foot.**

4. **When the player follows through with the pass, she makes contact in the center of the ball with her little toe.**

One-touch pass

Players call upon one-touch passes when they're tightly marked by the opposition or when they're pressured and in danger of losing the ball that's headed their way if they don't distribute it to a teammate quickly. The steps for executing a one-touch pass are similar to the push pass (see Chapter 9):

1. **The player's nonkicking foot is planted alongside the incoming ball.**

2. **His hips and shoulders are squared up to the teammate that he's delivering the ball to, and his kicking foot is open to expose the inside of the foot to the oncoming ball.**

3. **The instep of the foot makes contact in the middle of the ball with an abbreviated follow-through.**

   Using a short, jabbing motion on the moving ball allows for better control and accuracy.

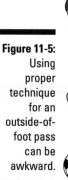

Figure 11-5: Using proper technique for an outside-of-foot pass can be awkward.

Wall pass

The wall pass is one of the most basic combination plays in soccer. Also referred to as the give-and-go, it's a good tactic for a pair of attackers to take advantage of a single attacker in the area and create chaos with the defense.

The give-and-go has many combinations. Here's how it generally works: The player with the ball beats the defender (see Figure 11-6) by utilizing a teammate to bounce the ball behind the defender, much like bouncing the ball against a wall. One of the best opportunities for utilizing a wall pass is when the attacking player is able to make the defensive player commit to guarding him. Use the following steps to teach your players the wall pass:

1. **When the attacking player is able to make the defensive player commit to guarding him, the player with the ball (A) delivers a pass to the second attacker (B).**

2. **Player B executes a one-touch pass to the open area behind the defender and then runs forward to join the attack.**

3. **Player A runs around the defender and meets the ball at the open spot on the field.**

Some other points to keep in mind when teaching the wall pass:

- ✔ **Push it:** The push pass, because of its accuracy, is the best method to deliver the ball to the wall player.

- ✔ **Targets:** Defenders who are slow-footed, who have a tendency to guard players with the ball very closely, or who keep their eyes glued on the ball and aren't paying close attention to what's going on throughout the rest of the field are susceptible to the wall pass.

- ✔ **Practice:** It works only when both offensive players recognize the opportunity. Although practice drills help with the timing of the one-touch passes into open space, this type of pass is best learned during games, as players learn to recognize when situations call for it. Besides that, you need sufficient space behind the defender to pull off this type of pass; otherwise, it likely results in a turnover.

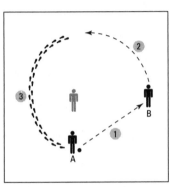

Figure 11-6:
A simple
give-and-go.

Banana kick

After players develop sound fundamentals on kicking the ball straight and pretty accurately, you can introduce them to the banana kick, whose name may get a chuckle or two from younger players. It's also referred to as a *bending ball kick*. This type of kick can be a great offensive weapon when players are able to curve the ball around defenders to get the ball to their teammates. Here are some helpful tips to use when teaching the banana kick:

- ✔ **Approach from the side:** The ball bends, or curves, when a youngster delivers the kick by coming across the ball (see Figure 11-7) rather than straight on.

- ✔ **Go low to get it high:** In order for the ball to curve, it has to be put in the air. Players must make contact with the ball at its bottom half.

- ✔ **Inside of foot:** As the youngster approaches the ball, he strikes it with the inside of his shoe and above his big toe, and drives across the ball.

Figure 11-7:
The banana
kick is an
advanced
offensive
technique.

Chapter 12

Coaching Defense 101

- -

In This Chapter

▶ Putting the "D" in your defense

▶ Testing types of tackles

- -

Sure, you have great fun watching your team delivering precision passes up and down the field, creating quality scoring chances, and keeping the scoreboard operator busy tallying all those goals on game day. But what about when your team doesn't have the ball? How do your players respond when the ball is deep in their end of the field, and they're under attack from the opposing team? What do they do when they turn the ball over at mid-field? What defensive style should you be teaching them?

In soccer, just like any other team sport, playing defense is a major element of the game. During games, roughly half of your team's time is spent playing defense, so players who know and understand the techniques involved in defending derive more enjoyment and success from the game. Learning defensive skills may not be as glamorous as learning offensive skills, but slowly, your players begin savoring the ability to derail and disrupt an opponent's attack. Being able to do so on a consistent basis is the mark of a well-coached team that understands how to play a complete game of soccer.

Building a Solid Foundation

Your team spends approximately half of every game on defense, so don't neglect this area of the game during your practice sessions.

Marking: The framework of sound defense

The foundation of all good defensive play begins with *marking*, which simply means that the defending player is between the attacking player and his own goal. Marking is guarding an offensive player to prevent him from dribbling or passing the ball, or slowing his progress while the defense is under attack.

Marking, also sometimes referred to as *backs on,* is where you simply assign your left and right fullbacks to follow specific attackers on the opposing team wherever they go on the field. This tactic typically works well with younger kids learning the game, because you can assign everyone a player to mark, and you can keep track of who loses their player relatively easily. This style of play also ensures that your players don't become bored or lose concentration during the game, because they have to stay focused on sticking with their assigned player. This system can also be effective at creating turnovers, because your players are always right on top of the player dribbling the ball, as well as guarding others tightly, which cuts down passing lanes.

Here are some points to keep in mind when teaching marking:

- ✔ **Get close:** The closer a defender sticks to the attacking player, the more difficult it is for that player to maneuver the ball, deliver a pass, or get off a shot.

- ✔ **Be aware:** Youngsters are in good defensive position only when they're between the player they're marking and their own goal — and they have sight of where the ball is. Whenever a player loses sight of where the ball is, his ability to defend is weakened.

- ✔ **Notice tendencies:** With older and more experienced players, stress the importance of paying attention to tendencies. Does the player always dribble with her right foot? If so, making a slight adjustment of sliding a small step over in coverage makes a big difference in how effectively you mark the player. By overplaying to one side, your players give themselves more chances to make a steal. Does the player look down a lot when she's dribbling? If so, she's susceptible to steals, and it's probably a sign that she's not totally comfortable with dribbling, which means that by putting tight defensive pressure on her, your player may be able to force a turnover.

A bunch of other key defensive principles

Regardless of what type of defense you choose for your team to play, the following are some basic defensive principles that any team, at any age or level of experience, should adhere to:

- ✔ **Protect the scoring area:** The area in front of the net is the prized piece of real estate. Keeping the opposing players out of this area drastically reduces the number of legitimate scoring chances they get against your squad.

- ✔ **Help out:** The essence of team defense is lending support when needed. When a player nearby gets beaten by the dribble, teammates need to recognize the importance of sliding over to help defend that player and preventing a clear shot on goal.

✔ **Beat the ball:** The more players you have between your goal and the opposing team when it has the ball, the more likely your squad is to make a successful defensive stand. When your team turns the ball over, your chances of derailing the attack go up as more players rush back and put themselves between the ball and their own goal.

✔ **Clear out:** Teach your defenders — and really, any player who gains possession of the ball in front of the net — to clear it out quickly. *Clearing out* refers to kicking the ball away from your own net to clear away the chances for the opposing team to get shots on goal.

These kicks should never be played across the front of your own net, where an interception can quickly lead to a quality scoring chance for the opponent. Rather, they should be played to the nearest sideline to help ensure that defenders can't get their foot on the ball or that if they do, they have limited options available to them.

✔ **Cover the dribbler:** Any time your defensive player finds himself outnumbered, such as in a 2-on-1 situation, he must always take the player who has the ball. You never want to give the player with the ball an easy and direct route to the goal. At least by covering the dribbler, you force him to make a pass, which produces a greater chance of a miscue and losing possession of the ball.

✔ **Don't lunge:** Defensive players who lunge for the ball instead of sticking to sound tackling fundamentals make it drastically easier for attacking players to maneuver the ball down the field. When a player lunges for the ball, she manages to take herself right out of the play and allows the attacking player the opportunity to continue dribbling, take advantage of the open area to get a clear shot on goal, or deliver an unobstructed pass to a teammate. Whenever you spot a player lunging during a drill in practice, immediately correct the mistake, and demonstrate what type of tackle is best to use in that particular situation. Check out the "Kicking the Defensive Skills up a Notch" section, later in the chapter, for tackling instruction.

✔ **Maintain proper depth:** Your defenders shouldn't be lined up straight across the field. All the attacking team needs to beat this type of alignment is one good through pass, which is a lot easier to convert when defenders are in a straight line. If your defensive players are staggered at different depths in the field, the attacking team encounters greater difficulty in executing its plays.

✔ **Angle approaches:** Your defensive players should always approach an attacking player from an angle instead of going directly at them. Taking an angle forces the attacking player to send a pass backward or to a specific area of the field, because the angle eliminates a lot of his passing options.

When a youngster makes a great defensive play, make sure you recognize the effort with a verbal comment during the game or a high-five when she comes to the sidelines for a breather. Kids understand the importance of defense, and give you a strong effort in that area of the game, when they sense that you put equal importance on it. If the enthusiasm you exhibit for a goal your team scores matches your enthusiasm when your squad stops a great scoring opportunity from the opposing team, your team is on its way to being well rounded.

Also, while the team is performing any type of drill, you may easily get caught up in watching the offensive player and his passing or shooting mechanics. Don't forget to devote an equal amount of attention to the defensive player. Pay attention to whether he uses the appropriate tackling method, which we cover later in this chapter.

Different Types of Defenses You Can Run

As we discuss in Chapter 11, you can utilize a variety of offensive styles, and the same goes for implementing defensive systems. The methods you choose for your team are based on several factors, most notably how much experience the youngsters have playing the game.

The most commonly used defensive style of play at the youngest age levels is man-to-man, which is exactly what it sounds like — a player is responsible for guarding a specific player on the opposing team. As kids gain more experience, you can introduce them to the zone defense, which tends to be a bit more complex to comprehend, because players are responsible for an area of the field rather than a particular individual. Of course, you can get really creative with your defense and incorporate aspects of both styles into your approach. Any defensive style can be altered to fit your team's strengths.

Man-to-man defense

Man-to-man is the most basic style of defense to teach beginning soccer players, because they have a fairly easy time understanding that they're responsible for following number 12 wherever he goes on the field. If you have any players who have participated in other team sports, such as basketball, they've probably been exposed to this concept and have a head start on some of your more inexperienced youngsters. With this defensive approach, your player covers the opposing player regardless of where he is on the field, and when you have possession of the ball, your player joins the attack.

One of the advantages of going with a man-to-man defense is that you can easily tell who's accountable for each of the opposing players. For example, if one of the opposing players is continually dribbling down the field, you clearly see who she's beating with her moves, and you can make an adjustment in who's responsible for that player, which usually remedies the problem.

Throughout the course of a game, your youngsters may lose track of the player they're guarding, or the opposing player may be faster and may beat the defender down the field with the ball. The element of defensive support comes in here. Introduce this aspect of the game to youngsters, and work with them to pay attention to what's going on throughout the field. Teach them to recognize that when one of their teammates is beaten defensively, the nearest defender is responsible for lending support and putting pressure on the attacking player who has broken free.

Lending this support can be a pretty difficult endeavor with youngsters at the beginning levels of play, who are easily distracted. But as players progress in the sport and gain experience playing games, they start to become familiar with those situations that require them to vacate their positions on the field and help provide defensive support to one of their teammates.

With the man-to-man defense, you can make various modifications to fit the needs and abilities of your players. For example, you can choose an aggressive defense that brings more risk into the picture, or you can opt to go with an approach that involves a lot less risk but also allows the opposing team to control much of the action.

Fore-checking

Fore-checking is a term you may have heard used in hockey, but it also applies to an aggressive defensive approach in soccer that is employed to regain possession of the ball as quickly as possible whenever you turn the ball over. The signature of this type of defense, which focuses on a high-pressure style of play, is that after a turnover:

- ✔ One and sometimes even two players always immediately pressure the dribbler in an effort to force turnovers, stall the attack, and handcuff the opponent's ability to get the ball moving downfield.

- ✔ The other defenders press forward to help cut down the number of options available for the player to get passes off to teammates.

It can be a fun style of play for kids who enjoy going after the ball. When operating this type of defense, you have to instill in the kids that as soon as the ball is turned over to the other team, their sole focus is to regain possession as quickly as possible before the other team even has a chance to set up and compose its attack. The biggest weakness associated with this type of defense is that it leaves the team highly vulnerable to a counterattack, because you have all your players pressing forward.

Falling back

At the other end of the spectrum from fore-checking is *falling back,* a low-pressure style of play. With this approach, when the team turns the ball over, players quickly move back to prevent any type of deep penetration by the attacking team. It's a great style of defense for protecting leads, because the attacking team has to execute at a very high efficiency in order to enjoy any results. One of the drawbacks of this approach is that the attacking team dictates play and has plenty of time to set up any specific plays it wants to run or to survey the defensive setup before attacking. And because your opponent's ball handlers aren't under any defensive pressure, they're able to scan the entire field.

You have plenty of room to make modifications with this approach. For example, you can have one player taking an aggressive approach and providing immediate pressure on the ball handler, which provides a few extra, and very valuable, seconds for the rest of the team to get back and set up in its proper positioning. Or you can choose to have a couple of players provide the defensive pressure as soon as your team turns the ball over and make the other players responsible for retreating toward their goal.

Zone defense

When youngsters have been involved in soccer for a couple of years and have a basic understanding of the principles of good defense, you can begin teaching the zone defense to them. Basically, a zone defense makes players responsible for a specific area of the field. Figure 12-1 shows which area of the field each player is responsible for in a 3-5-2 alignment. (We go into

Defending individual standouts

If you're facing a team that has a player who's highly talented and poses quite an offensive threat, you may want to consider using what is called *point marking,* or *man marking,* with your defense. With this approach, you designate one of your players to totally commit to stopping this offensive player, and even when your team has possession of the ball and is on the attack, this player hangs back so that he's always in position to defend the talented player if your team turns the ball over.

greater detail on the advantages and disadvantages of different alignments in Chapter 16.)

In the zone-defense approach, any time an attacking player enters a defensive player's zone, he is immediately marked. When the attacking player moves out of that defensive player's zone, you have two options:

- ✔ Instruct the defender to continue marking him, even though the player has to leave his zone to stick with the player and the ball. With this approach, nearby players have to rotate over, if necessary, to defend the area that has been vacated.

- ✔ Transfer the responsibility of marking him to the defensive player of that respective zone.

Coaches use both approaches, so it's up to you to find out which technique works best with your squad.

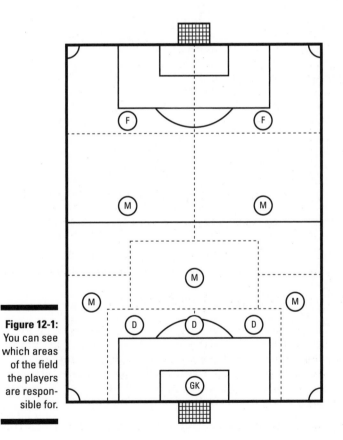

Figure 12-1:
You can see which areas of the field the players are responsible for.

Kicking the Defensive Skills up a Notch

Players on the attack must have a wide range of skills and moves to choose among to enhance their chances of being successful, and the same goes for youngsters on defense. A child who is resourceful and has an assortment of defensive techniques to utilize keeps the attacking players off balance, disrupts the attacking team's rush, and increases the likelihood that his team will regain possession of the ball. You can teach your team a smorgasbord of individual defensive techniques, including the various tackles we cover in this section. (Check out Chapter 16 for the more advanced slide-tackle technique.)

When conducting drills to practice all the tackling techniques covered in this chapter, be sure that you put the kids in a wide range of situations that force them to use both their left and right legs. For example, if you practice the shoulder tackle only coming from the right side, and in a game, one of your players needs to perform it coming from the left side, you really can't expect him to pull it off.

Block tackle

The best time for a defensive player to resort to a *block tackle,* often referred to as a *ground tackle,* is when the opposing player is dribbling the ball directly at him (see Figure 12-2a). In order to execute a successful block tackle, the defender moves directly toward the player and uses his entire body to tackle the opponent. The defensive player blocks the ball by applying steady and even pressure to it with the inside of his leg (see Figure 12-2b). He should also tense all the muscles of his leg, which helps protect the knees.

When teaching the block tackle, keep the following tips in mind:

- ✔ **Staggered:** As the defensive player moves toward the attacking player, one foot should be slightly ahead of the other, and he should be focused on the player's chest.

- ✔ **Crouched:** The defender should be slightly crouched, which enables him to be properly positioned to react to the dribbler moving to either her left or right.

- ✔ **Attacking the ball:** When the defender is ready to attempt the steal, he must go after the ball, not the player. He should use the inside surface of his foot and keep it firm as he drives it into the ball and blocks it so that the attacking player is unable to continue moving forward.

Figure 12-2:
The defender uses the block tackle against the player coming directly at him.

a   b

Shoulder tackle

Although soccer is a game played primarily with the feet, players who understand how to use their entire bodies to their advantage while on defense enjoy increased levels of success. The *shoulder tackle* (see Figure 12-3) is an excellent defensive technique to use when a defender finds herself running alongside an attacking player as she's chasing the ball. During games, you see a lot of contact among players, and players are usually allowed to make contact with an opponent's shoulder if they keep their elbows close to the body and the ball is in close proximity. Of course, this rule depends on the type of league you're playing in. Some leagues instruct their officials to call games closely and frown on any type of contact, while other leagues want the officials to call games more loosely and not whistle every infraction that occurs.

Figure 12-3:
Successful shoulder tackles rely on using the entire body.

a   b

If your league allows some contact, take a look at the keys to executing a successful shoulder tackle:

- ✔ **Leverage:** The key to making a shoulder tackle is being able to use the entire body to gain a better position to make a play on the ball. The player who gets her shoulder *in front of the opposing player's shoulder* (see Figure 12-3a) without being called for pushing, is at a distinct advantage.

- ✔ **The feet:** When the players arrive at the ball, the player who has the advantage in shoulder position uses the foot that is farther away from the defender to make a play on the ball (see Figure 12-3b). Using the inside foot makes it easier for the opponent to take the ball away. Using the outside leg and the outside portion of the foot makes it extremely difficult for the opposing player to have any chance at the ball.

Side tackle

You can use a *side tackle,* which is also referred to as a *poke tackle,* when a defender finds herself running alongside an attacking player who's dribbling the ball and looking to penetrate for a shot on goal or deliver a pass to a teammate. Executing a side tackle requires the defender to be right next to the attacking player. When the attacking player is about to pass or kick the ball (see Figure 12-4a), the defensive player reaches her leg in, extends her foot, and knocks the ball away by using the toes of the foot nearer the opponent (see Figure 12-4b).

After the ball is poked away, if no other players are in the vicinity, whoever can react faster is able to make a move on the ball. Players who carry out the side tackle shouldn't be satisfied with simply knocking the ball away from the opponent; encourage them to complete the play by hustling to gain possession of the ball for their team.

Remind players that they must be right next to the attacking player to pull off this type of tackle. If a defender isn't close to the offensive player when attempting this move, and she extends her leg, she isn't able to make contact with the ball, and the offensive player can scoot past her before she has a chance to recover, giving the attacking team a big advantage.

Figure 12-4: This player attempts to knock the ball away from her opponent with a side tackle.

a   b

Hook tackle

The *hook tackle* is similar to the sliding tackle in that the defensive player drops to the ground to carry it out. The biggest difference between the two is that hook tackles are done when the attacking player is dribbling right at the defender. The following are the steps to carry out a successful hook tackle:

- **Wait for commitment:** After the attacking player commits to going left or right, the defender can begin to make a play on the ball (see Figure 12-5a).

- **Get low:** As the attacking player moves to her right (see Figure 12-5b), the defender drops his body low to the ground and uses his right hand for balance. A common mistake many youngsters make when learning this technique is that they fail to get low to the ground right away. When they don't, they're often off balance and wind up lunging for the ball rather than making a hooking motion with their leg.

- **Top leg hooks ball:** While bending the bottom leg, the player's body connects with the ground, and he swings his top leg in a hooking motion to steal the ball (see Figure 12-5c). Teach youngsters to focus on making contact with the ball with the tops of their shoelaces. As your players become more experienced with this technique, some will actually be able to hook the ball and immediately gain control of it themselves.

a   b

Figure 12-5:
A player
uses the
hook tackle
to steal
the ball.

c

Chapter 13

Coaching Restarts

In This Chapter

▶ Mastering offensive opportunities

▶ Making a defensive stand

Shooting, passing, and tackling are some of the basic skills youngsters must have a good command of in order to excel on the field, but other areas of the game deserve your attention too. In this chapter, we introduce you to those aspects of the game that make playing soccer so truly unique and exciting — and coaching it constantly challenging and fascinating.

Efficiently executing direct and indirect free kicks, penalty kicks, corner kicks, and throw-ins — all those skills that come in handy following a stoppage or interruption in play — provides enormous advantages for the attacking squad. Helping your youngsters learn how to capitalize on these opportunities enhances their skill set and hopefully their already-growing enjoyment of the sport. Furthermore, developing their ability to make defensive stands when the opposing team is in attack mode can be equally rewarding.

Initiating Offense

During your games this season, the majority of your team's scoring chances may come in the form of throw-ins, direct and indirect kicks, and penalty kicks. Being prepared to take advantage of these opportunities when they arise can have a major impact on the game. For a basic description of the rules associated with these techniques, check out Chapter 3. And for associated drills, see Chapter 14.

Throw-ins

When the ball crosses the sideline during the course of action, play comes to a brief stop. The team that knocks the ball out of bounds loses possession, and its opponent gets to throw the ball in to start play again.

Put the throw-in into play as quickly as possible to gain the advantage if the opposing team isn't in proper position to defend it.

The steps for executing a throw-in are the following:

1. **The youngster must begin by holding the ball behind his head, with his body facing the direction in which he's throwing the ball (see Figure 13-1a).**

   When the ball goes behind the head, the child's elbows should be pointing out to the side to ensure that he gets the most power behind his throws.

2. **The player throws the ball with a continuous forward thrust until the ball is released in front of his head. When the player follows through with the throw-in, he should snap his wrists.**

   The player must use both hands to throw the ball and keep his feet on the ground. He isn't allowed a running start or a jump in the air to try to get more force behind the ball.

   Make sure the player drags the toes on his rear foot hard enough so that he can hear it. This habit helps ensure that he's never called for an illegal throw-in during the game for lifting his foot (see Figure 13-1b). More advanced players don't rely on dragging the foot and can generate enough force on their throws by standing with their feet close together.

3. **The player should deliver the ball at the feet of a teammate so she can easily control it and the team can begin its attack.**

   If the player throws the ball at head or chest level, it's more difficult to control, and defensive players have more opportunities to come up with steals.

Figure 13-1:
This child demon-
strates the
appropriate
way to start
a throw-in.

Some things to keep in mind when dealing with throw-ins and younger players include the following:

✔ Teach them to always throw the ball in the direction of the other team's goal. If the ball is thrown toward your own goal, and it's misplayed, your team has handed over possession of the ball to the opposition closer to your own goal. See Figure 13-2 for the way in which the most basic throw-in shakes out.

✔ If the ball has a lot of spin on it, the referee may rule that the player used one hand too much, and the opposing team will be given a throw-in. Stress to youngsters to follow through with both hands at their target, which helps prevent their stronger hand from having a more dominant role in the throw.

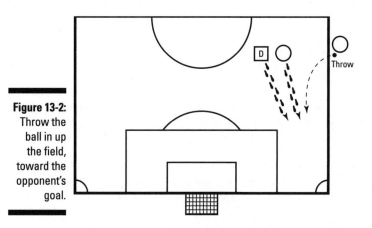

Figure 13-2:
Throw the ball in up the field, toward the opponent's goal.

During a game, having a throw-in at the opponent's end of the field represents an excellent opportunity to run some plays to help create scoring opportunities. The following is a basic Screen-and-Roll play your team can use. (See Figure 13-3.) Here's how it works:

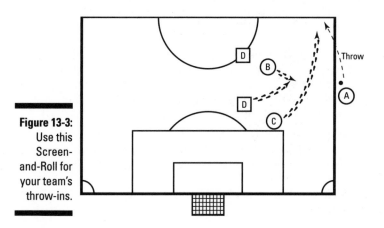

Figure 13-3:
Use this Screen-and-Roll for your team's throw-ins.

1. **Player A tells Player B to be ready for the pass.**

   This statement makes the defensive players think the ball is going to Player B, and they may relax their coverage a little bit on the other attacking players.

2. **Player B moves forward as though he's receiving the pass.**

3. **Player C sprints down the sideline.**

   Player B, moving forward, creates a partial screen to help enable Player C to get free to receive the pass.

4. **Player A throws the ball to Player C.**

Penalty kicks

The referee awards a *penalty kick* to the attacking team when a defensive player commits a penalty inside the penalty area. These kicks are golden opportunities to score a goal, because the goalie is at an overwhelming disadvantage. A penalty kick is a free shot that's taken from a spot 12 yards in front of the goal.

The penalty-kick spot is a lot closer for younger players in beginner leagues. Know your league's rules (as we remind you in Chapter 2). You may be embarrassed if your team has been practicing penalty kicks from 12 yards away during the week, only to earn a penalty kick on game day and find out that you can take these kicks from 7 yards away.

During the kick, the goalie must have his heels on the goal line. He can move side to side as long as he doesn't leave the line until the ball is kicked. All the other players must stand out of the penalty area. The more experienced your players are, the more exactly you want them to aim their shots when they're awarded penalty kicks. Ideally, you want them to aim at a spot within approximately 4 feet of either goal post. Depending on the age of your team, you have two options for what kind of shot to take:

- ✓ **Push pass:** At the younger levels of play, you may want your players to take the shot by using a push pass. As we discuss in Chapter 9, using the inside of the foot delivers a more accurate shot than an instep kick from this short distance, and the youngster should be able to get enough force behind the ball to beat the goalie.

- ✓ **Instep kick:** At the more advanced levels of soccer, players are able to utilize powerful instep kicks, because over the course of playing several seasons, they usually develop pretty good accuracy with this type of kick.

A good way to help young players hone their penalty-kicking skills is to set up a pylon behind the goal line in the net about 2 feet away from each goal post. If players are comfortable hitting the target (in this case, the pylon), they're sure to enjoy the same amount of success with a goalie standing in their way. A well-placed penalty kick with a decent amount of pace behind it is virtually impossible for a goalie to stop at any level of play. Having kids aim at a pylon in this drill helps them learn to pick out a spot inside each goal post that will be an extremely difficult shot for any goalie to stop.

Corner kicks

When a team knocks the ball past its own goal line, the opposing team is awarded a *corner kick* from the corner arch on the side of the field where the ball went out of play (see Figure 13-4). During the kick, defensive players must be at least 10 yards from the player kicking the ball, while the teammates of the youngster delivering the corner kick may position themselves anywhere they choose.

Generally speaking, the more players positioned in the goal area, the more difficult the goalkeeper's job of fielding the ball amid all the traffic around him. Ideally, you want the players to position their kicks about 5 yards in front of the net, which makes moving on the ball more difficult for the goalie. You can employ a number of tactics on a corner kick, depending on the age and skill level of your team:

- ✔ **Assist a header:** If you have a height advantage over the other team, you can send a high corner kick to the front of the net that your taller players can attempt to head into the goal.

- ✔ **Short corner kick:** Inexperienced players, or those players who don't have the leg strength to boot the ball toward the goal, can execute a short corner kick. Here, the ball is simply passed to a teammate positioned a short distance away, and the attack begins from there. This play is highly effective when the player receiving the ball is a skilled dribbler who can help work the ball into the opposition's penalty area to get off a shot or deliver a pass to a teammate to generate a scoring chance.

- ✔ **Back pass:** Here, the youngster sends the ball back toward midfield. Taking this approach allows the team to set up and get its players positioned for the ensuing attack.

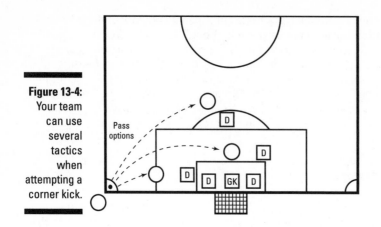

Figure 13-4:
Your team
can use
several
tactics
when
attempting a
corner kick.

One of the most effective techniques for teaching corner kicks is instructing the child to use her instep and kick low on the ball to get it airborne. The instep gives the child the most control over the ball. With older and more experienced players, you can work with them to come across the ball slightly as they make contact with it (check out Chapter 11, where we cover the banana kick), which generates spin on the ball — much like a golfer who draws (hooks) the ball on his tee shot (making it go right to left). This extra spin makes it more difficult for the goalie to handle the incoming ball. If you have a strong-footed kicker on your team who can deliver the ball to the farthest goal post, and a player who's pretty good at headers to make contact with the pass, they may be a potent tandem that your team can utilize to create scoring opportunities.

Free kick

The officials award two kinds of free kicks — direct and indirect — when players commit fouls. Free kicks are a great opportunity for your team to get organized, run a set play that you practiced during the week, and take control of the action on the field. The opposing players must be at least 10 yards away from the ball during a free kick. The most obvious difference between these two free kicks is that a direct free kick may be kicked directly at the goal, whereas an indirect free kick must touch another player before your team scores.

As you can see in the following sections, you're certainly at an advantage when your player with the strongest leg takes the direct kick and your best passer handles the indirect kick. But make sure that all the kids get plenty of work in these areas during practice. During the game, your strongest player may be at the other end of the field without time to run over to take the kick. Also, you should work closely with all your kids so that each one has enough confidence to take the kick, and regardless of how proficient the players are in this area of the game, all of them should have equal opportunities to try these kicks during the course of the game.

Direct free kicks

Direct free kicks (see Figure 13-5) provide the opportunity for you to get a little creative with your coaching. The more experienced and talented your players are, the more room you're afforded with your play calling, and the more options you have at your disposal. Working on a series of different plays in practice gives your team options to choose among on game day. Take a look at some key points to consider when taking a direct free kick:

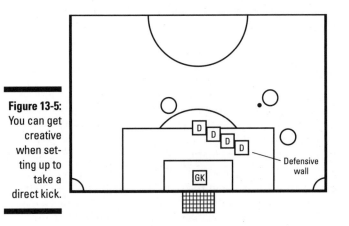

Figure 13-5:
You can get creative when setting up to take a direct kick.

✔ **The fewer, the better:** When your team sets up for a direct free kick in the vicinity of the opposing team's goal, the less time you spend on passes and the quicker you get the shot on goal, the better, because it translates into improved scoring chances. Using set plays that involve multiple passes provides the defense plenty of time to react and recover in order to make a steal or disrupt the play. During practices, teach the players to take a direct shot, or at least limit the team to one pass before shooting.

✔ **Attack quickly:** When setting up to take a direct kick, regardless of where it's from, do so quickly. These kicks are wonderful opportunities to begin a successful attack, and your team members enjoy greater success if they get play restarted quickly, before the other team has an opportunity to set up. If the defense has already gotten into position, don't rush if no tactical advantage exists. Get the team situated first and then proceed.

✔ **Use decoys:** These decoys are so-called trick plays that your team will, excuse the pun, get a real kick out of. They're fun to learn and practice, and when the deception translates into a goal on game day, everyone feels good seeing it all come together. For example, you can have a player charge up to the ball as if he's going to deliver a kick, but at the last second step over the ball and look to receive a pass from another player taking the free kick.

✔ **Good passer:** If you have a child on your team who has emerged as an excellent passer, you can take advantage of those skills by having her handle the free kick in a key situation. The ability to chip the ball over the wall of opposing players in front of the goal (see the "The wall — and other techniques for defending against free kicks" section, later in this chapter) is an excellent asset that can really put the defense on its heels and force your opponents to scramble to recover.

✔ **All areas:** Free kicks occur at random spots all over the field during games, not just in front of the goal, so vary the spots where you practice free kicks. Being prepared to take free kicks from all areas of the field and at different angles is crucial in order to exploit these opportunities to the fullest.

✔ **Direct shots:** The defensive team setting up a wall in front of it doesn't necessarily mean that your player handling the direct kick should look to pass rather than shoot. If your team is in a prime scoring area of the field, teach your players to take a good look at the wall before passing up a shot. The defensive team may have a wall set up that isn't technically sound, and your player can exploit it by executing a shot on net. If the player can get off a shot, strongly encourage him to do so.

✔ **Benders:** If the player is able to spin the ball, she can curve it around the wall, which creates all sorts of additional scoring chances. This type of shot can be particularly difficult for goalies to contend with, because they're screened from seeing the full shot. You can begin introducing kids to this type of kick after they have a little bit of experience playing the game.

Indirect free kick

Indirect free kicks are taken in much the same way as direct kicks, with the minor exception that another player has to touch the ball before you can score a goal. A good pass from the player handling the indirect free kick can create a good scoring opportunity for the team when it's in the vicinity of the opposing team's goal. Two basic plays you can run off an indirect free kick work like this:

✔ The player taking the kick sends the ball wide to a teammate and then takes off to get a return pass and catch the defenders off balance, because a lot of times, they converge on the player with the ball and neglect the other players. (See Figure 13-6a.)

✔ The player taking the kick sends the ball to a teammate positioned far enough past the wall that he can get an immediate shot on goal. (See Figure 13-6b.)

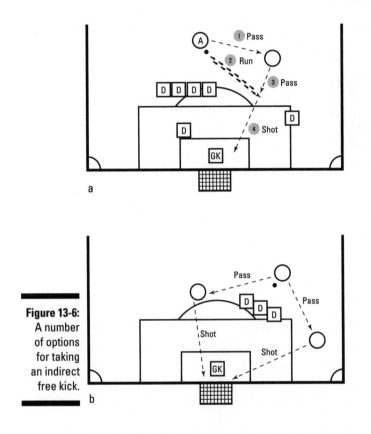

Figure 13-6:
A number
of options
for taking
an indirect
free kick.

Initiating the attack with your goalie

Although goaltenders are primarily thought of as defensive specialists, they can also play very important roles within your team's offense.

Goalie clearing kicks

A properly executed *clearing kick,* also referred to as *punting* the ball, can provide a couple very important things:

- ✔ **Defensive relief:** If your team is under an enormous amount of pressure from the opposing team's attack and playing much of the game in your end of the field, the clearing kick can give your team a reprieve from the assault.

- ✔ **Extra scoring chances:** A clearing kick that connects with a teammate quickly eliminates a portion of the field that the team has to negotiate, which can translate into extra scoring chances for the squad.

Take a look at the steps to executing a successful clearing kick (see Figure 13-7):

Figure 13-7:
The goalie
can help
your offense
by exe-
cuting a
successful
clearing
kick.

1. **Have the goalie focus on striking the center of the ball with the top of her shoelaces.**

2. **She should point the toe of her kicking foot and lock her ankle.**

3. **She should take a step forward with her nonkicking foot while dropping the ball on the kicking foot.**

   Some children, when beginning to learn this skill, have a tendency to throw the ball at their foot instead of letting it drop out of their hands.

Goalie throws

Another key skill for a goalie's arsenal is the throw. Punting is the most effective way to make the ball travel a long distance, but when a ball is booted that far, the other team has a chance to take possession.

Whenever possible, your goalie should throw the ball to a teammate to help start an attack. The throw is much easier to control than the punt, and it's much safer when you're trying to maintain possession.

The following steps teach your youngsters the art of throwing the ball to a teammate:

1. **A child begins by holding the ball with both hands.**

2. **As the child brings the ball over his throwing shoulder, he should spread his fingers, which provides added control of the ball.**

   Younger kids, with their smaller hands, encounter greater difficulty hanging onto the ball, which sometimes requires using both hands while bringing the ball over the throwing shoulder.

3. **The goalie steps forward and follows through toward his intended target (see Figure 13-8).**

Playing Defense

Although corner kicks and direct kicks can provide some fantastic scoring opportunities when your team has possession of the ball, they can be problematic when your team finds itself on the other side and is faced with trying to stop them. Taking away even the slightest advantage the offensive unit has is key to performing well when confronted with defending in these situations. Making a big defensive stop can provide your team a boost of confidence and dramatically shift the momentum of the game in your favor.

Defending throw-ins

When defending a throw-in, one of the main points to keep in mind is that the opposing team is probably going to run a set play that it worked on in practice. It may even be one of the same plays that your team runs or something similar that you quickly recognize. Regardless, work with your team to keep the following points in mind on defending throw-ins:

✔ **Maintain the advantage:** Don't put a defensive player on the youngster who's handling the throw-in, because it gives away the slight advantage you have with more defensive players in the field than offensive players. The player making the throw-in can't touch the ball until someone in the field of play does.

✔ **Don't get picked off:** Many teams run screen plays where players criss-cross back and forth (see the section on throw-ins in "Initiating Offense," earlier in this chapter, for one such play). Your best defensive bet may be assigning players to be responsible for a certain area of the field so that a lot of the confusion of trying to stick to an individual player is eliminated.

✓ **Keep an eye on the best player:** When the game gets under way, you and your team are going to have a good idea of who are some of the best players on the opposing squad. Throw-ins represent wonderful opportunities for teams to get the ball to these players. Consequently, consider putting your best defensive player on the team's most dangerous player, and have him shadow the player all over the field to help ensure that she doesn't break free with the ball following the throw-in.

✓ **Don't worry about offsides:** Your team must constantly be aware during throw-ins that an attacking player won't be called for being offsides. (For more details on the tricky offside rule, check out Chapter 3.) That means that your players have no reason to ever allow a player from the opposing team to break free while receiving a throw-in.

✓ **Don't forget the player who threw the ball in:** After this player throws the ball in, he must be accounted for. If not, he can race down the sideline and receive a return pass from the player he just threw the ball to. Keep an eye on this player, because he poses a risk after the ball is in play.

Defending penalty kicks

Winning the lottery. Never getting sick a day in your life. Stopping a penalty kick. All involve enormous odds stacked heavily against you. After all, a well-struck soccer ball can travel from the penalty mark to the goal in less than a second, which means the goalie is basically left guessing which direction the shot is headed. Often, the goalie's best option is to simply guess which side the player is kicking to and dive in that direction at the moment the player makes impact.

As your goalie becomes more skilled and masters the basic techniques of playing in front of the net, you can begin working with her on the difficult aspect of contending with a penalty shot. If the player taking the penalty shot and the goalie are both equally talented in their respective positions, the player kicking the ball has a distinct advantage. So any little thing the goalie can do to help minimize that advantage is key in her efforts to make stops on penalty shots. The goalie should try to:

✓ **Watch the other team during warm-ups:** A lot of teams have their designated shooter practice during warm-ups. Try to pick up any tendencies in terms of the type of shot and placement that you can.

✔ **Pay attention prior to the shot:** Teach the goaltender to pay close attention to the player before the shot. Maybe he can pick up something in the way the youngster takes a warm-up swing with his leg before the shot that gives away what type of shot he's taking.

✔ **Take a cue from the kicker:** Have your goalie get used to checking out the direction the kicker's plant foot is pointing and even the posture of the kicker's body. Try to read her as she approaches the ball. Is the player already looking at a certain part of the net and unknowingly giving away where she intends to kick the ball? Is she approaching the ball at a certain angle to get a better shot at one side of the net? Although a goalie certainly won't be able to pick up all that information in the short amount of time he has to work with, he may pick up on one tidbit of information that he can use to his advantage.

✔ **Use game knowledge:** If the penalty kick takes place in the second half, your goalie may already have a feel for the player taking the kick. Perhaps she has already had to make some plays on this youngster's shots, so she may know that the player has a tendency to aim all his shots to the left or right. Is he a finesse or power player? Have all his shots been either low to the ground or in the air? These factors can help the goalie make a big stop for the team.

Defending corner kicks

Teams delivering corner kicks are in a great position to create scoring opportunities. Experienced soccer teams score the bulk of their goals off corner kicks from headers. Therefore, guarding the front of the goal line with three defensive players is important. With this setup, the defenders have a good chance to gain possession and quickly clear the ball or put together an attack of its own if the ball enters their penalty area.

Position one defender directly in the goal area near or next to the goal post while making sure that he doesn't obstruct the goalie's view. Position the second defender at the goal post at the far end. If the goalie is forced to leave the box, the defenders can collapse to the middle of the goal area to protect both halves (check out Figure 13-4 earlier in the chapter). The third defender marks the player taking the corner kick so that he isn't able to roam free once he puts the ball into play.

Midfielders can also be utilized to play the posts, which allows defenders more freedom to move about and converge on the ball when play unfolds.

The wall — and other techniques for defending against free kicks

Free kicks can present real problems for defenders, especially at the more advanced levels of soccer, where players have the ability to kick hard, accurate shots from long distances. This type of player poses a big threat, and if your team isn't prepared, these kids quickly exploit your defensive weaknesses and put goals on the scoreboard. Assembling a wall and positioning it properly are vital for establishing that first line of defense against a free kick.

The wall is your team's best weapon against free kicks that take place at your end of the field. *The wall* is exactly what it sounds like — a wall of stationary players lined up to serve as an obstacle to the opposing player taking the free kick. When the attacking team is in range to get a good shot on goal, get a wall set up to help block the shot or disrupt the play the offensive team is attempting to run.

In a full-scale soccer game of 11-on-11, the wall is usually comprised of 3, 4, or 5 players who are stationed 10 yards away from the ball. In smaller-scale games of soccer involving kids at the beginning levels, such as 6-on-6, the wall can be as small as 1 or 2 players. As we discuss in Chapter 2, your league's rules on how far away the wall must be from the ball can vary greatly from the official rules of soccer. In smaller-scale games with younger kids, the distance can be as little as 5 yards.

One of the main purposes of the wall is to cover the near-post half of the goal (see Figure 13-9), while the goalie's primary responsibility is on the other half of the net. (The *near post* is the post closer to the shooter.) On direct and indirect free kicks, the players comprising the wall must remain still until the ball is kicked. Here are a few other tips to keep in mind when it comes to the wall:

Figure 13-9: When players form the wall, they help the goalie defend against a shot.

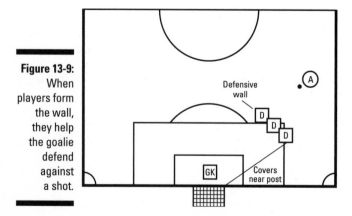

✔ **Be quick:** The players need to get lined up quickly so that the offense isn't able to get an advantage. With younger teams, you may want to designate ahead of time a player or two who will be in the wall so that you always have a couple players rushing to get set up, and then, depending on their positions on the field, other teammates can join in quickly.

✔ **Choose the number of players:** With more experienced teams, you can rely on the goalie to choose the number of players for the wall. With less experienced teams, you need to take a more vocal role in helping select the number of players for the wall. The goalie is also responsible for instructing the wall to move in whatever direction is most effective, with the end player lined up with the post.

✔ **Don't move:** Inexperienced players who aren't accustomed to standing still while a ball is kicked toward them have a tendency to turn their backs on it. This tendency is a bad habit for players to get into for a couple of reasons. One, turning sideways creates unwanted gaps for the ball to slip through, and two, the players are at a disadvantage because they aren't able to see where the ball is and react quickly.

✔ **Height matters:** The tallest player in the wall should be lined up with the near post. The remaining players comprising the wall should stand shoulder to shoulder — from tallest to shortest — with no gaps between them.

When a direct or indirect kick takes place far from your own goal, you have no special defensive tactics to rely on. Basically, you want your defenders to move quickly and maintain their proper positioning between the ball and the goal. On an indirect kick, the overwhelming majority of the time, the attacking player delivers a short pass to a teammate to the left or right of the wall. Because this scenario is most often used, defensive players should already be focused on marking their opponent so that they don't allow the attacking team any advantage going down the field.

Chapter 14

Taking Practice Drills to the Next Level

*Y*ou've reached that point in the season where your team is starting to get a fairly good grasp of the basics of passing and receiving. Your goalie has become pretty proficient at making the routine saves. When your team is pressured deep in your end of the field, your players enjoy their share of success in halting the attack. You've even had a couple players get off a header in a game. Your team is learning and making progress, and that should bring a smile to your face. To ensure that the learning and skill development don't come to a grinding halt, you need to kick your practice drills up a notch.

So now what? You have to match your team's increasing skill level with drills that continue to challenge, motivate, and excite the players. A successful drill you used during the first week of practice doesn't carry the same type of benefits for a team that's been together for quite awhile. Dig into some fun new drills in this chapter to reenergize your players' enthusiasm and continue pushing them down that path of learning and skill development.

And for those players who have been lacing up their spikes for several years now, you can use these drills to enhance their skills and turn them into more proficient players in all areas of the game.

Offensive Drills

Young soccer players love scoring goals, but you need a lot of good offensive techniques to get to that end result of goal-scoring. The following sections explore drills for attacking, passing, ball handling, heading, and — yes — scoring. For the basics of coaching offense, see Chapter 11. For more advanced offensive strategies, see Chapter 15.

When conducting drills, you want every child actively involved. Standing around and waiting in line drains the fun out of their participation, and the amount of learning taking place is drastically reduced.

Attacking

The ability to create quality scoring chances, particularly when your team has the advantage of outnumbering the defense, is the mark of a well-coached team. Although your team isn't always going to put up a goal in these situations, generating good scoring opportunities pays dividends over the duration of the season.

2-on-1

This drill helps youngsters learn to exploit a 2-on-1 advantage to the fullest and generate a quality scoring opportunity.

What you need: Area of field with goal. 4 players. 1 ball.

How it works: Position an attacking player on each side of the goalie, who begins the drill holding a ball. (See Figure 14-1.) Also position a defensive player about 10 yards in front of the goalie. The two attacking players move away from the net, and the goalie delivers a pass to one of them. Then the attacking pair turns around and works to beat the lone defender and get a good shot on net.

Coaching pointers: Observe the goalie to ensure that he uses proper form while delivering the outlet pass, and monitor the placement of the pass. Also, monitor the offensive pair to see whether either player takes a shot too early in the drill or makes quality passes to fully capitalize on the pair's man advantage. The defender should try to force the action to one side to limit the opportunities of the offense.

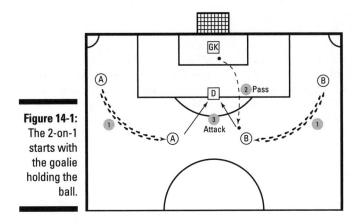

Figure 14-1:
The 2-on-1 starts with the goalie holding the ball.

3-on-2

This drill teaches youngsters to take advantage when they have an extra player on the attack. This setup also allows players to work on their throw-ins, as well as their passing, receiving, and shooting skills. By being outnumbered, the defensive players have to be quick on their feet in reading the play.

What you need: Area of field with goal. 6 players. 1 ball.

How it works: Set up an offensive player on the sideline to throw the ball in. (See Figure 14-2.) Position two more attacking players in the area you have for the drill, along with two defensive players and a goalie. When the player throws the ball in, she should look to create space to stretch the two defenders out. The player who receives the ball can either press forward and take a shot on net or pass to one of his teammates flanking him, depending on how the defenders handle the play.

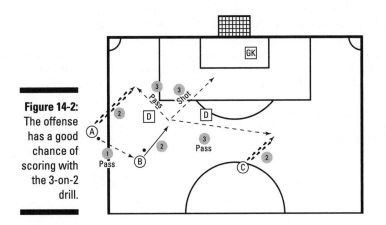

Figure 14-2:
The offense has a good chance of scoring with the 3-on-2 drill.

Coaching pointers: Initially, make sure that the child makes a legal throw-in and drags her foot while releasing the ball, which we discuss in greater detail in Chapter 13. Kids with plenty of soccer experience can handle throw-ins by placing their feet close together and generating strength in their throws from their arm and abdomen muscles. Focus on the offensive player who receives the throw-in to make sure that he dribbles with his head up and delivers a pass if a teammate is open, or gets off a shot if that turns out to be the best scoring opportunity.

Passing

You may have a number of players who are proficient at putting the ball in the net, and that's a great asset. But if few teammates can get them the ball when and where they need it, the number of scoring chances your team generates is going to sink. These drills can hone those all-important passing skills and put some sizzle in your team's attack.

Fancy Foot

Fancy Foot develops the kids' less-dominant feet so that they become comfortable passing and receiving with either foot.

What you need: 10- x 30-yard grid. 3 players. 1 ball.

How it works: Set up a basic 2-on-1 drill. The object is for two offensive players to try to work the ball down the field against a lone defender. The twist is that one of the two offensive players can pass and receive the ball only with his less-dominant foot. A player that is right-foot-dominant should be on the left side so he can practice receiving passes with his outside foot and sending passes back to his partner. On the return trip up the field, switch roles so the other player can practice with his less-dominant foot.

Coaching pointers: Kids may be frustrated when learning to use their less-dominant foot, because during games, they naturally use their stronger foot. So be patient; provide lots of encouragement; and help them understand that when their feet are equally skilled, they're that much more of an offensive threat or that much stronger a defender.

Diagonal Passing

This drill works on the accuracy of the players' short and long passes, their ability to get the ball airborne when the situation requires, and their ability to receive and gather under control different types of passes. *Diagonal passes,* also known as *crossing passes,* are typically played while attacking and are used to generate scoring opportunities at the opponent's end of the field. Check out Chapter 11 for more details.

What you need: 10- x 20-yard grid. 4 players. 4 balls.

How it works: This drill can be run simultaneously with the entire team broken into groups of four. (See Figure 14-3.) Position 2 players about 10 yards apart, and position 2 more players about 20 yards away. Each player starts with a soccer ball.

1. **The two players nearest each other exchange passes.** One player must send a push pass along the ground, while the other player delivers a chip pass that gets the ball in the air so the balls don't collide.

2. **After receiving the passes, the players deliver long passes to the player downfield who's across from them.** Again, one player delivers a pass along the ground, while the other sends one in the air. Rotate the types of passes the players are using so everyone gets practice doing both.

Coaching pointers: Make sure the kids are following through toward their intended targets. When they know they have to react quickly to receive an incoming ball, they may have a tendency to cut their follow-through short in preparation for receiving a pass.

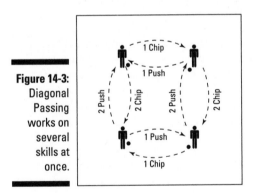

Figure 14-3: Diagonal Passing works on several skills at once.

Shooting

Choose a variety of shooting drills that challenge your players to work on their accuracy, distance, and technique. In game situations, kids have to shoot the ball from different angles and distances; using the drills in this section gets them prepared to take those shots on game day.

Bending and Chipping Balls

This drill works on a youngster's shooting skills with both feet and getting off shots at challenging angles with a defensive player in the way. For more information on teaching these shooting techniques, see Chapter 11.

What you need: Area of field with goal. 4 players. 3 balls.

How it works: Position 2 offensive players about 30 yards away from the goal, with one player the designated shooter and the other the passer. Also, have a defensive player out about 10 yards in front to serve as an obstacle that the shooter has to work the ball around. The drill begins:

1. **The passer delivers the ball to the shooter (♦), who gets off a shot while the ball is rolling. (See Figure 14-4a.)**

   With the defensive player between the shooter and the goal, the shooter either has to chip the ball over the player's head or, if she's more advanced, work on using side spin to bend the ball around the player.

2. **The shooter receives a diagonal pass that forces her to go to her left and take a shot with her other foot, while the defensive player slides over to cut down the shooting angle (see Figure 14-4b).**

3. **The shooter has to cut back to her right to receive another pass and get off a shot at a sharp angle, with the defensive player again standing in the way (see Figure 14-4c).**

Coaching pointers: Watch to see whether the passer puts the ball in the most advantageous position, whether the attacker takes the right angle for the shot, and whether the defender and goalie work together to prevent the player from getting a quality shot off.

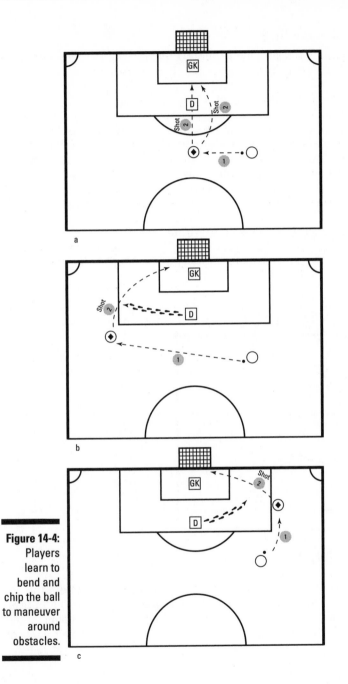

Figure 14-4:
Players
learn to
bend and
chip the ball
to maneuver
around
obstacles.

Zig Zag

The Zig Zag helps kids work on their shooting technique and accuracy from a variety of distances and angles.

What you need: Area of field with goal. 4 players. 3 balls.

How it works: Begin with the shooter (♦) about 30 yards away from the goal. (See Figure 14-5.) Position a passer (A) about 10 yards away from him with a ball, as well as another player (B) by the side of the net with 2 balls. The drill begins with the Player A giving the shooter a slow-moving ball that he connects with and shoots while running straight ahead. The passer at the side of the net (B) follows with a diagonal pass and then another pass at a sharp angle.

Coaching pointers: On the initial kick, make sure the player gets full force behind the shot and follows through at the net. Watch the positioning of his plant foot on the other shots, because he may use a sloppy technique if he isn't used to taking sharp angle kicks.

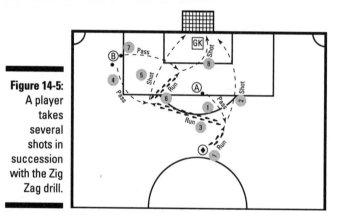

Figure 14-5:
A player takes several shots in succession with the Zig Zag drill.

Ball handling

Good ball handling plays a prominent role in a team's success at both the offensive and defensive ends of the field. Players who can dribble out of trouble while pinned back near their own goal save their goalie from being forced to make a bundle of saves. Also, players who don't turn the ball over while on the attack apply additional pressure on the opponent, which can translate into extra scoring chances.

Musical Soccer Balls

This drill helps youngsters learn to handle the ball in tight spaces while being pressured by a defender.

What you need: 15- x 15-yard grid. 5 players. 3 balls.

How it works: Mark off a playing area of about 15 yards by 15 yards. Place three soccer balls in the center of the playing area, and have 5 players positioned around the outside of the area. On your command, the players run in and battle for possession of the ball. Run the drill for a minute or two. The object is to see who can maintain possession of the ball when time runs out. This drill is fun for kids of all ages, and if you begin counting down out loud with 10 seconds left, the competitive juices really get flowing as the kids try to make a last-second steal or try to cling to possession of their ball.

Coaching pointers: With several players in a tight area, keep a close eye on them to make sure players aren't committing penalties by trying to steal balls or by trying to protect them illegally.

Gridlock

Works on ball-handling skills in both a 1-on-1 setting and in those difficult 1-on-2 scenarios.

What you need: 15- x 40-yard grid. 3 players. 1 ball.

How it works: An offensive player starts at midfield with the ball. For about 20 yards, she dribbles downfield against a defender. If she reaches the 20-yard marker that you've designated with a pylon, she continues trying to move on for another 20 yards, but this time against 2 defenders. If, while going 1-on-1, she loses possession of the ball, she starts over from the spot where the ball was taken and continues until she reaches the first marker. After the player reaches the first marker (and in some cases, there may be several turnovers before she gets there), she goes against the 2 defenders.

Coaching pointers: Match up players of similar abilities during this drill. You don't want your least-skilled ball handler going up against your best defender and not being able to get to the marker.

Heading

Well-rounded soccer players are able to utilize all parts of their body to move the ball where they want. Using the ol' noggin can be a great weapon for scoring goals, as well as clearing the ball out of danger. The following are some drills to get your kids thinking and using their heads.

Head 'Em Up

This drill helps players zero in on an incoming ball, and learn to make quick adjustments and head a pass to an open teammate.

What you need: 5- x 5-yard grid. 2 players. 1 ball.

How it works: Position a player about 10 yards in front of you. Toss a ball up in the air to him, and as he's getting into position to make a header, take a few steps to the left or right. The player must adjust to your movements and head the ball back to you, preferably at your feet.

Coaching pointers: Make sure the child keeps a close eye on the ball and relies on his peripheral vision to locate in which direction you're moving. Otherwise, he won't be able to make solid contact with the ball, and his headers will be off target.

Cross and Head

Cross and Head works on heading, delivering accurate crossing passes, and helping goalies learn to defend against headers.

What you need: Area of field with goal. 3 players. 1 ball.

How it works: Position one player (A) to the side of the net and the designated header (♦) about 18 yards away from the goalie. (See Figure 14-6.) The drill begins with the player at the side delivering a crossing pass to be headed at the net. The goalie, who either makes the save or retrieves the ball, then distributes the ball on an outlet pass to the passer, who delivers a ball in the air to be headed again. The goalie then sends a pass along the end line, and the player delivers another crossing pass to be headed.

Coaching pointers: If the crossing passes aren't on target, watch where the youngster's foot is making contact with the ball. On headers, remind the player to follow through with his head at the target to get the maximum force behind his shots.

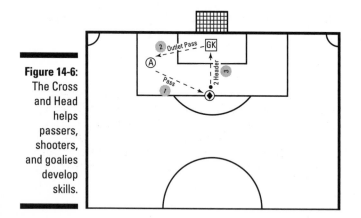

Figure 14-6:
The Cross and Head helps passers, shooters, and goalies develop skills.

Restarts

Take a look at some drills you can incorporate into your practices to teach your team these restart related skills — many of your scoring chances will come from these situations — and how your team can best take advantage of them. For more information on teaching the techniques, see Chapter 13.

Throw-In Competition

A good throw-in drill to incorporate into your practices is to stage a mini-tournament with your players. Here's a sample of one that works for any age group.

What you need: Half the field. Ball and cone for each player.

How it works: Place a cone several yards away from the sideline, and have each youngster take five throws. Record who gets the ball closest to the target or who hits the target the most. To avoid having the kids stuck in lines waiting to throw, set up several cones around the field at the same distance from the sideline so that a number of kids can throw simultaneously. You can also stage a throw-in competition by seeing who can throw the ball the farthest and with the most accuracy.

Coaching pointers: When conducting these mini-competitions, make sure that the team uses proper form on every throw-in. Any time the players use an incorrect technique, the throw doesn't count in the competition, even if it hits the target.

Shooting in the Spotlight

Youngsters often feel a little more pressure than normal when taking a penalty shot because all eyes are on them, so devise drills that incorporate that factor into the equation.

What you need: Area of field with goal. Entire team. 1 ball.

How it works: At the end of practice, have each player take a few penalty shots on the goalie with the entire team watching to get them comfortable performing the skill while people watch. Turn it into a fun contest so that every time a player notches a goal, you have to do a pushup. Shooting in the Spotlight is an exciting way to help the players work on honing their shots while also giving your goalie some great practice for those situations where she's called upon in a game to face down a penalty shot.

Coaching pointers: Some kids are going to be uncomfortable performing a skill like this with the entire team watching, so be sure that they focus on the ball and make solid contact with their shots, rather than worry about what their teammates are doing.

Corner-Kick Challenge

Corner kicks represent wonderful scoring opportunities for your team. The more comfortable and proficient your players become delivering them, the more goals you're likely to generate.

What you need: All four corners of the field. Entire team. 4 balls.

How it works: This drill can be run simultaneously in all four corners of the field to eliminate standing-around time.

1. **Position a player about 10 yards in front of the net.**

2. **The player delivering the corner kick must try to get the ball in the air.**

3. **The player receiving the ball can either work on his heading skills and attempt to head the ball into the net or work on his receiving skills by gaining control of the ball and then taking a quick shot on goal.**

With this drill going on in all corners of the field, the goalie also has to react quickly and make several saves in succession. The difficulty of the drill can be increased by adding a defensive player to the mix, which makes the drill more gamelike.

Coaching pointers: Make sure your players aren't sending the ball too close to the front of the net when making corner kicks.

Defensive Drills

In much the same way that offensive players work on different ways to control the ball and negotiate down the field, defensive players work to master the skills required of their position. You must help them learn different techniques to swipe possession of the ball and find ways to prevent the opposing players from capitalizing on a scoring opportunity when they have a player advantage on the attack. As we discuss in the preceding chapters, you can use a number of available methods. Now take a look at some drills to enhance some of those skills.

Tackling

Nothing disrupts the flow of an attack quicker than defenders who are skillful when it comes to taking the ball away. Sound tackling techniques are a necessity for any team at any level.

Chase and Catch

The Chase and Catch drill helps players learn to use their entire bodies, and specifically their shoulders, to take possession of the ball from an opposing player.

What you need: Area of field with goal. 3 players. A coach. 1 ball.

How it works: Position 2 players about 10 yards apart, with a coach between them with a ball. The coach sends the ball downfield. The two players flanking her run and try to gain possession of the ball. The player who gains control of the ball continues and tries to score a goal, while the other player takes a defensive role, trying to poke the ball away and prevent a shot on goal.

Coaching pointers: Make sure the kids keep their elbows tucked close to their body, because they may have a tendency to use them to muscle the opponent off the ball. If they do that, they're called for a penalty that results in turning the ball over to the opposing team.

Pressure

Pressure teaches kids to receive a throw-in and to gather the ball under control and maintain possession of it while they're facing heavy pressure from a defender.

What you need: 10- x 10-yard grid. 2 players. 1 ball.

How it works: Pair your players up, and give a youngster in each twosome a ball. The drill begins with the pairs facing each other with about 10 yards between them. At your command, the kids with a ball deliver a throw-in to their partners. After delivering the throw-in, they immediately charge toward their partners and try to steal possession of the ball. Run the drill for 5 or 10 seconds, or keep it going until possession of the ball is lost. Keep rotating who delivers the throw-in to start so players get practice in both scenarios.

Coaching pointers: Make sure the children receiving the ball are watching it into their bodies. Kids sometimes have the tendency to look at the player charging at them, which disrupts their ability to control the ball.

Race to the Cone

Race to the Cone gives defensive players a lot of tackling practice in a short period of time, with offensive players rapidly moving all around them. They also work on how to take the right angle to attempt stealing a ball from a player.

What you need: 20- x 20-yard grid. 5 players. 3 balls. 4 cones.

How it works: Select 2 players to serve as defenders. Position 4 (or more) cones at random spots around the playing field, and give each of the other 3 kids a soccer ball. (See Figure 14-7.) The object of the game is for the 3 offensive players to dribble their balls from cone to cone without losing possession. The cones represent safe spots, where defensive players can't swipe the ball. Allow players to remain at the safe spots for only a few seconds to keep the game moving. Rotate the players often so that everyone gets chances to be an offensive and defensive player.

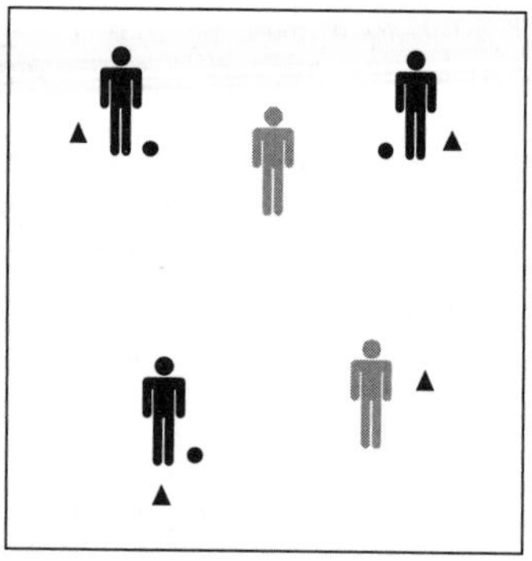

Figure 14-7:
Rotate players during Race to the Cone so that they all play offense and defense.

Coaching pointers: Although this drill also promotes ball-handling skills, be on the lookout for defensive players using proper tackling techniques. Build the foundation of good defense so your players don't receive unnecessary penalties during games for being too rough.

Defending

The better your team becomes at defending, the happier your goalie is going to be. Besides giving him less work, the more proficient the team becomes in this area of the game, the more likely the team is to spend more time in its opponent's end of the field.

Taking on 2-on-1s

This drill gives defenders work in a number of areas, including battling for balls 1-on-1 and disrupting 2-on-1s from close range.

What you need: Area of field with goal. 4 players. 1 ball.

How it works: Position 2 attacking players near the penalty arc, 1 defensive player at the top of the goalie box, and the goalie in the net (see Figure 14-8). From off to the side of the net, send a high ball between the 2 attackers and the defender. Force the defensive player to make a quick decision: Is the ball in range for him to go for it, or is the play too risky? If the play is too risky, he ends up being out of position and leaves his goalie in a precarious situation. The drill continues until an attacker scores a goal, the goalie makes a save, or the defensive player clears the ball out of the area.

Coaching pointers: Deliver balls at a variety of angles and distances so that youngsters get a real taste of what game action is like. On balls that you deliberately kick long, make sure the defensive player isn't going after them. Reinforce to him to go after only balls that he has a realistic shot of making a play on so he doesn't put his team at an unnecessary disadvantage.

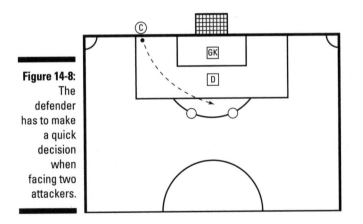

Figure 14-8: The defender has to make a quick decision when facing two attackers.

Tackling 3-on-2s

This drill rewards strong defensive play in a gamelike setting and forces the attacking team to make quick decisions under the pressure of the clock.

What you need: Area of field with goal. 6 players. 1 ball.

How it works: Play a series of 1- or 2-minute games in which the attacking team tries to score a goal in this 3-on-2 setup. Award the attackers 2 points if their players score a goal and 1 point if they get a shot on goal. Award the defenders 2 points if their side is able to prevent any shot from reaching the goal. With this setup, both sides have multiple opportunities to register points, which keeps the drill action packed.

Coaching pointers: Make sure the defensive players aren't overcommitting on a play, which creates an even bigger advantage for the attacking team. Also, make sure the attacking players are aggressively working for a shot, because they have little time to work with.

Goaltending

Manning the goalie position is no easy task for youngsters, who are challenged to make stops on kicks coming at them from all sorts of angles and distances. The ability to make saves, both on the ground and in the air, takes plenty of practice.

Diving One-Handers

This drill gets goalies comfortable — and confident — with making one-handed saves in those situations where they just aren't able to get both hands on the ball.

What you need: A goalie. 2 offensive players. 2 balls.

How it works: Position 2 players about 15 yards away from the net and at an angle. Give both players a ball. The first player takes a shot, and the goalie must dive and attempt to block the shot with one hand. Then, getting up quickly and beginning at the other post, she dives in the opposite direction to make a save from the other kick.

Coaching pointers: Make sure that the goalie is stretching out fully in order to make it as difficult as possible on the shooter. When she makes a save and is lying on the ground, see whether she cradles the ball like a puppy and protects it with her body.

Mystery Saves

Mystery Saves improves the reaction skills of your goalie.

What you need: Goal and space 10 yards out in front of net. 3 players. 2 balls.

How it works: Position 2 players in front of the net, about 10 yards away from each other. Give each player a ball. You stand out of the goalie's view and, without her knowledge, signal which player actually takes the shot on net. On your whistle, both players approach their balls at the same time, but only one player delivers a shot on net. This approach forces the goalie to really concentrate on each ball and react quickly to the incoming shot.

Coaching pointers: Make sure the goalie follows the shot all the way into her hands and doesn't allow the ball to bounce away for a dangerous rebound.

Punting Partners

To help your goalies get a good feel for properly connecting on their kicks, here's a great drill to help them on their way.

What you need: A quarter of the field. 2 goalies. 1 ball.

How it works: Position 2 goalkeepers approximately 10 yards apart. The purpose of the drill is for the players to punt the ball to their partners. By starting the players close together, you make them focus on making contact with the ball in the center. After they become proficient in punting the ball back and forth to each other, you can start moving them farther apart. After they have their accuracy down, they can start punting for distance. Another benefit of this drill is that by catching their partner's punts, they're building their hand–eye coordination and getting some great practice fielding high shots.

After your goalies have the proper punting technique down cold, you can have them practice punting into their own net, which gives them a high number of repetitions in a short period of time. Plus they don't have to chase the ball all over the field.

Coaching pointers: Make sure the goalie is watching his foot make contact with the ball. Kids sometimes have a tendency to look up before their foot connects with the ball because they're eager to see how far they've booted it.

Putting It All Together: Sample Practice Session

Now that you're armed with a new set of drills that you can incorporate into your practices, it's time to put them together. A well-structured session that features new drills for the players to perform keeps their attention levels high and continues their progression in the sport. Take a look at Table 14-1 for a 1-hour sample practice plan that you can use with your players, utilizing the drills covered in this chapter.

Table 14-1		Intermediate Practice Plan
Duration	*Activity*	*Comments*
10 min.	Warm-up	Stretching, calisthenics, and several minutes of moving with the ball. This activity can involve dribbling around the field in a light jog or breaking the team into twosomes and having them dribble against their partners, who apply light defensive pressure before the players switch roles.
5 min.	**Chase and Catch**	Split the squad in half, performing the drill at both ends of the field.
15 min.	**Diagonal Passing** **Zig Zag** **Diving One-Handers**	Break the team up into three groups. In the center of the field, run the Diagonal Passing drill, and run the other drills at opposite ends of the field. Rotate players every 5 minutes so they go through each of the drills during this 15-minute segment. Players rotate to work on the various offensive and defensive skills during each drill, while the goalies work on the different aspects of making saves that are part of each activity.
5 min.	**Musical Soccer Balls**	Keep the team broken into the same three groups, and run three games of the Musical Soccer Ball drill. It's a fun, yet highly competitive, game that puts a smile on the kids' faces right in the middle of the practice.
10 min.	**Tackling 3-on-2s** **Mystery Saves**	The first half of the practice has been devoted to working on individual skills, so now is a good time to get the kids working together on game-type situations. Incorporate each drill at one end of the field. As players go through the 3-on-2 drill, interchange them with the players involved at the other end of the field to give everyone a chance.
10 min.	**Taking on 2-on-1s** **Corner-Kick Challenge**	At one end of the field, use the Taking on 2-on-1s drill, and at the other end, have players work on their corner kicks in both corners of the field. After 5 minutes, rotate.
5 min.	Scrimmage	Conclude the practice with a scrimmage game that has proved to be popular over the season. A quick game of the kids against the coaches and parents, which we cover in Chapter 6, is always a winner and a great way to send everyone home happy and looking forward to returning for the next practice.

Part IV
Advanced Soccer Strategies

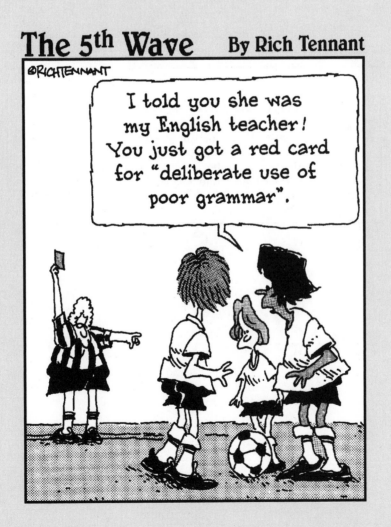

The 5th Wave   By Rich Tennant

@RICHTENNANT

I told you she was my English teacher! You just got a red card for "deliberate use of poor grammar".

In this part . . .

Soccer is more than kids running up and down the field, chasing the ball, and waving at grandma in the stands. In this part, we offer up some additional insights to help take your team's offensive and defensive play to the next level.

Chapter 15

Coaching Offense 201

· ·

In This Chapter
▶ Figuring formations
▶ Upgrading offensive skills

· ·

Choosing a formation for your team to run is sort of like trying to decide on dessert after a meal at a fancy restaurant. You have so many options, and they all look good. You can introduce a variety of formations to your team when the players have the basics of the game down. Some formations cater to an attacking style of play, while others lean toward a more defensive approach.

In this chapter, we delve into those formations that are designed to produce high-quality scoring chances. Try these offenses when your players are able to maintain possession of the ball while dribbling and make accurate passes to their teammates. (In Chapter 16, we take a look at more defensive-oriented systems.) We also take a closer look at upgrading your players' skills in delivering crossing passes and heading those crosses, as well as using a wide range of feints to negotiate through defenders and create shots on goal.

Upgrading the Offense

A *system of play* is the basic style of play a team uses. It assigns explicit responsibilities for every position. Systems can either be offensive or defensive, depending on the formation and what you're trying to accomplish. A *formation* is how the players are aligned on the field. Offensive formations feature more players at the attacking end of the field, while defensive formations have more players set up near their own goal. Whatever system you choose to use with your players, every player has to do his best to fulfill his responsibilities in order for the system to operate as smoothly as possible.

Because you have a number of formations at your disposal, introducing your team to several of them is a good idea. You may come across one that really seems to fit the team's personality and players; you'll never know if you don't experiment a little. Some formations will work, and some won't be nearly as successful. Go ahead and experiment with them to see what your players enjoy and what works best for them, and then go from there.

In the name of a formation, the first number represents the number of defenders, the second number is the number of players who are positioned in the midfield area, and the last number is the number of players at the front of the attack. These numbers always add up to 10 (because the goalie isn't mentioned in any formation alignment). Of course, these types of formations are appropriate only for games of 11-on-11.

2-3-5 formation

This heavily offensive system generates lots of scoring chances and keeps the ball in the opponent's half of the field, because the bulk of the players are on the front line. You have five attackers playing the forward position with a striker (the center forward) flanked by two forwards (a winger and insider) on each side (see Figure 15-1). Take a look at the players' tasks in this setup:

- ✔ **Defenders:** The players manning these positions play behind the midfielders and are also referred to as the *sweeper* and *stopper*. The stopper is always positioned in front of the sweeper, whose main job, as the position's title suggests, is to sweep all balls out of the goal area. These players are the last line of defense before the goalie, and the majority of the team is positioned away from the net, so your team is likely to enjoy more success from this system of play if the defensive players are good at handling offensive pressure from the opposing team.

- ✔ **Midfielders:** The center midfielder orchestrates the attack after the team has possession of the ball. Her duties include gathering the ball from her defensive teammates and moving it up the field with an accurate pass to the forwards. The left and right midfielders move the ball up to the forwards, and when the ball is in the opponent's half of the field, they move forward, well past the center line. They're also responsible for making sure that the opposing team's wingers don't push the ball past them down into the corner-kick areas when the opposing team has the ball.

- ✔ **Forwards:** The focus of the forwards is to work the ball along the sidelines, toward the corner-kick areas, and to deliver centering passes to teammates in the goal area. The *inside forwards* (or *insiders*), the players positioned between the center forward and the left and right forwards, distribute the ball to the other forwards. The primary responsibility of the center forward — or *striker*, as he's often called — is to get the ball in the net. In the more competitive levels of youth soccer, the player handling this position must be an excellent dribbler and have an accurate shot for this system to truly be successful.

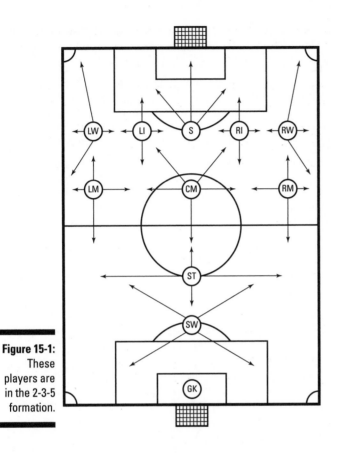

Figure 15-1:
These
players are
in the 2-3-5
formation.

TIP

If your team has some very good defensive players, it may be in your best interest to increase the number of players that you're using on the attack in the front line by having the center midfielder taking a more aggressive role downfield.

4-2-4 formation

This formation is the most balanced you can use, because the numbers of players on offense and defense are equal (see Figure 15-2), with four attackers and four defenders, as well as two midfielders. Here's how it works:

✔ **Defenders:** The defense is comprised of the right and left fullbacks, the sweeper, and the stopper. The left fullback's job is to monitor the right winger on the opposing team and help prevent her from maneuvering into the penalty area and getting a dangerous shot on net or creating a scoring opportunity for a teammate. The right fullback does the same against the left winger. When the defense is under an enormous amount of pressure, the midfielders also retreat to provide support.

- ✔ **Midfielders:** Each of the two players handling these positions has a defined role as either the offensive or defensive midfielder. As the name suggests, the offensive midfielder plays more with the offense than the defense, and vice versa. Regardless of which role they play, they both have to return to their positions on the field as soon as they're done either assisting with the offensive attack or providing defensive support.

- ✔ **Forwards:** In this style of attack, the left and right wingers look to move the ball down the sideline toward the corner-kick areas or to work a pass into the middle of the field if any openings present themselves. One of the two strikers pulls double duty in this system, because he attacks when his team has possession of the ball and falls back to assist in the midfield area when the team is on defense.

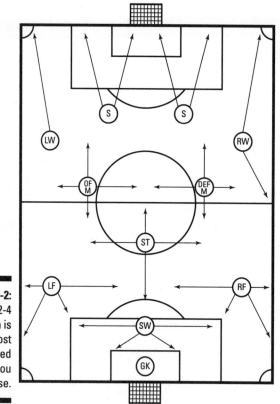

Figure 15-2:
The 4-2-4
formation is
the most
balanced
offense you
can use.

3-3-4 formation

This system places greater emphasis on offense than the 4-2-4 because it has four attackers, along with three midfielders and three defenders (see Figure 15-3).

- ✔ **Defenders:** The three players handling these responsibilities — the right, left, and center fullbacks — are positioned in the penalty area and rarely stray from their positions within the box as they provide support for the goalie.

- ✔ **Midfielders:** The system is similar to the 4-2-4 system we cover earlier in the chapter. If you're using a 4-2-4 alignment, you can simply move one player from defense up to midfield to make the 3-3-4. In this system, the right midfielder takes a more offensive-minded approach, while the left midfielder's role is more defensive.

- ✔ **Forwards:** The front four consists of the right and left wingers, along with the two strikers.

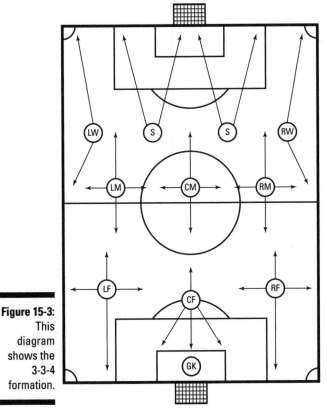

Figure 15-3:
This diagram shows the 3-3-4 formation.

TIP

If you're coaching an experienced team that has a good handle on formations and systems of play, you can make adjustments during the course of the game to fit your needs. If you're struggling to generate scoring chances, you can infuse the offense with a bit more firepower by switching to a more offense-oriented system. Of course, use only formations that you've practiced so the kids understand their new roles and responsibilities and can make a quick transition.

3-5-2 formation

This system (see Figure 15-4) evolved from the 4-4-2 system that we cover in Chapter 16, which emphasizes controlling the play in the middle of the field.

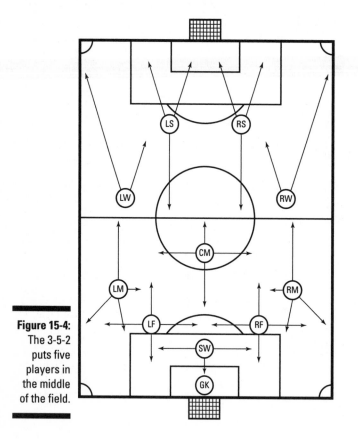

Figure 15-4:
The 3-5-2 puts five players in the middle of the field.

Because of the tight, five-player formation in the midfield area, the 3-5-2 is an excellent formation to use if you want to use a counterattack or fore-check (see Chapters 11 and 12, respectively).

- ✔ **Defenders:** The left and right fullbacks patrol the area in front of the penalty box, the center of the field, and the sideline nearest them. The sweeper is positioned in the penalty-box area and is responsible for moving laterally and getting the ball out of the penalty-box area.

- ✔ **Midfielders:** When you clog the center of the field with your offensive players, the opposing team faces greater difficulty generating passes through the midfield area. Consequently, they're susceptible to a counterattack, because this formation generates turnovers. The key to the success of using this formation is to ensure that the five midfielders (the left, right, and center midfielders, along with the left and right wingers) are working together and constantly communicating.

- ✔ **Forwards:** The left and right strikers carry a heavy load of responsibility in this formation. Besides being counted on a great deal for getting shots on goal, they are required to do a lot of running back and forth between the opponent's goal and midfield line to provide defensive pressure and support when the opposing team has possession of the ball.

3-4-3 formation

This formation is rather popular at the younger age levels because it provides balance at the offensive and defensive ends of the field (see Figure 15-5).

- ✔ **Defenders:** The left and right fullbacks are responsible for controlling the area in front of the penalty box, as well as the sideline nearest them. The sweeper is positioned in the penalty-box area and is responsible for moving laterally and getting the ball out of the penalty-box area.

  Midfielders: If you happen to have several youngsters on the squad who are quick on their feet, this formation can be used to your advantage, because in the midfield, they can be aggressive on the fore-check and quickly join the attack at the opponent's end of the field.

- ✔ **Forwards:** The left and right wingers are responsible for moving the ball down the sideline and sending crossing passes to the striker. Only three players are in the front row of this alignment, so the bulk of the scoring responsibility falls on the striker's shoulders.

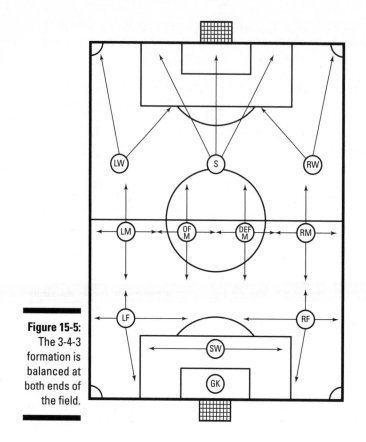

Figure 15-5:
The 3-4-3 formation is balanced at both ends of the field.

Introducing New Offensive Skills

As your team gains experience moving the ball down the field and attacking during games, it will encounter a variety of defensive styles and techniques. Having the ability to call on different moves and use different offensive approaches to help generate scoring opportunities for the team is a real asset. The positions of the defenders during that particular moment in the game dictate, to a large extent, what type of offensive approach works best. In this section, we take a peek at three areas that can bolster your team's offensive prowess and clear the way for more goal-scoring opportunities: crossing passes, heading crosses, and feinting.

Delivering crossing passes

A soccer team that's able to continually execute sound crossing passes in enemy territory will ensure that more of its trips are rewarded with decent scoring opportunities. You have a number of crossing options available to choose from. A player with the ball on the sideline (see Figure 15-6) has the option of delivering the ball to:

✔ The area around the near post (the goal post nearest the passer)

✔ The central area, which is the region between the posts

✔ The area in front of the far post (the post that's farthest from the passer)

✔ The cut-back area, which is that area of the field that comprises the penalty spot and reaches to the edge of the penalty box

No set rules exist when determining which type of crossing pass is the most appropriate to deliver. Each game situation poses a number of challenges for the players. Whenever a crossing-pass opportunity presents itself, the player has to take into account the situation as it unfolds and examine how the defense is positioned, all while dribbling the ball. From there, he has to determine which is the best option for getting the ball to his teammate in the desired zone. He may have to chip the ball over a defender to his attacking teammate positioned on the far post, or out of the corner of his eye, he may spot a teammate trailing the play and cut the ball backward to him for a quality shot on net.

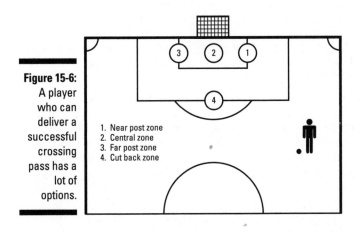

Figure 15-6:
A player who can deliver a successful crossing pass has a lot of options.

1. Near post zone
2. Central zone
3. Far post zone
4. Cut back zone

WARNING!

One of the most common mistakes young players make when delivering a crossing pass is failing to recognize the defensive player positioned at the near post. If balls aren't delivered with enough pace on them, the defender can easily step out and intercept them. Also, if the offensive player doesn't loft the ball high enough in the air when attempting to send it to the far post, the defender can head it out of danger rather easily. (In Chapter 17, we take a look at some crossing drills that you can incorporate into your practice sessions to help ensure that your team is making the most of its opportunities at this end of the field.)

When a ball is crossed, the attacking team is rarely able to make a play on the ball without a defender to contend with because the ball is typically in the air for several seconds, which allows defenders some time to react. So constantly encourage your players to go after the ball when receiving a crossing pass. They can't afford to wait for the ball, because that allows defenders the opportunity to converge on the ball and quash the team's goal-scoring opportunity.

Heading crosses

A youngster's head can be equally as potent a scoring weapon as her foot when your team is on the attack. Players who have the header in their bag of offensive moves are going to pose quite a threat to opposing teams. When a youngster is jumping up to deliver a header on a crossing pass from a teammate, keep the following tips in mind:

- ✔ **Open the eyes:** Many youngsters have a tendency to close their eyes as their head is about to make contact with the ball, which wreaks havoc with the accuracy of their headers.

- ✔ **Protect the body:** Attempting a header in the penalty area is difficult for a number of reasons, most notably because the player is dealing with all the traffic in the vicinity. While players are jumping into the air to deliver the header, they need to use their hands to help protect their head from colliding with any body parts of players on the opposing team. Remind players that they can't be pushing or grabbing opponents, because they will be called for a penalty, but they can use their hands as a barrier for additional protection.

- ✔ **Attack the ball:** When a crossing pass is headed toward a youngster, she needs to respond aggressively in order to take full advantage of the pass. This aggressiveness means attacking the ball with the forehead. Sometimes, youngsters fall into the trap of allowing the ball to hit them on the top of the head instead of taking the initiative to go after it and deliver a solid blow with the top of their forehead.

When working with youngsters on heading drills that involve delivering shots on goal, be sure to help them learn to direct those shots both up into the air and on the ground. Often, a more difficult shot for a goaltender to stop is one that's directed at the ground near the goal line.

Sometimes, the crossing pass isn't up in the air but closer to ground level, which requires the player to leave her feet and execute a dive header. This header is extremely difficult to pull off and should be taught only to older and experienced players, because it involves diving and landing on the ground with the full force of the body. To execute a proper dive header, the player launches herself toward the incoming ball (see Figure 15-7). As the player makes contact with the top of her forehead, she should be almost parallel to the ground. She lays her arms out with her palms facing down to help cushion her body as it hits the ground.

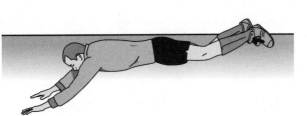

Figure 15-7:
You should
teach diving
headers
only to
experienced
players.

The actual dive is the tricky part of learning this skill, but you can take a clever approach that the team will have plenty of fun with. To get kids used to diving and getting airborne, lie on the ground, and have the kids practice diving over you without a soccer ball involved. We said you were going to have a lot of fun with the kids during the season, and this drill is guaranteed to put smiles on your players' faces! After the kids are comfortable diving, introduce the ball into the mix. You can continue lying on the ground or, better yet, recruit a parent or assistant coach to hit the ground so you can monitor the heading.

Feinting

When your players have gotten pretty good at dribbling, spotting open team-mates, and delivering the ball to them fairly accurately, help them work feint-ing into their arsenal of offensive skills. *Feinting* is when the ball handler fakes doing something in an effort to get the opponent to believe that he's doing one thing when he's actually doing something completely different. For example, a player may fake like he's going to be dribbling to the left when he's actually going to attack to the right.

During games, your players may encounter situations on the attack when they're unable to fend off a defensive player who's stuck to them tighter than their own shadow. And to make matters worse, no teammates are available to rescue them. In these situations, your players benefit by being able to resort to any number of faking techniques to help get the defender off balance, create a little space to work with, and gain a one- or two-step advantage on the attack. Feinting is often all it takes to initiate a goal-scoring opportunity.

The ability to fake out an opponent is a valuable skill to have, particularly because it can be utilized in all areas of the field. Near the opponent's goal, when your player is squeezed in tight along the sidelines by a defender, the feint can get that defender leaning off balance for just a split second, which may be enough time to get off a quality shot or find an open teammate with an excellent scoring opportunity. Or perhaps on a turnover, your team needs a little extra time to get properly positioned for its attack, and a feint can be used to buy a couple of extra seconds of dribbling time.

Having players who can use feints to their team's advantage is a real luxury, particularly because the risk is low and the payoff is high. Using them doesn't jeopardize your team's possession of the ball by risking a pass or dribbling into defensive traffic. It's simply a 1-on-1 move that allows an offensive player to escape trouble. The basic feints are shooting, heel, turning, passing, and body feints, all of which we cover in the following sections.

Shooting

A player who's being closely guarded in the vicinity of the opponent's goal can rely on a shooting feint to get a shot off if no good passing options exist at the moment. During the shooting feint, the player plants her left foot and bends her right foot back just like she would while delivering a shot (see Figure 15-8a). As she does this, the defender is likely to stick out his left foot (see Figure 15-8b). The attacking player stops the swinging motion of her right foot and uses the inside of the foot to move the ball to the defender's right (see Figure 15-8c). This split-second when the defender is leaning off balance to his left gives the offensive player a chance to get a shot off.

Ideally, the player should now deliver the kick with her left foot, which is farther away from the defender. We discuss in Chapter 9 the importance of working with your players to become comfortable using both feet for dribbling, passing, and shooting, and this example is certainly one of those situations when being comfortable shooting with either foot comes in handy. Because the feint usually creates only a small window of opportunity — usually just a second or so — the defender is still nearby, and you don't want your player to waste a good feint by using her right leg to kick the ball. That may allow the defender to lunge at the ball, poke it away, and make a nice defensive recovery for his team.

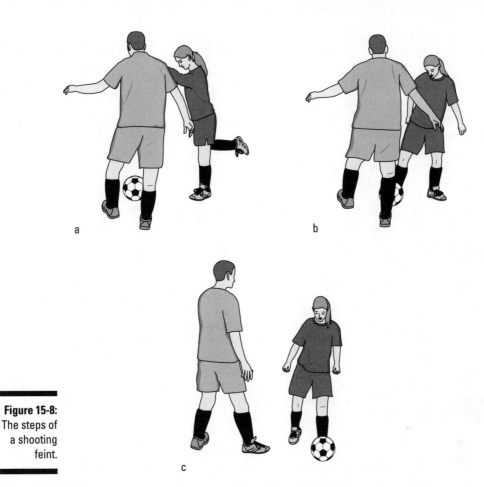

Figure 15-8:
The steps of
a shooting
feint.

Heel

Players who are being tightly challenged running down the field find the heel feint a valuable resource to help shake off that defensive pressure. When a player dribbling the ball has a defender running side by side with her, or even a half-step behind her (see Figure 15-9a), she actually steps over the ball with her right foot and uses her heel to cushion the ball and bring it to a stop (see Figure 15-9b). The heel feint should be used with the foot farther away from the defender. So when the defender is on the attacking player's left side, she relies on her right foot for the heel feint. As the player steps over the ball, the defender, who has been running at top speed to stay even with the player, typically isn't prepared to stop as quickly as the attacking player did.

Figure 15-9:
The heel
feint works
when the
defender is
behind or
next to the
dribbler.

a   b

The attacking player, with this momentary advantage, has a couple of options at her disposal. She can use the extra seconds to survey the field and deliver a pass to a teammate, or she can resume pushing the ball forward by using the time the defender has taken to stop to resume running at full speed herself.

All feints take lots of practice, but this one requires even more, because it can be quite challenging keeping a rolling ball under control by using just the heel.

Turning

Turning feints are typically used at the defensive end of the field to protect the ball before getting an attack under way. When an opponent is on a player's back, the turning feint can be used to shed the player. As the player is dribbling with his back to the defender, he leans slightly to the left (see Figure 15-10a) and brings his right foot toward the ball, giving the indication that he's headed to the left. As the defensive player also begins moving to his left, the offensive player swings his foot over the ball and, with the outside of his right foot (see Figure 15-10b), moves the ball to his right (see Figure 15-10c). This type of maneuver usually creates at least a step or two of extra space.

Passing

The passing feint — similar to the shooting feint — is especially useful when a defender is headed at an attacking player straight on. In this situation, the attacking player spins to the right as though she's going to deliver a pass in that direction (see Figure 15-11a). As she brings her foot down toward the ball (see Figure 15-11b), she sweeps it around to the side and moves the ball to her left (see Figure 15-11c), while the opposing player has probably lunged to block the pass. From this position, she creates several options for herself, including continuing moving the ball forward with her left foot.

Figure 15-10:
This player fakes to his left and moves the ball to his right.

a   b   c

Figure 15-11:
The attacker spins as though she's going to deliver a pass to her right.

a   b   c

Body

The body feint involves using any part of the body in an exaggerated motion in the opposite direction from which a player intends to move. As your players gain more experience, encourage them to be creative when working on these moves until they find those feints that they're comfortable using and that tend to work well for them during games.

Although the previous feints are the basic ones that your team will benefit from learning, when they have those down and are comfortable using them in game situations, encourage them to work on their own. You may be surprised at some of the moves the kids come up with that actually prove to be quite effective during games. As youngsters learn to incorporate their own special touches into their skills, their enjoyment of the sport — and playing for you — will skyrocket.

Chapter 16

Coaching Defense 201

In This Chapter

▶ Determining defenses

▶ Upgrading skills

*A*s the seasons roll along, you begin noticing that many of the youngsters in your league are adding all sorts of offensive skills to their arsenal. You observe them becoming more dominant with their dribbling, more efficient with their passing, and more accurate with their shooting. Although we hope this improvement is occurring on your own team as well, it can present some new and exciting challenges for you and your squad at the defensive end of the field. The ability to kick your team's defensive skills up a notch or two translates into greater enjoyment of the sport. Your players derive additional satisfaction by consistently being able to spoil an opponent's attack.

As you begin upgrading your defensive efforts, you can introduce systems of play that best match your team's playing skills and abilities; you can start teaching techniques such as moving out and the offside trap, which are key components of strong defensive play; and you can share with your team the basics of clearing, which are essential if you're not going to surrender an avalanche of goals during the season.

Defensive Approaches

Choosing a defensive system of play to use with your team really isn't a whole lot different from shopping for a new car. You have a lot of styles and options to choose among, and usually after looking around and taking some test drives, you settle on the one that best fits your needs and turns out to be the most comfortable. The same goes for determining the best defensive system for your squad. With so many different systems of play out there, including several offensive-oriented approaches that we discuss in Chapter 15, the only way you can discover the most comfortable fit for your team is to try them out during practice sessions or in scrimmages with other teams.

Although you won't want to spend the entire season forcing the kids to play a single defensive style, understanding the merits of these approaches can prove valuable at different points in the season. Whether your team finds itself going against a high-scoring team that needs to be slowed down or simply trying to protect a one-goal lead in the closing minutes of a game, properly executing a defensive system of play can be enormously valuable for all involved.

In a formation's name, the first number represents the number of defenders, the second number is the number of midfielders, and the last number is the number of forwards. The goalie is always in the play but unaccounted for in the formation's name.

4-3-3 formation

This formation (see Figure 16-1) is one of the most popular in youth soccer, because it happens to be one of the easiest for teams to learn and operate in. This system of play works well for teams that don't have a lot of tactical experience playing the game, which is why it's often used with younger and more inexperienced players.

✔ **Defenders:** This style of play features a very balanced setup, particularly along the back line, with four defenders: a left and right fullback, a sweeper, and a stopper. The primary responsibilities of the left and right fullback are to defend their area of the field and clear the ball whenever an opposing player brings the ball into their territory. Although the players manning these positions can sometimes join the attack, they must exercise extreme caution so that they aren't caught by a team's counterattack. Their top priority, though, remains clearing the ball out of danger.

The player you choose to handle the sweeper responsibilities must be a jack of all trades. He should be fast, confident, steady under pressure, and have a firm grasp of the style of play you're employing. The sweeper's main job is to control the back area of the field and coordinate the defensive unit. So when an opposing player is racing down the left side of the field, he has to slide over in that direction to serve as an extra layer of defensive support in the event that the player maneuvers past the left fullback. Besides serving as the defensive anchor while the opposing team is on the attack, he has to have the skills to boot clearing kicks when the ball gets close to the goal or to use headers to knock the ball out of danger if the situation calls for it. He's also responsible for working in conjunction with you in setting up the defensive alignments for corner and free kicks.

The stopper provides additional support to the defensive unit. Her basic responsibility is to clear balls out of her area before the opposing team can strike. Any mistakes made by this player can result in a good scoring chance by the opposing team, particularly if the sweeper is forced to provide assistance to one of the two fullbacks.

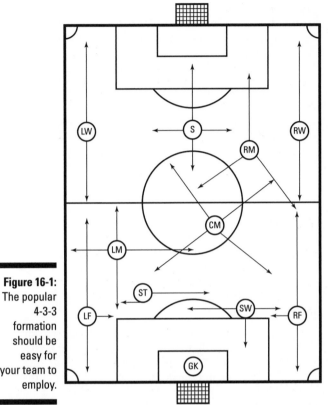

Figure 16-1:
The popular
4-3-3
formation
should be
easy for
your team to
employ.

✔ **Midfielders:** The left and right midfielders do a large amount of running, because they step up when the team is on the attack and must race back on defense to lend support to the fullbacks along the outer edges of the field. The center midfielder has a smorgasbord of responsibilities. Most notably, he's vying for loose balls in the middle of the field all game long. The more successful he is at outdueling opposing players for the ball, the more offensive chances he generates for his team.

✔ **Forwards:** The center forward probably takes the bulk of the team's shots on goal, so players who have the ability to take accurate shots from a variety of distances and angles are best suited for this position. The outside forwards are the playmakers of the unit; they have the job of continually looking to move the ball down the sides of the field and looking to create scoring opportunities for either themselves or the center forward.

4-4-2 formation

This style of play is even more defense oriented than the 4-3-3 we mention in the previous section, because one of the forwards steps back to the midfield, while you retain the four defenders (see Figure 16-2). This system works if you have players who have good tactical skills and can easily adapt to switching back and forth between the midfield and forward positions. It's also an effective system to use for squaring off against an explosive offense, because the bulk of your players are situated in the midfield area. Even if your team isn't creating a lot of scoring opportunities, maintaining possession limits the number of offensive chances the other team enjoys.

- ✔ **Defenders:** In this setup, the defenders form somewhat of a diamond shape in front of the goal, with the sweeper directly in front of the goal, the two fullbacks off to each side, and the stopper several yards ahead. The sweeper's focus usually isn't on any single player but strictly to oversee the play coming toward her and to move side to side to lend support to quash the opposing team's goal-scoring chances. The stopper is generally entrusted with marking the opponent's center forward or center midfielder. The fullbacks are responsible for derailing attacks taking place on their half of the field.

- ✔ **Midfielders:** The four midfielders in this alignment are staggered across the playing field. Simply spreading them out across the field in a straight line allows the opposing team to easily negotiate past them. The outside midfielders do large amounts of running as they join the attack and move down the field. They're also expected to provide strong defensive support when the opponent has possession of the ball.

- ✔ **Forwards:** These players' scoring opportunities are limited most of the time, simply because with this style of play, they can't rely on having a lot of available players for assistance in joining the attack. The youngsters handling these positions run considerable distances, but if they're speedy and excellent ball handlers, they may be able to create scoring chances for themselves.

4-5-1 formation

This system of play (see Figure 16-3) isn't used a lot in the youth soccer ranks, but it can be an effective approach to use occasionally in an effort to slow an offensive team that turned in a strong first half that produced a lot of good scoring opportunities.

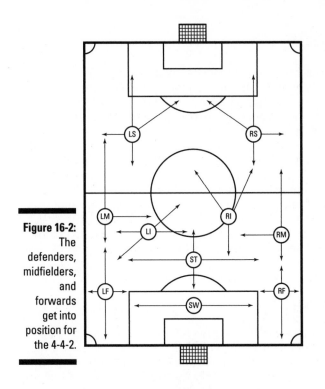

Figure 16-2:
The defenders, midfielders, and forwards get into position for the 4-4-2.

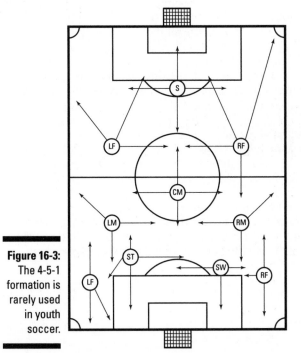

Figure 16-3:
The 4-5-1 formation is rarely used in youth soccer.

Clearing Strategies

Soccer is a complex game, but when you peel away the outer layers, you see that the team that spends more of the game on the opponent's end of the field than on its own is generally going to produce more goals and wins. So a team's ability to extricate itself from trouble by effectively clearing the ball out of the area in front of its goal is crucial to its success.

Clearing out is simply kicking the ball away from your own net, preferably aiming it toward the sidelines rather than the middle of the field, to clear away the chances for the opposing team to get shots on goal. Fending off the opponent's attack doesn't require magical moves or Houdini-like maneuvers from your players. Simply teaching the kids some basic clearing principles involving your goalie and the sidelines should be enough to help them move the ball out of danger and begin mounting an attack of their own.

Clearing to goalie

During the heat of competition, when your team is under attack and struggling to clear the ball out of its own end of the field, players can easily forget that their goalie can be a huge asset in helping bail them out of trouble. For example, if your stopper has possession of the ball but is limited in where he can dribble upfield due to all the attacking players in the vicinity, he can turn to the goalie. And if your fullback has possession of the ball, but all her passing options to teammates moving toward the midfield area are cut off, she can turn to the goalie.

A pass back to the goalie, also referred to as a *safety pass,* can bring the opponent's attack to a halt. When the goalie has the ball, he can survey the field and look to deliver a pass to a teammate.

Reinforce to your players that they should use a safety pass only when opposing players have no chance of intercepting the ball. Also, although the pass back to the goalie should be firm, it shouldn't be so hard that it actually challenges the youngster in the net to make a save from one of his own players.

Mastering this play takes a little time before youngsters are comfortable resorting to this type of pass during an actual game. They eventually learn, through their game experience, to remember to look behind them to utilize their goalie if that turns out to be the best option to derail the opponent's attack.

Work with your goalies during scrimmages or any type of drills that you're running to be vocal and let their teammates know that they're available for the safety pass if they sense the team struggling to move the ball, and they don't see any other options open downfield. Players often forget during the excitement of games that the goalie is there to help them, if needed. A simple verbal reminder from the goalie lets her teammates know that she's ready to receive a safety pass. Communication among your players is a vital asset in stopping an offensive attack.

Clearing to sidelines

When your team is under pressure, one of the best escape routes to teach is playing the ball toward the sidelines, which involves the least amount of risk. Players, especially the relatively inexperienced ones, are always tempted to move the ball straight ahead, either dribbling or passing, and that usually moves them directly into trouble.

The center of the field represents the most dangerous territory to a defensive team looking to clear the ball. One poorly timed pass or turnover while dribbling can be costly. Always instruct your players to look to the nearest sideline for a teammate to clear the ball to. Even if the ball happens to be intercepted in that area, the opposing player doesn't have nearly as many options to maneuver the ball as he does if the ball is coughed up in the middle of the field. Good offenses find ways to get the ball into the middle of the field; good defenses work the ball to the sidelines.

As players begin learning to get the ball in the air, they're gradually tempted when delivering clearing passes to simply kick the ball over the head of an oncoming opponent. This move can be problematic simply because it's a risky play that can produce an immediate scoring opportunity for the opposing player if the ball isn't put high enough in the air. Remind your players, especially your fullbacks and players positioned near the net, to try to pass the ball around opposing players to minimize the threat of turning the ball over in the vicinity of their own net.

Introducing New Defensive Skills

As your players begin getting comfortable with different playing styles, you can start introducing them to additional defensive tactics that they can employ. Helping them upgrade this area of their game allows them to enjoy more success in their 1-on-1 battles for the ball and also enhances the team's overall play at the defensive end of the field.

Moving out

Moving out is a key defensive concept that plays on the *offside rule* that keeps opposing players from lingering near the goal awaiting a pass (see Chapter 3 for a complete onside/offside discussion). When the opposing team has the ball, an attacking player can advance toward the goal in only a couple of ways. He can move in when the ball is closer to the goal than the player is or when one of your defensive players (excluding your goalie) is closer to the goal than the offensive player. Teach your defensive players not to back in toward the goal and bunch up near the goalie. If your players are hovering around the goal, the opposing players can too. You want your fullbacks to focus on staying upfield, because that ensures that the forwards on the opposing team can't advance farther than where they're situated on the field without the ball. Keep in mind, though, that your defensive players must begin retreating as the ball approaches, because everyone can advance at least as far as the ball.

Offside trap

You can use the *offside trap* to gain possession of the ball (see Figure 16-4). Your defensive player, who's downfield of the ball, runs beyond the attacking player on the opposing team. As soon as the attacker receives the ball, if no other players on your team are between the attacker and the goal (excluding the goalie, of course), the referee calls offside and awards the ball to your team for an indirect free kick. At the more advanced levels of youth soccer, or at least with a team that has many players who have been around the game for several years, this play is used often to stem an opponent's attack and take possession of the ball. When attempting an offside trap, keep the following in mind:

> ✓ **Fullback awareness:** If you signal your team to attempt the offside trap, make sure that all your fullbacks are aware of the situation. If all your defenders haven't run past the opponent who receives the pass, he isn't offside and suddenly has a golden scoring opportunity landing in his lap because your entire team wasn't aware that the play was on.

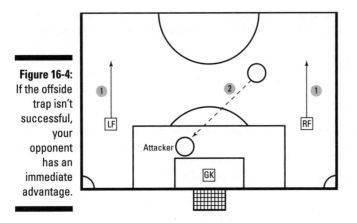

Figure 16-4:
If the offside
trap isn't
successful,
your
opponent
has an
immediate
advantage.

> ✔ **Dangerous:** If your fullback is attempting to run past the opponent but is a step or two slow when the opponent receives the ball, your defense has put itself in a highly compromising position. The attacking player may have already been moving forward when he received the ball, and now he can either continue in on net or fire off a shot.

> ✔ **Referee factor:** Youth soccer officials are out there doing the best they can for the kids and calling the game as fairly as they possibly can. But the offside trap is one of the tougher calls to make. You always take the chance that the referee may miss the call or simply deem that the team isn't offside. In either case, the result is going to be an immediate advantage for the opponent. You may want to consider working with your players to raise their hands to get the referee's attention when you're attempting to use the offside trap so that the ref is aware of it — without giving away your intentions to the other team. Tell your team to keep playing whether the call is made or not. Regardless of what type of calls the officials make, your players should respect them at all times — even during those instances when calls don't work out in your favor.

Sliding tackle

The *sliding tackle* is used by defenders who have been beaten by the attacking player and are in danger of giving up a good scoring opportunity. In many youth soccer leagues, slide tackling isn't permitted because of the injury risk involved for both the attacking and defensive players. As we discuss in Chapter 2, get a handle on your league's rules — you don't want to devote practice time to a technique that isn't allowed. In the more advanced levels of youth soccer, the sliding tackle is part of the game, and it's one of those skills that need to be taught correctly to minimize the injury risk for your players.

In programs in which this type of tackle is allowed, your team should use it sparingly and call on it when no other defensive options are available. That's because if a sliding tackle isn't successful, the defensive team is at a real disadvantage: The defender who attempted the tackle is on the ground and has a difficult time recovering and helping out against the opponent's attack. So the sliding tackle is not only one of the more difficult tackles to teach young players, but also one of the riskier ones to pull off during a game. While teaching youngsters this technique, stress the importance of making contact with the ball first; otherwise, a tripping penalty is likely to be called.

Take a look at how it's done:

- ✔ **The approach:** When the defender has been beaten or is trying to catch up to an attacking player dribbling downfield, he has to approach from the side (see Figure 16-5a). He has to be close to the player, or the attacking player can dribble out of range when he begins the sliding motion.

- ✔ **Sliding leg:** As the defender nears the player, he drops his lower body and begins the sliding motion with the leg closer to the player (see Figure 16-5b).

- ✔ **Top leg:** As the defender's leg makes contact with the ground, he bends and tucks it underneath him while extending the top leg straight out (see Figure 16-5c).

- ✔ **Knock away:** With the top leg, the defender knocks the ball away from the attacking player with as much force as he can generate so that the opponent isn't able to track the ball down while he's still lying on the ground (see Figure 16-5d).

Because the sliding tackle is one of the most difficult tackling techniques to master, start with a stationary ball. Have the kids run up alongside the ball, perform the slide, and make contact with the ball. Learning to gauge when to begin the slide against a moving player takes lots of practice and plenty of repetitions. So focus on proper sliding technique with just ball, and when the players start progressing in that area, you can incorporate a moving offensive player into the drill.

Figure 16-5:
The sliding tackle is an advanced defensive technique.

a

b

c

d

Chapter 17

Implementing Advanced Drills

*O*ne of the best indicators that you're doing a pretty good coaching job is team members who are gobbling up your instructions, putting your feedback to good use, and really developing as young players. Now, more than ever, is the ideal time to take full advantage of this momentum. Unveiling new — and even more challenging — drills is just what the kids need to propel them to higher levels of play, and you can find those drills in this chapter.

We also address the issue of conditioning — one of those topics that makes kids cringe and instantly puts horrible images in their heads of excruciating drills and nonstop running. Although conditioning is important in all youth sports, it arguably takes on even greater importance in soccer, where running is the foundation of the game. We shed some light on this topic and show you why it doesn't have to have an unpleasant label attached to it.

Conditioning Your Players

Just how important is conditioning in a sport like soccer? Well, think about it this way. A highly skilled player who hasn't been properly conditioned and tires easily doesn't enjoy the sport as much, and isn't an asset to the team, if she's gasping for air midway through the game and can't chase balls or keep up with opposing players. Clearly, less-skilled players who have plenty of stamina, and are just as effective late in the second half of games as they are at the start of games, are more beneficial to the team over the long term and derive far more satisfaction from their participation.

Because soccer involves lots of continuous running mixed in with short bursts of high-intensity sprints, youngsters need a combination of aerobic and anaerobic fitness to perform at their maximum level all game long. Don't worry — we're not going to turn this section into a discussion that takes you back to your high school science-class days. We just give you a brief recap of the two, which you may already be familiar with:

- *Aerobic stamina* refers to the level at which youngsters can take in and use oxygen. The stronger a youngster's heart and lungs are, the longer he's able to run up and down the field without tiring.

- *Anaerobic fitness* pertains to how long a youngster can perform at high intensity, which includes sprinting after a ball.

Because the positions in soccer are so varied and require such diverse skills, the conditioning needs for each are quite different as well:

- **Midfielders:** A midfielder has the responsibility of covering a lot of territory, and because the position requires a large amount of continuous running, she's better prepared to handle those duties if she has strong aerobic fitness.

- **Forwards:** Much like midfielders, players handling these positions do large amounts of running. The more aerobically fit they are, the more success they are likely to enjoy.

- **Defenders:** You count on defenders to do far less nonstop running. Because these positions entail short bursts of speed to cover attacking players, their bodies are better able to fulfill their responsibilities if they possess strong anaerobic fitness.

- **Goalkeepers:** Clearly, the goalie position doesn't entail much running compared with the other positions on the field. Yet goalies are required to move with short bursts of speed to make plays when under attack.

Youngsters who are fatigued are much more likely to suffer injuries than those players operating on a full tank of energy, because they become sloppier in their technique. So keep an eye out during games for players who are tiring. Giving them a breather for a few minutes is usually enough for them to catch that second wind and get back on track.

The most effective conditioning takes place when you incorporate it into your practices and the kids don't even realize it's happening. If you played sports growing up, you probably remember the end of practice, when your coach announced that it was time for conditioning. You and your teammates let out a groan, and you began running endless laps around the field until you heard the whistle blow. Having kids run laps around the soccer field gets them into shape — and probably makes them dread coming to practice, too. Some may even decide to conserve energy toward the end of practice so that they fare better in the running, which compromises their development. Utilize drills that emphasize constant movement and eliminate standing around, and the youngsters on your team will emerge as well-conditioned players.

Challenging Drills

Are you looking to add some flair and excitement to your offensive drills? How about giving your players some situations that really test their defensive abilities? The following drills are designed to push players who have already become pretty proficient in the sport to the next level.

Wall Pass–Heading Combination

This drill (see Figure 17-1) has it all: throw-ins, ball handling, dribbling, passing, and heading.

What you need: Area of field with goal. 5 players. 1 ball. 2 cones.

How it works: Use the following steps to run this drill:

1. **Player A, on the sideline, begins the drill with a throw-in to Player B.**

2. **After Player B receives the throw-in, he dribbles to the center of the field and delivers a pass between a pair of cones to Player C.**

3. **Player C executes a wall pass back to Player B.**

4. **Player B sends a long pass to Player D, at the top of the goal arc.**

   While all this movement takes place, Player A, who delivered the throw-in, runs the length of the field to play defense against Players C and D.

5. **Player D sends a side pass to Player C, who executes a chip pass that Player D attempts to head into the net.**

Figure 17-1:
This drill gives five players the chance to work on their skills.

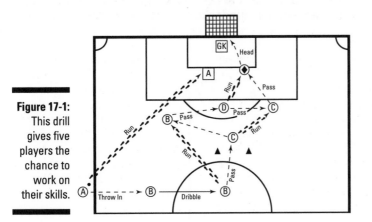

TIP

You can increase the difficulty of the drill by incorporating another defender into the mix to make the passing that much more complicated to pull off.

Coaching pointers: Begin by keeping a close eye on the youngster executing the throw-in. Your team should never turn over possession by committing an illegal throw-in. Stress the importance of executing this drill at full speed, mimicking a game situation. You may even want to let them know that you're giving them only 10 seconds to perform the drill to reinforce the emphasis on being fast with the ball and making quick decisions.

Near and Far Post Crosses

This drill (see Figure 17-2) helps players become proficient at delivering cross-ing passes to both the near and far posts while facing defensive pressure.

What you need: Area of field with goal. 4 players. 1 ball.

How it works: Use the following steps for this drill:

1. **Player A starts with a ball at the top of the penalty area and delivers a pass to Player B, who is moving toward the end line.**

2. **After Player A delivers the pass, she moves toward the near post and receives a crossing pass from Player B.**

   Player B has to focus on making an accurate pass that can't be inter-cepted by the defensive player stationed in the penalty area.

3. **After Player B delivers the crossing pass, and Player A attempts to head the ball into the goal, Player B sprints to the corner-kick area.**

4. **Player B delivers a corner kick to the far post that Player A attempts to head into the net while dealing with the defensive player.**

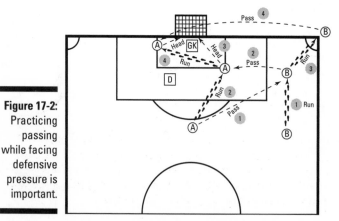

Figure 17-2:
Practicing
passing
while facing
defensive
pressure is
important.

Coaching pointers: This drill can get pretty competitive with older and more skilled kids who battle for position in front of the net to get off headers or defend them, so keep a close watch to make sure that they aren't pushing illegally or committing penalties.

Spin and Shoot

This drill helps players, while dribbling the ball, make quick and accurate ball-distribution decisions when a goal-scoring opportunity presents itself.

What you need: Area of field with goal. 5 players. 1 ball.

How it works: Use these steps for Spin and Shoot:

1. **Position a sweeper in the penalty area to put extra pressure on the attacking players to make an accurate pass.**

2. **The drill begins (see Figure 17-3) with you (C) throwing a high pass to Player A, who must trap it with his chest and gain control of it.**

3. **The players on Player A's left and right near the top of the penalty box execute spin moves and head toward the goal.**

4. **Player A immediately sends a pass to hit one of the two players in stride.**

5. **The player who receives the pass dribbles forward and either takes a shot on goal or passes to the other attacking player for a shot on net.**

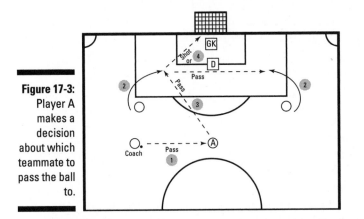

Figure 17-3:
Player A makes a decision about which teammate to pass the ball to.

Coaching pointers: Work with the attacking players to make sure that they don't spend too much time dribbling the ball. Players sometimes have a tendency to want to use too many 1-on-1 moves when, in a situation like a 3-on-1, they need to learn to take advantage of having the defense outnumbered and pass to a teammate to generate a better-quality shot on goal.

Move and React

Move and React gives players chances to work on their 1-on-1 moves while being closely defended, as well as to work on their shooting and passing skills.

What you need: Area of field with goal. 4 players. 1 ball.

How it works: Player A begins with the ball outside the penalty area (see Figure 17-4). Player B, who is on the attack with her, is at an angle outside the penalty box, facing Player A. A defender starts a couple of yards behind Player B. Use the following steps for this drill:

1. **The drill begins with Player A sending a pass to Player B.**

2. **After receiving the pass, Player B executes a spin move to either her left or right.**

3. **Depending on whether she's free from the defender, Player B takes a shot on goal or looks to pass to Player A, who is trailing the play.**

4. **If Player B shoots, and the ball rebounds, Player A is there for the follow-up.**

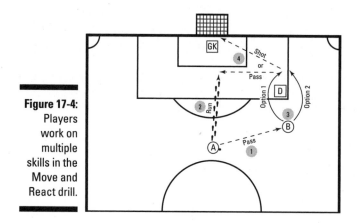

Figure 17-4: Players work on multiple skills in the Move and React drill.

Coaching pointers: Kids naturally love taking shots on goal, so watch Player B's execution closely, and make sure he's distributing the ball to Player A if his spin move doesn't produce an opening to get off a quality shot. If he should pass the ball instead of shooting, don't hesitate to interrupt the drill. Show him that a better opportunity for a goal existed by demonstrating where Player A was without a defender near her.

Specialties Galore

This drill is good for conditioning because it's fast paced and allows little time for recovery. Besides helping players work on specialty skills like throw-ins and corner kicks, it generates a game-type atmosphere with 2-on-2 and 3-on-2 play.

What you need: Area of field with goal. 6 players. 1 ball.

How it works: Position two attacking players and two defensive players in the penalty area (see Figure 17-5). Put an additional attacking player on the sideline. In this drill, you have a total of three mini-games. To keep the drill moving, allow only 15 seconds of play. You can award 1 point to the attacking players if they get a shot on goal (2 points if they score a goal) and 1 point for the defensive team if it prevents a shot on goal. Keeping score helps keep the kids' interest and ensures that they're competing as hard as they would in a game situation.

1. **The attacking player on the sideline begins the drill with a corner kick.**

2. **The other two attacking players attempt to score a goal while the defenders try to clear the ball out of danger.**

3. **While this play is going on, the player who delivered the corner kick rushes up the sideline, picks up a ball, and delivers a throw-in, which produces a game of 2-on-2.**

4. **The drill concludes with the player who began the drill rushing up the sideline again, delivering another throw-in, and joining the action for a 3-on-2 opportunity.**

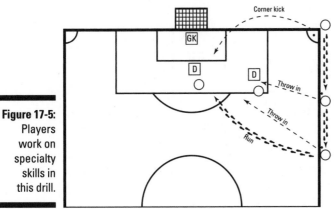

Figure 17-5:
Players
work on
specialty
skills in
this drill.

Coaching pointers: Particularly with the 3-on-2 portion of this drill, make sure that the attacking trio is maintaining proper spacing. Whenever the team has a tactical advantage with an extra player, you don't want to minimize that advantage by bunching up close together, which makes it much easier for the defensive team.

Crisscrossing

This drill puts a premium on good ball handling and passing, and also gives both offensive and defensive players work on their 1-on-1 play, which occurs all game long all over the field and plays a big role in how successful the team is.

What you need: Area of field with goal. 5 players. 1 ball.

How it works: The following steps set up the Crisscrossing drill:

1. **Player A starts at midfield (see Figure 17-6) and dribbles the ball against a defender to a predetermined spot.**
2. **Player A executes a square pass to Player B.**
3. **Player A runs at an angle toward the penalty area.**
4. **Player B gains control of the ball and sends a pass forward to connect with Player A.**
5. **Player B moves diagonally to the outer edge of the penalty box.**
6. **Player A sends a pass to Player B in the penalty-box area, and Player B now must beat the defender there and get a shot on goal.**

Figure 17-6: The defensive players try to break up the crisscrossing pattern of passes.

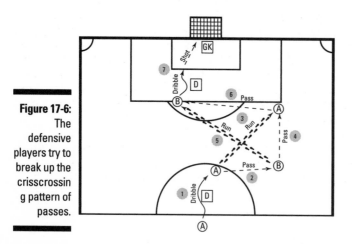

Coaching pointers: No matter what the age level or ability of your players, always stress the fundamentals when passing and receiving. You never want your players to get into the habit of straying from the fundamentals, which only prove more difficult to correct later.

Goalie Tester

Goalie Tester gives your goalie, regardless of his age or ability, the chance to hone his skills and receive a lot of quality practice in a short period of time.

What you need: Area of field with goal. 1 player. Multiple balls.

How it works: Use the following steps for this drill:

1. **The goalie takes his normal position in front of the net. You take a spot approximately 10 yards from the goalie and kneel with a large supply of balls at your disposal.**

2. **You begin the drill by throwing balls at the net one at a time, so that the youngster is forced to make the save and then quickly return to his starting position to stop the next ball.**

   By kneeling, you're able to send a wide variety of balls at the goalie. You can roll them, bounce them, or throw them in the air.

A lot of times in drills, goalies aren't really tested and forced to extend far to their left and right to make saves. By delivering the balls with your hands, you ensure that the goalie gets work making all types of saves that he'll be called upon to make in actual games.

You can increase the difficulty level of this drill in a couple of ways. One, you can place a defender a few yards in front of the goalie to serve as a screen so that the goalie is challenged on his sight lines, which often happens during a game with players battling for position around the net. And two, you can position players to the left and right of you, and periodically, instead of throwing a ball at the net, you can roll one to your left or right for a player to take a shot on goal. Again, this unpredictability forces the goalie to really be alert and react quickly to all sorts of situations, which is exactly what he confronts during an actual game.

Coaching pointers: Footwork and form are the key elements to successful goalkeeping. Watch that the youngster uses proper form when he reaches high for a ball or is forced to get low to scoop up a rolling ball.

Part V
The Extra Points

In this part . . .

What your team does before it takes the field can have a major impact on how well it performs. In this part, we serve up some pre- and post-game routines, including warm-ups and nutritional tips that will fuel your players, and examine how you can best protect your team from annoying injuries. And, in the event you have to deal with a problem parent or child, we provide some useful solutions. For those of you interested in tackling the more challenging role of coaching a travel or select team, you find all sorts of useful information here, too.

Chapter 18

Keeping Kids Healthy and Injury Free

In This Chapter

▶ Preventing and recognizing injuries
▶ Staying safe when bad weather threatens
▶ Fueling young bodies

*B*eing a well-rounded soccer player requires a lot of skills in many areas. The same goes for being a well-rounded soccer coach. Besides teaching kids the basic skills, techniques, and strategies of the game, you need a handle on the aspects of the game that often slip under the radar of most volunteer coaches: injury prevention, recognition, and treatment, as well as the dos and don'ts of pre- and post-game nutrition.

Although you certainly don't need a medical background or expertise in the sports nutrition field, you should at least be familiar with these topics and how they influence kids' performances on the soccer field. Being healthy and injury-free makes a big difference in how much your players enjoy the game — as well as how successful you are in helping them have fun fulfilling their potential. Dig in to this chapter to see how you can help your kids remain injury-free and fuel their young bodies to perform at their maximum capabilities.

Injury Prevention

You simply can't get around the fact that any youngster who steps onto the soccer field — regardless of age, level of ability, or experience playing the sport — is vulnerable to suffering an injury. Although you can't eliminate the threat of injuries occurring during practices or games, you can take several steps to help reduce the chance of a child suffering an injury. Having your team follow a sound stretching regimen — both before and after games and practices — goes a long way in not only promoting better flexibility, but also providing added protection against unwanted aches and pains.

Keep the following points in mind when leading your team in stretching:

- ✔ **Cover all the muscle groups.** You want the pre-game warm-up to involve all the major muscle groups that the kids use during the game. That means stretches for the hamstrings, calves, neck, and back.

- ✔ **Make it soccer-related.** Exercises that focus on soccer-related movements serve the dual purpose of getting the kids loosened up and simulating game action. One simple way to do this kind of exercise is to have each child pass a ball back and forth between his feet, using the inside of each foot. Doing this while jogging in place builds ball-handling skills and warms up the body in the process.

- ✔ **Keep the exercises light.** You want the kids to get loosened up gradually. Remind them to go at no more than half speed in the beginning. You don't want them going full speed throughout the entire warm-up so that by the time the game begins, they're fatigued and gasping for breath.

Proper warm-up for practice and games

Stretching the muscles enhances a youngster's agility and flexibility, improves his range of motion and soccer technique, and reduces his chances of being injured. Setting aside a period of time to get the heart rate up and the muscles loosened up before practice and games clears the way for a productive session.

For younger kids, your warm-ups don't need to be elaborate. Simply having the kids perform a soccer-related activity to get their hearts pumping and their muscles loosened up gets them ready for action. Have each player place her ball in front of her and alternate putting her right foot on top of the ball, and then her left foot, to get her heart pumping. Have the kids start slowly and gradually build up a little bit of speed. You can also have all the kids dribble their balls in a designated area while maintaining a slight jog. By confining them to an area, you force them to dribble around their teammates so their bodies are getting warmed up and comfortable moving in all directions. It also provides good dribbling practice because the kids have to keep their heads up to scan the area so they don't bump into one another.

With older children, you want to ensure that they loosen all their muscles properly, because they rely upon all of them during the course of the practice. Stretching the hamstrings, the quadriceps, the calves, the neck and upper back, the lower back, and the area around the waist are all important, so make sure your warm-up touches on all those areas. Here are some tips to keep in mind when it comes to stretching:

✔ **Passive stretching:** This is the most beneficial type of stretching for children. Rather than bouncing and straining to reach a desired position, which can result in injury, you slowly move to the desired position, just slightly beyond discomfort, holding that position for a short period of time and then relaxing. Remind kids that mild tension — not pain — is what they need to be striving to achieve on any type of stretch. For example, they want to slowly bend down and touch their toes, count to five, and then relax and return to an upright position.

✔ **Hands on:** During any stretching exercises, make sure you have 1-on-1 contact with all the kids. This contact is particularly important for youngsters who are new to soccer or new to the whole concept of stretching before participating in an activity. For example, when a child is stretching out his hamstrings, place his hand on the back of his leg so that he can feel the exact area of his body that's being stretched and prepared for competition. This technique also helps ensure that the kids are following proper form.

Stretching out

Maintaining and improving a child's flexibility is essential for not only preventing injuries, but also for giving him the solid foundation of strength, balance, and coordination needed to reach his full potential. Incorporating a variety of stretches and strength-building exercises is a key component for preparing youngsters for the rigorous demands of soccer. Take a look at several different stretches that can be utilized during your warm-ups to help prepare a youngster's legs for practices and games:

✔ **Standing squats:** The child holds the soccer ball in the center of her chest with her elbows flexed. Her feet should be about shoulder width apart. In a slow and controlled manner, the child squats into a deep bend at the knees, with her body weight centered over the heels. After a one-second pause, she lifts up, keeping the upper body steady.

✔ **Backward lunges:** The child begins by holding the ball in front of his chest with flexed elbows. Next, he steps backward, landing on the ball of his foot, while his stationary knee is in line with his ankle. He lowers his body by bending his knees. Using the rear leg, he lifts the stationary leg back so his feet are together. Then he repeats, using the opposite leg.

✔ **Alternating leg raise:** The child lays face down and places her elbows under her shoulders with her forearms on the ground. She places her legs hip-distance apart and curls her toes under while lifting her body onto her elbows and toes. Keeping her back straight, she alternates leg raises from the hip with a straight knee.

✔ **Calf stretch:** The child stands in a lunge position with his front knee bent, though that front knee shouldn't extend past the ankle. The child places his hands on the front of his thigh and presses forward, keeping his back leg straight while pressing his rear heel down.

✔ **Knee bends:** While the child is seated on the ground, she bends her left knee and places her left foot flat on the floor. She follows by placing her right foot and ankle on her left thigh just above her knee. She places her hands on the floor behind her hips and presses her chest toward her knee and foot. Her upper torso, neck, and shoulders should remain open and straight; don't let her round her upper back.

✔ **Hip-flexor stretch:** The child stands with his feet in a lunge position and his front knee slightly bent. He briefly pushes up onto the toes of his back foot. He also presses his hips forward while tightening his buttocks and then slowly lowers his body until he feels a stretch in the front of his hip. While he performs this stretch, his upper body remains upright and centered directly over his hips.

✔ **Hamstring stretch:** While sitting, the child assumes the hurdle position by extending her right leg fully and bending her left leg, placing the inside of her foot along her right calf. While keeping her back straight, she slowly leans forward, bringing her chest toward her knee and reaching with both hands toward her toes. Depending on how much flexibility the child has, she either places her hands on the floor alongside her legs or holds her toes. Have her hold the stretch for a few counts and then release. Make sure she isn't lunging for her toes. She also shouldn't feel any pain — just a slight stretch in her muscles.

✔ **Quadriceps stretch:** In the same position used earlier for the hamstring stretch, have the child lean slightly back to stretch the quadriceps on the leg that's bent.

✔ **Groin stretch:** The child sits on the ground and places the soles of his feet together with his knees off to the sides. Leaning forward, the child slowly presses forward until he feels a mild tension in the groin.

✔ **Waist/lower-back stretch:** The player stands with her feet beyond shoulder width apart, arcs her right arm over her head, and points to the left while her left arm rests against her left knee. Have the team perform a few repetitions in each direction.

✔ **Neck stretch:** The child stands and slowly turns her head all the way to the left and then all the way to the right. Then have her tuck her chin to her chest to help stretch out the back of her neck.

✔ **Upper back:** The player stands and stretches both arms behind his back while puffing his chest out. Have him hold for a few seconds and then release.

Your kids have vastly different characteristics and levels of ability, which includes their levels of flexibility. Some kids are extremely flexible; others don't even come close to being able to touch their toes. Make sure the team knows that when the warm-up period is complete, anyone can spend a few extra moments doing some additional stretching if they don't feel sufficiently loosened up until they're comfortable and ready to proceed with the game.

Here are a few other warm-up tips to keep in mind:

✔ **Don't allow any horseplay during these exercises.** Keep the kids' attention focused on the specific stretch they're performing.

✔ **Emphasize slow movements.** Younger children can complete just a couple of repetitions of each stretch. This repetition also helps ingrain in them at an early age the importance of always stretching before performing an activity.

✔ **Join in.** As the coach, you're running around teaching and instructing during the course of the practice, so joining the kids for the stretches is a good idea for you and your assistants. This participation further instills the importance of warming up to the youngsters and helps you avoid being sidelined with a strained or pulled muscle. As we cover in Chapter 6, if you're conducting a scrimmage or any exercises that also involve the parents, get them out on the field to warm up with their child, too.

✔ **Be consistent.** Always start practice with a warm-up. Repetition is important, and if youngsters know that at every practice they stretch, they'll understand that stretching is an important part of the game.

Breaking a sweat

Because soccer obviously requires large amounts of running with players moving almost continuously throughout the game, you don't want to send your players out on the field without first getting their bodies warmed up and their hearts pumping for this type of strenuous activity. During your warm-up period, you want the kids to get loosened up with some jumping jacks or some light jogging while dribbling a soccer ball or performing other soccer-related movements that they use in the game.

For example, you can have the kids dribble a soccer ball down the field to help get their hearts beating a little harder and get them ready for running at full speed during the game. Or, you can have the players jog down the field in pairs, dribbling the ball and passing it back and forth. Incorporating skills that the kids use in the game into the warm-up is doubly effective. You want to avoid doing a lot of 1-on-1 exercises that put kids in a competitive situation where they tend to exert more energy than you want them to. You want them working at about 50 percent of their normal speed during this phase so that they have a full tank of energy to call on throughout the game. Here are a few other tips to keep in mind:

- ✔ **Keep moving:** When the players are warmed up, make sure that their bodies don't have a chance to cool down before they step on the field. Sometimes the game preceding yours runs long, and your warm-up loses a lot of its effectiveness if kids wind up just standing on the sidelines for several minutes, waiting to take the field. The same goes for those youngsters who aren't starting the game. You don't want them planting themselves on the bench when the game begins. Encourage players to keep moving around, lightly jogging in place, and doing light stretches to keep their legs loose and their bodies warm.

- ✔ **Pay attention to conditions:** If the weather is extremely hot, you may want to shorten the warm-up. And if your team is involved in a tournament and may be playing several games that day or over the course of a weekend, you should reduce the amount of time the players spend warming up because they're going to expend more energy than they're accustomed to.

Proper cool-down for practice and games

Although the warm-up usually gets all the attention because the focus is on preparing kids for games, post-practice and post-game cool-downs are equally important for the long-term health of your team. Doing some light stretches that you used for the pre-game warm-up helps prevent the tightening of muscles that accompanies vigorous exercise. The cool-down helps reduce muscle soreness, aids circulation, and helps clear waste products from the muscles.

Youngsters should get in the habit of going through the cool-down process every time they participate in a practice or game. The cool-down doesn't have to be quite as focused as the warm-up session, because the purpose is to wind down from the activity rather than build up to one.

Following a game, you can make the cool-down period fun for the kids by talking to them about the game while they go through the exercises. Joke with them about anything unusual or funny that may have happened in the game. Point out how well they executed a 3-on-2 or how well they defended an attack. Ask them what they enjoyed most about playing.

Injury Recognition

Eliminating the threat of injury during practices and games is impossible, but how you handle injuries when they do pop up has a significant impact on how the children view their future soccer participation. First things first: Be sure you have a well-stocked first-aid kit, as we describe in Chapter 6.

Preparing yourself for an emergency or first-aid situation

If a serious injury occurs, are you prepared to handle it? Much like you spend time practicing corner kicks, practicing how you respond in an emergency situation is important. How you respond — and how quickly — can make the difference in saving a youngster's life. The following are some steps to keep in mind:

- **Know where you're playing:** Be aware of the name of the facility where you're playing, as well as the address. In the event that you have to call 911, being able to provide as much accurate information as possible in a quick manner helps ensure that emergency medical personnel arrive as quickly as possible at the proper location.

- **Have each child's emergency information on hand:** Those important forms we discuss in Chapter 4 are crucial in the event that medical personnel need to know whether the child is allergic to any type of medication, for example. Always carry those forms in your first-aid kit and have them easily accessible in the event of an emergency.

- **Provide first aid:** While awaiting the arrival of medical personnel, provide only the first-aid care that you're trained to perform.

- **Comfort the ailing child:** If the child is conscious, comfort him by talking in a calm and relaxed voice. Let him know that he's going to be okay and that medical help is on the way.

- **Make sure phone calls are made:** If the child's parents aren't in attendance, one of your assistant coaches should have the responsibility to call them to let them know what's going on. Your foremost responsibility at a time like this is to the child, so if you've already designated someone else to make that initial call to the parents, you don't have to waste unnecessary time when all your attention needs to be focused on the youngster.

Keeping good records

Any time a child suffers an injury that you provide any type of treatment for, be sure to write down exactly what you do, and regardless of how minor the injury is, always be sure to inform the child's parents. In your practice planner or in a separate logbook, write down the nature of the injury, how it happened, and what treatment you provided. Do so the same day, while the event is still fresh in your mind. Unfortunately, we live in a litigious society, so having an accurate account of everything that transpired that day — in case you need to recount what happened — helps protect you in a court of law. Don't discard these records after the season is over. Keep these accounts, along with your dated practice plans and notes, for several years.

Having detailed notes of everything that happens is critical to protect yourself from unwarranted accusations. In addition, detailed practice plans, with dates, are evidence that you safely and properly taught your players specific skills, and they protect you against ridiculous and totally unfounded lawsuits.

You always want to proceed cautiously when dealing with any type of injury, and that's particularly true any time you're dealing with an injury that involves the head, neck, or spine. Never attempt to move a player who's lying on the ground with such an injury, because doing so is likely to cause further damage. Medical assistance should always be called immediately whenever you deal with a serious injury.

Being able to assess sports injuries is an integral part of coaching youth soccer. You must be prepared for any type of injury, including when a child goes down and may have lost consciousness. The acronym COACH is a handy reminder of how to respond:

- ✔ **C:** Determining whether the child is *conscious* is always the first step.
- ✔ **O:** Is the child breathing and getting *oxygen?* (If the answer is yes to these first two questions, move on.)
- ✔ **A:** *Ask* the youngster where he or she is hurt.
- ✔ **C:** *Control* the area that's painful.
- ✔ **H:** What type of *help* is required? Decide whether you need to call for immediate medical assistance and have the child taken to the hospital.

When you're approaching an injured child, be sure to keep this sequence in mind. Look at her lip color, feel her chest, or put your cheek next to her nose to see whether she's breathing. If she isn't breathing, and you don't see a palpable pulse in her neck or wrist, you must immediately initiate CPR and have some-one call for immediate medical assistance. If a child sustains an injury to the head or neck, calm her down and restrain her in the position you found her in while emergency medical assistance is responding.

We strongly recommended that anyone working with children in sports be cer-tified in CPR. All youth soccer coaches should receive CPR and first-aid train-ing from the American Red Cross or other nationally recognized organization. (You can find the Red Cross in your neighborhood by going to www.red cross.org.) At every practice and game, you're responsible for the safety and well being of every single player. Do your team and yourself a huge favor — take the time to go through the class. You'll be glad you did.

Treatment for common injuries

The overwhelming majority of injuries you're likely to encounter during your soccer coaching career involve "minor" bumps, bruises, cuts, and twisted ankles. But although they may seem minor to you, these injuries may seem pretty major to a child who suddenly sees blood on his leg or feels unfamiliar ankle pain when he tries to walk. By acting quickly and administering the proper treatment for a routine injury — while comforting the youngster — you help the child bounce back and return to action fairly quickly.

Cuts and scrapes

Cuts and scrapes can produce major tears with young players but, luckily, are minor injuries that you can treat quickly and effectively with the materials in your first-aid kit. Keep the following pointers in mind:

- **Wear latex gloves:** Any time one of your players suffers a cut or has an open wound, the first thing you should do is grab a pair of latex gloves or use some other type of blood barrier to limit your contact with the blood.

- **Apply direct pressure:** You can stop the bleeding by applying direct pressure to the wound with a clean dressing. If you have trouble stop-ping the bleeding, elevate the child's injured area above her heart while maintaining the pressure.

- **Clean it:** After you stop the bleeding, clean the wound. Premoistened towelettes can be used for cleaning minor cuts and scrapes, or you can use over-the-counter alcohol swabs or antibiotic creams.

- **Cover it:** Use a bandage or piece of sterile gauze to cover the cut, and be sure to secure it tightly in place, particularly if the child is interested in continuing playing.

✔ **Discard trash:** Place your gloves and any other materials that may have blood on them in a sealed bag, and place the bag in the trash so that no one else is at risk of coming into contact with the materials.

Although being fearful of HIV/AIDS is certainly understandable, it should never be a factor in providing help to an injured player on your team. You're at risk only if you allow the blood of an HIV-positive person to come into contact with an open wound that you have. If one of your players has AIDS or is HIV positive, his parents certainly should make you aware of this fact during the preseason parents meeting that we discuss in Chapter 4. Whether you're aware of the player's HIV status or not, however, the latex gloves provide the protection you need in order to treat the injured child.

Twists, sprains, and strains

Soccer is a physically demanding sport that requires players to run, make sudden stops and starts, and execute sharp turns while often coming into contact with other players in the process. These movements — and some of the collisions that accompany them — can result in muscle strains and sprains. Because much of soccer is played below the waist, the majority of these types of injuries involve the ankle and knee.

When a player strains a muscle or twists an ankle, keep in mind the RICE method for treatment:

✔ **Rest:** Immediately get the child to the sideline so that he can rest the injury. If the child has twisted his ankle, for example, have an assistant coach or a parent from the stands help you carry the child off the field so that he doesn't put any additional pressure on the injured area.

✔ **Ice:** Apply ice to the injured area. The ice helps reduce the swelling and pain. Don't apply the ice directly to the skin. Wrap the bag in a towel and then place it on the injured area.

✔ **Compress:** Compress the injured area by using athletic tape or any other type of material to hold the ice in place.

✔ **Elevate:** Have the child elevate the injury above his heart to prevent blood from pooling in the injured area.

After any swelling, discoloration, or pain subsides, you can allow the youngster to return to competition. If any symptom is present for more than a couple of days, a physician should examine the player before you allow him back on the field. You never want a child to return to the field when his injury hasn't completely healed, because it puts him at greater risk of reinjuring the area and missing an even greater amount of action.

Other injuries

At the more competitive levels of soccer, as the players become bigger and stronger and are capable of kicking the ball with tremendous force, the door opens for the possibility of other types of injuries. Take a quick look at some of these injuries and how you should respond:

- ✔ **Concussion:** A *concussion* is a jarring injury to the head, face, or jaw resulting in a disturbance of the brain. Concussions are classified as mild or severe. Symptoms include a brief loss of consciousness, headache, grogginess, confusion, glassy-eyed look, amnesia, disturbed balance, and slight dizziness. Immediate care includes rest on the sidelines with an adult in attendance to provide careful observation. If you see any evidence of something more serious, such as prolonged unconsciousness, change in the size of eye pupils, or convulsions, take an immediate trip by ambulance to a hospital for further observation. Mild concussions may require up to a week for recovery, and the decision to return must be made by a physician. Severe concussions require at least four weeks of recovery, and permission to return should be given only by a specialist.

- ✔ **Foreign object in the eye:** Any foreign body lodged in the eye, such as a fleck of dirt, needs attention. Usually, this kind of injury is just a nuisance, but if the irritation doesn't go away, it needs to be evaluated by an eye specialist. Symptoms are tearing, pain, and redness. Most objects can be easily removed with a cotton swab and saline wash. If the surface of the eye isn't seriously injured and vision isn't impaired, the youngster can return to competition as soon as the object is removed.

- ✔ **Injury to the eyeball:** A direct injury to the eyeball is an immediate medical emergency. Symptoms are extreme pain, loss of vision, hazy vision, double vision, change in vision colors, or obvious lacerations or abrasions of the eye. If the vision loss is the result of a direct eye injury rather than a head injury, a dry, sterile eye patch or piece of gauze should be applied to the eye, along with a bag of soft, crushed ice. The youngster should immediately be taken to an emergency facility.

- ✔ **Poked in eye:** When a youngster is poked in the eye, examine the eye. If the youngster isn't in significant pain, and you see minimal redness and no discharge or bleeding, simply clean the area out with cool water and allow the athlete to rest before returning to play. If you see any type of discharge or blood coming from the eye, get the child to a doctor immediately.

- ✔ **Orbital fracture:** An *orbital fracture* is a fracture of the bony frame around the eye. All orbital fractures are serious and require expert medical treatment. Symptoms include severe pain with possible double vision or other vision problems. It may be accompanied by cuts, abrasions, bleeding, and black-and-blue marks. Any youngster who suffers significant injury to the area around the eye should be transported to a facility where she can be x-rayed to determine whether a fracture has occurred.

✔ **Shin splints:** Shin splints are common in a sport like soccer where repetitive running is involved. The primary cause of the injury is related to the weight pounding down on the shin. Other factors that can contribute to the injury are muscle weakness, poor flexibility, improper warm-up and cool-down exercises, and improper footwear. Symptoms are typically easy to identify because the athlete has pain in the shin. The four stages associated with shin splints are pain after activity; pain before and after activity without affecting performance; pain before, during, and after activity, adversely affecting performance; and constant pain that prohibits activity. The early stages of shin splints are relatively mild, but later stages can become much more severe. If the injury isn't properly managed, it can result in a stress fracture. If a player develops shin splints, use ice to reduce pain and swelling and eliminate any weight-bearing activities to allow the affected area time to heal.

✔ **Wind knocked out:** A youngster who has the wind knocked out of him for the first time is likely going to panic when he has trouble breathing. Comfort the youngster, and have him take short, quick breaths and pant like a puppy until he's able to resume breathing normally again.

✔ **Tooth knocked out:** If a child has a tooth knocked out, retrieve the tooth, place it in a sterile gauze pad with some saline solution, and have the child immediately taken to a dentist.

✔ **Nosebleed:** Nosebleeds are fairly common in youth soccer. Gently squeeze the nostrils together to stop the bleeding. If the bleeding doesn't stop after a couple of minutes, get the child to a doctor, because it could be a more serious injury, such as a nasal fracture.

What to do with the kids during an injury stoppage in play

Kids are obviously very curious about what happens to a teammate who's injured, but they should be kept away from the injured child. You don't want the entire team crowding around the injured child, which can make her more panicked than she already is if she sees everyone hovering over her and staring at her with concerned looks on their faces.

During a serious injury to a player on the opposing team during a game, you want your team to return to its sideline. You need to immediately check on the injured child with the other coaches and provide any assistance that's needed. You don't want your players to be a distraction or unnecessarily get in the way while treatment is being provided.

Watching the Weather

Mother Nature and her tremendous power should never be taken lightly. Severe weather poses a great risk to youngsters, and your responsibility is to get them off the field before trouble arrives. During a game, don't rely on the league administrator or the official to stop the game when bad weather approaches. Never try to squeeze in another minute or try to get the game in so you don't have to deal with the hassle of rescheduling. Think about it. Endangering the safety of your players simply to finish a game is never worth the risk. Be aware of the following potential weather problems:

- ✔ **Lightning:** Lightning is a big concern simply because it can show up so quickly. If a storm moves in on you unexpectedly, and lightning is in the area, safe places to retreat to with the kids are enclosed buildings, fully enclosed vehicles with the windows up, and low ground. Be sure to stay away from trees, water, wide-open areas, metal bleachers, light poles, fences, or any other metallic objects.

- ✔ **High winds and tornadoes:** If for some reason your team is caught in severe weather that involves a tornado, you should move your players inside a building immediately if one is available. If not, get the kids into a ditch and lie down, or move to some other low-lying area where they should use their arms to protect their head and neck.

- ✔ **Heat:** Children don't acclimate to heat as well as adults do, so you need to consider several points. You should be aware that certain temperatures present an extreme stress to kids. As a general rule of thumb, when the humidity rises above 70 percent and the temperature is above 80 degrees, you need to exercise extra caution with your team. Encourage the kids to drink extra water and wear lighter clothing. When the temperature rises above 90 degrees with the humidity between 70 and 80 percent, heat illnesses may occur. When these types of conditions are present, practices or games should be suspended or at the very least significantly curtailed. The kids should wear only cool, porous clothing, and you should never withhold water as a form of discipline, no matter how serious the infraction or broken team rule.

- ✔ **Sun:** Exposure to the sun is an often-overlooked health risk in youth soccer. Our skin is an excellent recordkeeper of our time outdoors, and every moment we spend in the sun adds up, accumulating like money in the bank. Unfortunately, the payoff is often skin damage and skin cancer. The best defense to protect your athletes from the sun is to encourage them to use a sunscreen with an SPF of 30. Make sun safety a priority with your team.

Following a Healthy Diet

You can teach kids the proper way to head a ball, deliver a corner kick, or make a tackle, but if they aren't eating the right foods before arriving at the field, their performance is going to be compromised. Although you can't control what your team eats before practices and games, you can spend some time during the season discussing the importance of following good nutritional habits in order to maximize performance.

Discussing nutrition with your players (and even their parents) and how fueling the body can improve performance by giving them energy and added strength can make a difference and carry over to general eating habits. Television commercials sing the praises of candy bars packed with caramel centers and covered with great-tasting chocolate shells, but nutrition is found in the four basic food groups, not in candy bars. Children bring home ideas from many sources, and they can bring home healthier eating habits from you if you take the time to explain it to them.

The two primary ingredients for fueling a child's muscles during practices and games — and which get used up the longer the activity goes on — are

- ✔ **Fluids:** Kids lose fluids through perspiration, which is why water is such a vital ingredient to keep a child's body temperature from rising during exercise. The longer children exercise without replacing lost fluids, and the more extreme the temperatures and conditions are, the less effective their performances are and the worse they feel.

- ✔ **Glucose:** Although we don't intend to give you flashbacks to your seventh-grade science class, you may recall that *glucose,* a sugar derived from carbohydrates, is an important muscle fuel. It's carried to the working muscles through the bloodstream and stored in the muscles in long chains called glycogen. With all the running, stopping, and starting that's required in a game, a child's glycogen stores are steadily depleted. The more carbohydrate fuel children lose during competition, the less energy they have to perform at their peak.

What your child eats and drinks before, during, and after games impacts her performance, as well as how quickly she recovers before the next outing. The following sections cover what should be going into those young mouths before the shin guards are strapped on; share this information with your team.

Talking to kids about how today's food can affect their health years from now is ineffective. But if you frame your discussion in terms of how their meal this morning affects their performance in the game this afternoon, your chance of grabbing their attention is much better, and the team is much more interested in what you have to say on the topic.

What to eat — pre-game

When your players show up at games without eating or after having devoured a burger, fries, and a soda, their energy levels are down, and they have trouble performing and concentrating. Although often overlooked, a nutritious pre-game meal clears the way for the children to execute at their optimum level. Youngsters who eat a healthy meal — or at least some healthy snacks — comprised of plenty of carbohydrates have the muscle energy to play and play well.

The pre-game meal needs to be comprised of foods that have most of their calories from carbohydrates, because they convert into energy quicker and more efficiently than other nutrients. For the most nutritional punch, youngsters should opt for pastas, breads, cereals, and whole grains, along with fruits or vegetables. Good pre-game snacks are bagels, yogurt, dried fruit, fresh fruit, energy bars, fruit granola bars, and whole-grain crackers with peanut butter or cheese. Stay away from candy, cookies, doughnuts, and regular and diet sodas.

Players should consume their pre-game meal 2–3 hours prior to the game. They should avoid eating within an hour of game time, because their bodies will spend the first half digesting their food, which detracts from their performance.

If your players feel sluggish in the second half of games or really seem to tire and not perform as well as they do in the first half, their diets may be the culprit. Have them experiment by changing their eating habits on practice days. Have them consume some healthy snacks prior to a practice and see whether they notice any difference in their energy levels. If so, they can utilize that knowledge and feed their body those types of food prior to their games, too.

If your team has a morning game, and the kids simply aren't able to get up early enough to have a proper pre-game meal, make sure they focus on eating a nutritionally sound meal the night before, which helps prepare their bodies when they step on the field the following morning. This meal should be a big serving of pasta with some vegetables, chicken, or fish. Even the night before a game, kids should steer clear of candy, ice cream, and pop, which have the ability to rob them of much-needed energy on game day.

What to eat — post-game

What you say — and how you say it — following your team's game impacts each child's confidence and self-esteem. Similarly, what the players eat following a contest impacts their bodies and how they feel. Rewarding kids for a game well played with a tasty snack is fun, but giving them junk food sends the wrong message about the importance of following proper nutritional habits. The following are some post-game tips:

- ✔ **Think carbohydrates:** Foods rich in carbohydrates that also have some protein value are the most beneficial for youngsters. Ideally, the post-game meal or snack should look a lot like the pre-game meal, with the only difference in the portions, which should be a little bit smaller. Turkey sandwiches, fresh fruit, and crackers with cheese are great post-game foods to let your team chow on.

- ✔ **The sooner, the better:** The sooner your team digs into its post-game food, the better. Plenty of research out there indicates that foods packed with carbohydrates that are consumed within 30 minutes of a game or practice provide the most benefits for youngsters.

The importance of fluids

The importance of children consuming lots of fluids — and the right kinds — simply can't be stated enough. When kids are running up and down the field chasing the soccer ball and exerting energy, their body temperature rises. The younger the children, the less they sweat, because their sweat glands aren't completely developed at this stage in their life. This development is one of the reasons why their bodies soak up more heat when games are played in high temperatures and humidity. Children who don't consume adequate amounts of water during games, especially those contested in hot and humid conditions, are at increased risk of becoming dehydrated and suffering muscle cramps; heat exhaustion; or, even worse, heat stroke.

So how much water should kids be consuming? Well, this amount varies, because game conditions dictate whether they need increased water consumption to remain sufficiently hydrated. Also, with so many different body types, kids sweat at different rates and need different levels of fluids.

Generally speaking, you want kids consuming water whenever possible. This rule means drinking a glass of water with their pre-game meal, consuming water during the pre-game warm-ups, and taking sips of water whenever they come out of the game. When it comes to fluids, here are some additional tips to quench your knowledge:

- ✔ **Be specific:** With younger children, even though they hear you telling them to drink water, they probably aren't consuming enough. During a break in practice or during a timeout during a game, tell the players to take 10 sips of water, for example. This specific instruction helps ensure that the kids get enough fluids into their bodies.

✔ **Help internal organs:** After exerting themselves, kids need to consume lots of fluids to help replenish what they lose throughout the game. Giving the body water after a game helps the liver and kidneys push out all the waste, which is a key element in recovery.

✔ **Don't worry about too much water:** You don't need to worry about kids drinking too much water. Most kids drink based on need. It's a voluntary habit, and thirst is the mechanism that tells them to drink, so with plenty of water breaks, you don't have to worry about them sitting on the sidelines chugging too much water and not being able to perform on the field.

✔ **Encourage drinking even if they aren't thirsty:** Kids are often so immersed in the game that they don't even think about drinking any water. You have to encourage them to drink. During timeouts and at halftime of games, when you're providing encouragement and discussing game strategy, make sure you stress drinking water, too. Kids should be sipping water from their water bottles while you talk to them.

✔ **Encourage parents:** A great way to help ensure that kids are properly hydrated is to work with parents. On the car ride over to the game, the parents can have their children drink some water. Spreading the water intake out helps ensure that the body remains hydrated, and kids don't become bloated by trying to drink too much in one sitting.

✔ **Bring extra water:** Always have extra water on hand to refill any child's water bottle. Designate a couple of different parents each week to be responsible for bringing extra water; it's simply something you should never have a shortage of at any practice or game.

✔ **Say no to caffeine:** Beverages with caffeine in them act as a diuretic, which is exactly the opposite of what you're trying to accomplish in keeping the kids hydrated. Also, keep kids away from carbonated drinks, because carbonation discourages drinking.

Chapter 19

Dealing with Common Coaching Challenges

In This Chapter
▶ Communicating with problem parents
▶ Sharing the sidelines with a disagreeable coach
▶ Taming team troublemakers

*P*articipating in organized soccer provides children a lifetime of memorable moments — though unfortunately, some of those memories may not turn out to be happy ones. Although every child who laces up a pair of soccer cleats and straps on a pair of shin guards should be able to look back on her participation with fondness, inappropriate behavior by parents in the stands and opposing coaches on the sidelines can quickly quash the fun and ruin the entire experience for everyone.

Bad behavior by coaches, parents, and spectators should never be allowed to infringe on a child's soccer experience. The same goes for disruptive players on your own squad who impact their teammates' enjoyment level. Hopefully, you'll have few, if any, times when you need to discipline a youngster on your team or — even worse — deal with inappropriate comments by an opposing coach, parent, or spectator. In the event that you're forced into addressing an uncomfortable issue with another adult — or a challenging matter with one of your players — this chapter is here to lend a hand in helping you negotiate your way through the unpleasantness.

Dealing with Difficult Parents

A lot of the childish behavior at youth soccer games around the country doesn't take place among the kids on the field, but among the adult spectators in the stands and the coaches pacing the sidelines. Sure, minor conflicts arise throughout the course of a soccer season. You're bringing together a group of parents with different backgrounds, motivations, and sports experiences — and they're all looking for something different out of their children's sports experiences. Occasional problems will pop up.

Take the time to conduct a preseason parents meeting (which we cover in Chapter 4) to lay some of the key groundwork in preventing parental problems from escalating into something no longer manageable. During the meeting, detail your expectations of parent behavior during games, and clearly explain what constitutes appropriate and inappropriate behavior from the parents and their children during the season.

Laying out your expectations for parental behavior before the first soccer ball is ever kicked is important, but it's by no means a guarantee that every parent is going to be a model of good behavior all season long. So be prepared to step forward at the first indication of trouble. Any time you allow a problem to linger, it has the potential to blossom into something much worse.

The following sections take a look at some of the most common problems that you may deal with this season, and what approaches are best to implement to take care of them quickly and effectively before they negatively impact any child's experience.

The win-at-all-cost attitude

Parents invest a lot of time, money, and energy in their children's soccer experience, and they naturally want to see their kids excel in the sport and reap the benefits of participating. That means they may place unrealistic expectations on their child — and you — to perform at exceedingly high levels. Nothing less than a league championship is satisfactory in their eyes. This type of unhealthy behavior can place an enormous burden on you and your ability to work with all the youngsters. The additional pressure also infringes on some of the other kids' enjoyment of the game, and — most important — it puts the youngster whose parents have the skyrocketing expectations in a really uncomfortable and pressure-filled position.

Reviewing the scenarios

Blinded by their visions of shiny first-place trophies and postseason accolades, win-at-all-cost parents do whatever it takes to ensure that their child's team wins — and that their child looks good in the process. They shout disparaging remarks at referees. They even go so far as to try to intimidate referees into getting favorable calls, even when those referees are teenagers simply doing their best to call a fair game. These parents verbally criticize the opposing coach and the techniques his team is using, especially if the other team happens to be winning the game or doing a really good job of defending their child and not allowing him to show off any of his skills.

You're also going to be on their radar screen as a big target for criticism and questions about your coaching style whenever the outcome of a game doesn't turn out in your team's favor. These parents, regardless of the age level of the youngsters, are likely to confront you about the importance of playing the more athletic kids more often and benching the less-skilled players, all to help ensure that the team wins more games and their child receives more playing time. They critique your game strategy following losses, question your line-up, analyze your substitution patterns, and offer their unsolicited advice regarding your offensive tactics and defensive philosophy.

These win-at-all-cost parents equate wins with winning the lottery and view losses as catastrophes of truly epic proportions. This unhealthy outlook and what they're teaching the child at home about how important winning is go against everything you're trying to teach the kids regarding doing their best and having fun.

Dealing with the problem

Although you don't have a say in what the parents say to their child at home about the importance of winning, you do have a say in what's said while you're coaching a game. Look at the soccer field as a classroom where you're teaching the kids not only soccer skills, but also teamwork, good sportsmanship, and doing the best they can at all times. You can't allow outside influences to disrupt the messages that you're trying to get across.

Chances are that during the course of the season, some parents may begin adopting a rather intense interest in the outcome of games. You may start noticing that their comments and reactions during the game, or what they say to their kids afterward, are becoming problematic and counterproductive to what you're trying to teach the youngsters. Groaning when your goalie misplays a shot that results in a goal or stomping feet on the bleachers in disgust when one of your players fails to convert a golden scoring opportunity are clear signals that their behavior is taking on the tone of a professional or college game and not a youth game.

To help stem the competitive tide and prevent it from enveloping the other parents of your players, give a brief and friendly talk to the parents before your next game. Spending a couple of minutes talking to the entire group, reminding the parents that their children play in a recreational youth soccer league, and repeating that winning the game isn't the most important factor may help put them in the proper frame of mind. If the league has staff members who monitor the behavior of fans, point out to your parents that their actions are being observed, and you'd hate to see their child embarrassed if her parents were asked to leave the facility because they couldn't control themselves during the game.

If the group chat doesn't help, and the win-at-all-cost attitude continues to prevail, arrange to speak with the parent privately, and share your concerns that his comments are a real detriment to not only his child's development, but also that of the rest of the team. Be sure to reiterate that you're trying to help all the kids learn skills and that although winning the game is one of the objectives that you're striving to achieve, it's not the sole objective.

Let the parent know that if he isn't happy with your philosophy on coaching kids, perhaps he should consider coaching next season or look into signing his child up for a more competitive team. In the meantime, you need his cooperation. Share with him that you don't want him to be absent from this exciting time in his child's life, but if the improper behavior continues to detract from the values you're teaching, the only other recourse you have is to speak to the league director. Don't be confrontational in this discussion, but be firm in your stance, because you have the welfare of a group of kids to look out for. You may also want the recreation supervisor or league director present for the discussion to lend additional support.

Soccer = babysitting service

Most parents juggle chaotic schedules and try to maintain their sanity while gobbling up dinners at drive-through windows and herding their kids to all their assorted activities. A lot of times, parents view your practices — and even games — as a convenient babysitting service where they drop their youngster off and return an hour or so later.

Sure, today, when single parenting plays an ever-increasing role in family life, Mom or Dad simply may not have the luxury of being able to hang out at the soccer field. But ideally, you want parents to be — at least to some extent — a part of the practice regimen whenever possible and to be there on game day providing positive support and encouragement for not just their child, but also the entire team.

After a couple of weeks of practices and games, you start to get a pretty good sense of which parents simply can't be there all the time and which parents are taking advantage of you and using you as an unpaid babysitting service. During your interactions with the kids, begin gauging what type of family lives they have at home, and use your conversations with parents before practices and games to get a feel for what type of people they are.

 One of the best ways to get parents to stick around for practice is to include them in some of your drills, as we discuss in Chapter 6. When those parents who typically don't hang around after dropping their child off see all the fun that's taking place and how involved the other parents are with their children, they're going to start hanging around and wanting to be part of the action.

 A lot of parents may be unfamiliar with their roles and responsibilities in a team sport like soccer, and perhaps what you outlined for them at your pre-season parents meeting didn't sink in. A quick, casual conversation with parents when they arrive to pick their children up may be all you need to make a difference. Let them know that you think their children can really benefit from having them take a more active interest in soccer and being a part of practices and games. A child who scores a goal or makes a nifty defensive play derives a lot more satisfaction from the play if she's able to glance over to the sidelines and see a thumbs-up or a nod of approval and a smile from her mom or dad.

Share with parents that their presence, even during a routine practice during the middle of the week, can do so much for a child's confidence while also maintaining their interest in the sport. You can even mention an drill you've done in practice that their child has really taken a liking to and suggest that they can work on it with their youngster at home. Not only does working on this drill help the child improve that particular area of his game, but it also gets the parents more involved in their child's development, which is good news for everyone.

Playing-time complaints

A lot of parents track their child's playing time more closely than their investment portfolio. In youth soccer, playing time is like gold, and parents can't get enough of it. After all, many parents view their child's status on the team as a true reflection of their parenting skills. The more skilled their child is — and the more playing time he receives because of those skills — the better parenting job they assume they must be doing. In their eyes, their child's playing time becomes a status symbol among the rest of the team, as well as for the parents that whom sitting next to in the stands.

A lot of parents have ridiculously unrealistic expectations of their child's soccer ability. Every time they see their child sitting on the bench, they think her athletic future is being compromised and her soccer scholarship is being put in jeopardy. Despite the league rule that's most likely in place (especially at the beginning levels of youth soccer) regarding equal playing time for all kids — regardless of their ability — when the season gets under way, some parents aren't in agreement with this policy, not when they see their child taking her turn sitting on the bench.

Dealing with parents who are disappointed by the amount of playing time their child receives is pretty common in soccer, and it's fairly easy to handle. Here are some points to keep in mind:

✔ **Rely on league policy:** If your league has a policy on equal playing time for all the kids, and you explained that policy at the start of the season to all the parents, you have a pretty convincing case for why you're rotating the kids in and out of the line-up. Let the parents know that you enjoy coaching their children, and you want to provide more playing time, but you have to be fair to all your players. And after all, rules are rules.

✔ **Offer a reminder:** Remind the parent of your stated preseason policy that every child receives an equal amount of playing time — based on regularly attending practices and not ability.

✔ **Chart playing time:** If the parents question whether you're distributing playing time equally among all the players, hopefully, you can refer to your line-up to show them that you (or an assistant coach) very carefully monitor the playing time of each child to ensure that all players get an equal amount. Written documentation of the great lengths you go to make the season fair for everyone is usually enough to make your point.

At the other end of the spectrum, some kids may refuse to return to the game when you call upon them. Perhaps a child was kicked in the shin, and the pain hasn't subsided, or maybe she's matched against a highly skilled player and is frustrated by her lack of success. Whatever the reason for her reluctance to get back on the field, never embarrass the youngster or force her back out there against her will. If the child isn't comfortable explaining why she's hesitant to return, be sure to speak with her privately after the game to learn what happened and what you can do to ease those fears before the next game.

Trouble in the stands

Overinvolved parents who regularly wander across the line of good behavior have become increasingly common in youth soccer programs. Too often, loud-mouthed insults, cursing, ranting, raving, and frightening violence have found their way into an increasing number of soccer programs and youth sports programs in general. Why some parents act irresponsibly and behave poorly while watching a youth soccer game is difficult to figure out and probably involves a bunch of factors that are completely out of your control. But what is in your control is your ability to keep that type of negative behavior from embarrassing the children and disrupting the game.

If a parent displays inappropriate behavior, address it as soon as possible. Ignoring the actions of these parents or being afraid to step forward and address the situation sends a terrible message that this type of behavior is acceptable and that everything that you talked about during your preseason parents meeting was just a bunch of hollow words. Parents need to know that inappropriate words and actions aren't tolerated in any form whatsoever. Dealing with problems swiftly also lets the other team parents know that if they step or act out of line, you'll deal with them accordingly. The entire team of parents will appreciate your commitment to ensuring that each child on the team has a safe and fun-filled experience.

How do you handle a parent who has just shouted an embarrassing comment? What do you do when parents yell across the field at the coach who appears to be running up the score on your team? What do you do when tensions seem to be rising among parents who are suddenly not very happy with how the game is unfolding? In the following sections, we provide you some strategies to deal with such situations. And because you're only human, and such disruptions and confrontations are bound to get you steamed at times, we also advise you what not to do — don't let your emotions get the better of you.

What do to

The following are some approaches you can use to help keep everyone's temper in check and the game moving along without any unnecessary disruptions for the kids:

- ✔ **Provide a friendly reminder:** A lot of times, parents may not even realize that they're behaving inappropriately, and a firm — but friendly — reminder to keep their emotions in check and their comments about the game or the referee's calls to themselves may be all that's required.

- ✔ **Understand your league's parent policy:** As we discuss in Chapter 2, thoroughly knowing your league's rules is extremely important. An increasing number of soccer leagues around the country are instituting parent sportsmanship programs — both voluntary and mandatory — to help give parents a clear understanding of their roles and responsibilities. You may want to recommend to your league director adopting a program so all the parents work together to ensure meeting the best interests of all the kids.

- ✔ **Set a civil example:** You can quickly defuse a tense situation between yourself and an upset parent by maintaining a calm and friendly demeanor at all times. Setting a civil tone right from the start is a critical building block for a productive discussion. Granted, this civility may be difficult at times, particularly when the parent is unleashing a verbal assault accusing you of being an inept soccer coach with no sense of what's right for the kids.

- ✔ **Be prepared to listen:** If you're not willing to listen to what the parents have to say, how can you realistically expect them to listen to you? Focus as much on listening as trying to get your point across, and the parent is more likely to work with you and not against you.

- ✔ **Use the right tone:** Just as your tone and body language influence your interactions with the kids, they have the same impact on your dealings with parents. For example, if a parent poses a question to you about why her child only got to play in half the game, and before responding, you put your hands on your hips, she perceives you as being upset before you even respond to the question. Mixed body-language signals or a negative tone are quick routes to an unproductive and unhealthy conversation.

✔ **Remove abusive parents from the field only as a last resort:** Having a parent removed from the playing area is an extreme step to take — but sometimes, it's the only recourse available to ensure the safety and well being of the young participants on the field, as well as the other spectators in the stands. Being thrown out is certainly an embarrassment for the parent who's being removed, as well as for the child whose fun game of soccer is being interrupted.

Parents want the best for their children, so if they request a meeting with you and are willing to take the time to speak with you on their child's behalf, that shows that they're caring and concerned parents. Let them know that you understand that they want the best for their child, as do you. Acknowledge their child's attributes, and let them know how proud you are of how the child has developed so far this season, what a pleasure she is to coach, and what a valuable member of the team she is.

What not to do

Sometimes, as frustration levels mount regarding specific issues, you may be tempted to try all sorts of tactics to rid yourself of the problem. We advise steering clear of the following:

✔ **Don't fire back:** Many parents agree to meet with you about their behavior and then use the meeting as an opportunity to bombard you with accusations, complaints, and other negative comments. No matter how frustrated or upset you are, resist the urge to fire back at the parent in defense of your coaching abilities, because doing so accomplishes absolutely nothing.

✔ **Don't embarrass the parent:** Being the parent of a youth soccer player isn't easy. Parents want the best for their young players, and if they see their child knocked down or tripped by an opposing player, and the referee doesn't blow the whistle, keeping their displeasure to themselves can be extremely difficult. When you hear a comment shouted from the stands, sometimes you can just look over your shoulder at the offending parents. That brief eye contact with them lets them know that what they just said is unacceptable and that they need to tone it down.

Take the time to follow up and meet with the parent after the game — if you have an opportunity to speak with her alone — and remind her that negative comments detract from everyone's enjoyment of the game. For example, try something along the lines of "I know that tripping call the referee made against your son in the second half was a little shaky, but you know all the calls aren't going to go our way this season. Please remember that I need you and all the parents to set an example of good sportsmanship and that negative comments take away from all the kids' enjoyment. I know it's difficult, but please don't let it happen again."

- **Never punish the child:** No matter how poorly behaved a mom or dad is, never take out your frustration on the child. Remember, the youngsters on your team have no control over how their parents behave on game day, so don't trim down their playing time, shift their position on the field, or take any other drastic measures in an effort to rein in the emotional outbursts of their parents. Continue coaching the children, working with them, and applauding their efforts, and hopefully, your chats with the parents will help them control themselves. With luck, the remainder of the season will progress smoothly, with no more behavioral hiccups along the way.

- **Don't tolerate surprise attacks in the parking lot following the game:** When the parent is visibly upset, and tensions are running high, the situation isn't conducive to a mature discussion, and nothing good comes of it. Explain to the parents that you're happy to meet with them to discuss any concerns they may have at a time that's convenient for both of you and that isn't in front of their child or the rest of the team.

- **Don't physically confront a parent who refuses to abide by your request to behave:** Sometimes, the league policies stipulate that the coach contact a league director when problems arise, and he or she deals with them accordingly. Some programs have even resorted to hiring police officers who patrol the fields in case a verbal or physical altercation or threat occurs.

Dealing with Problem Coaches

Unfortunately, the odds are pretty good that at some point during your soccer coaching career, you're going to come across coaches who just don't get it when it comes to kids and soccer. Although you're more likely to see rude, out-of-control, and offensive behavior in the older age groups and more advanced levels of soccer, when the competition becomes more intense, you also find it at the beginning levels.

Improper behavior from opposing coaches

The best way to combat this type of behavior from an opposing coach is to maintain a level head and a calm demeanor while he's losing his. These situations test how well you can adhere to that coaching philosophy of yours (which we discuss in Chapter 2).

Your top priority at all times is to protect the best interests of your squad. The players on your team take their cues from you and how you act when the tension rises and blood pressures escalate.

Encouraging unsafe play

Ensuring the safety of your players should always be a top priority. Sure, in a contact sport like soccer, injuries happen, and you can't always avoid the normal bumps and bruises that occur during the course of a season. But if you find your team going against a squad that's being encouraged to use unsafe methods that put your team's safety and well being in jeopardy, you have to take immediate action. What steps should you take?

- ✔ **Talk to the referee:** Address your concerns in a respectable manner to the referee, and express that your players are being put at unnecessary risk. Be clear that you're concerned about the welfare of all the kids, not how the referee is calling the game. Never hesitate to address a safety issue. One of the referee's most important responsibilities is to ensure the safety of all the players, so by working with her — not against her — you can help make that happen.

- ✔ **Don't confront the opposing coach:** Utilize the referee as your intermediary to resolve the situation. Heading over to the other sideline typically just creates the potential for more conflict. It could also antagonize the coach, who may feel threatened that you've come over and put his coaching techniques in question in front of all the fans. The coach may react negatively and view it as a ploy to affect his team's play, particularly if he's winning the game.

- ✔ **Stop the game:** If, after speaking with the referee, you don't feel that the tone and nature of the game have changed enough and that physical and unsafe play continues to prevail, your only recourse is removing your team from the field. Certainly, you hope that the play never gets bad enough that you have to resort to this action, but completing a soccer game simply to get it in the books — at the risk of injury to a child — is never worth it.

- ✔ **Speak with the league director:** If a league director monitors games at the facility where your team plays and is on the premises, speak with him about your concerns before pulling your players off the field. If he's not available, meet with him as soon as possible to explain your concerns about the game and why you felt that terminating the game was in the best interest of your kids.

Modeling poor sportsmanship

You're in for quite a surprise if you head into the season thinking that every opposing team's coach is a mild-mannered individual who's going to be a model of good behavior and human decency. Some soccer coaches — hopefully, not in your league — do prowl the sidelines like hungry tigers. They wear out their lungs by screaming at their players to run faster and kick harder. They fire negative comments at referees, argue every call that goes against their team, and give their team members the perception that everyone is against them. These coaches behave like every game is for the World Cup, every call carries life-or-death consequences, and every victory is an affirmation of what a wonderful job they're doing.

What's the best way to combat opposing coaches who are sabotaging the experience for everyone involved? Here are a few tips to keep in mind when the game heats up:

- ✔ **Keep a level head:** Opposing coaches who operate with unsportsman-like behavior challenge your patience, test your poise, and wreak havoc with your blood pressure. You want to avoid retaliating and remain a model of good behavior for your team.

- ✔ **Use it as a teachable moment:** Point out to your team the type of boorish behavior taking place on the other sideline and that they have to rise above that and demonstrate that they can be much better behaved.

- ✔ **Meet with the league director:** Make her aware that a coach is really setting a poor example for the kids on his team and that he's not the type of individual who should be coaching in this league.

- ✔ **Tune out distractions:** Tell players to ignore the coach's shouting and to play their own game. Keep talking to them in a positive manner; keep their attention focused on the game and utilizing their skills, and don't allow them to be distracted by his loud-mouthed behavior.

Disagreements with assistants

As we discuss in Chapter 4, assistants play a vital role in the success of your team. They're extra sets of eyes and ears during games, and they can help provide instruction and keep drills moving during practices. But as we also mention in Chapter 4, exercising great caution before selecting individuals to hold these key positions is extremely important. What are some of the problems that you can run into with your assistant coaches? Take a look at the assistant who:

- ✔ **Wants his child to play more:** Perhaps this person had ulterior motives from the start and grabbed an assistant's role to help ensure that her child got extra playing time or was guaranteed a certain position.

- ✔ **Is a distraction during games:** Even the most laid-back, mild-mannered parents can turn into raving, screaming lunatics when the game begins. As soon as the scoreboard is turned on, you'd think a switch was flipped in their heads as they go into a mode of screaming and running up and down the sidelines.

- ✔ **Is a poor teacher:** You don't want to teach youngsters the wrong way to perform a skill or, worst of all, an unsafe technique that can put them at unnecessary risk and pose an injury risk for the kids they're playing against. You may have some great, well-meaning parents who raised their hands and volunteered to help you out, but if their knowledge of soccer skills is limited or nonexistent (which is often the case, because many of today's parents didn't play soccer growing up), it knocks open the door for all sorts of problems to occur.

✔ **Has a different philosophy:** During your preseason meeting with the parents, you (hopefully) stressed that winning was going to take a backseat to skill development and fun. Although all the parents may have nodded in agreement with those statements back then, you may discover that after the games begin and they start watching the standings, they don't exactly share those same views anymore. Basically, they bailed out on you and are preaching to the kids everything that you're against.

Your assistant coaches are an extension of you — which makes everything they say and do on your behalf extremely important to the overall success of the season. Keep an eye out, especially during your first few practices of the season, to closely monitor how your assistants interact and teach the kids skills. If they're not getting the job done or adhering to the philosophies you're looking to instill in your team, you need to have a 1-on-1 talk with them right away to reinforce what you want to accomplish this season. Usually, this chat is enough to get them back on the right track. If it's not, and problems continue, let them know that you think it's in the best interest of the team that they step down from their assistant duties. Be sure to thank them for their time and effort. The position is simply too important to let problems linger any longer than necessary.

Dealing with Discipline Problems on Your Own Team

Teaching kids the finer points of heading and how to deliver accurate corner kicks are just some of the areas of the game that challenge your coaching skills. Making sure that youngsters listen to your instructions, respect your authority, and abide by the team rules you set forth can pose a whole new set of challenges that you may not have been completely aware of — or prepared for — when you raised your hand to volunteer this season.

The chances are pretty good that at some point during the season, you'll have to discipline a child who steps over the line. A lot of times, children become disruptive because they're frustrated at their lack of progress in soccer, they feel like their contributions aren't valued by the coach, or they get a sense that their teammates don't value them or like them being a part of the team.

Reviewing some general advice

When dealing with behavior problems among your players, keep the following in mind:

✔ **Stay away from laps:** When a child mouths off, sending him on a lap or two around the field as punishment is tempting. But conditioning exercises should never be used as a form of punishment with players. Conditioning plays a very important role in soccer, particularly at the more advanced levels of play, where it becomes a major aspect of the game and impacts the play on the field. If children relate conditioning and running with punishment, they're more likely to develop a negative outlook on conditioning, which can be disruptive to their development.

✔ **Be true to your word:** When you outline to a particular player the discipline that will follow if she doesn't behave appropriately, you have to follow through with the punishment to maintain your authority, credibility, trust, and respect with the team.

✔ **Apply team rules evenly:** One of the most disastrous moves you can make when disciplining children is to play favorites and allow some kids to get away with certain behavior while punishing others for the same infraction. A youngster's ability to kick a soccer ball harder or more accurately than his teammate shouldn't generate a separate set of team rules for him. Doing so divides the team and causes resentment among players, which quickly sabotages team chemistry.

✔ **Make sure the punishment is fair:** Don't go overboard enforcing team policies. If a child forgets her water bottle at practice, don't view it as the same type of infraction as swearing during a practice or game.

✔ **Avoid the doghouse syndrome:** As soon as the discipline with the child is completed, sweep that incident to the side, and move on. Don't hold a grudge or treat the child differently than you did before the problem occurred. Keeping the child in the doghouse simply isn't fair when you've already punished him for his transgression. Forgive, forget, and focus on making sure the youngster feels like a valued member of the team again. This means recognizing when he does something well, which helps reassure him that you've forgotten the past problems.

✔ **Maintain a level head:** Shouting at athletes or losing your temper when disciplining distorts the discipline you're trying to enforce and sets a poor example for the team regarding acceptable behavior.

✔ **Don't discipline for playing miscues:** Never resort to disciplining a child who gives up a goal or makes an errant pass that results in the game-winning goal for the opposing team. But, if a player intentionally tries to injure another player by tripping her, for example, immediately remove him from the game. This type of behavior may warrant further disciplinary action on your part, depending on the severity of the action, the intent, and other factors that led up to the tripping incident.

Using the three-strikes approach

Addressing discipline problems at the first sign of trouble and resolving conflicts before they escalate and cause further disruptions are vital for maintaining team order and your sanity. An effective approach to rely on is a three-strikes technique that allows the children a little room for error and gives you time to restructure their behavior. It will probably do the trick for you in most scenarios that you encounter. Inform the parents of the procedure you'll be following before any problems ever materialize so that everyone fully understands how punishment will be handed out.

Strike one!

The first time a child displays behavior that you deem unacceptable, give her a verbal warning. This warning lets her know that you're not pleased with what she said or did and that if it happens again, you will punish her. Some examples of behavior that merits a strike-one warning include a child swearing during a game or displaying unsportsmanlike conduct, such as refusing to shake the hand of an opposing player following a game. In most cases, when a child knows that a stricter measure will be enforced if she repeats the same behavior, she isn't likely to do it again. Of course, kids are kids, and some aren't able to break their bad behavior habits or simply may have to test your authority to see whether you're serious about punishing them if they misbehave again. This approach is sort of like telling a child not to touch something because it's still hot, and she still proceeds to touch it, much to your disapproval. So be prepared, and don't allow a child to trample your authority. Be willing to go to the next discipline level.

Strike two!

If the youngster continues to disobey your instructions, and she's still swearing during games, for example, you have to bump up the severity of the punishment in order to derail this negative behavior before it becomes a total distraction to the team. Taking away a portion of her playing time in the next game sends a clear message that she has no room for negotiating and that if she doesn't stop this behavior immediately, she's not going to get back on the field. Let the player know in specific terms that if she misbehaves anymore, she's jeopardizing her future with the team. After a strike-two warning, meet with the parents, and let them know what took place. Let the parents know that you want their child to be a part of this team and that she won't face repercussions the rest of the season if she behaves in an appropriate manner. Relay exactly what you told the child so the parents can reinforce your message at home. This makes the child aware of the seriousness of her behavior and that she must take immediate action to continue playing on the team. Let the parents know that their child will be sitting on the bench for an extended period of time as punishment. If you happen to be coaching in a more competitive league, and the offending child is a starter, not allowing her to start is usually all you need to warrant a turnaround in her behavior.

Strike three!

Rarely do youngsters venture into strike-three territory. With this three-tiered approach to passing out punishment, and with coveted playing time at stake, most youngsters behave after the verbal warning is issued at the first hint of a problem. In the rare event where the child simply refuses to adhere to your instructions and her behavior continues to be unacceptable, you may have no recourse but to remove the child from the team. You have a responsibility to all the kids on your team, and you can't allow the behavior of one child to disrupt the experience of everyone else. Ideally, you never want to be in a position to force a child away from a sport, and before resorting to this measure, meet with the league director to detail what's happened so far. In order to give the child every opportunity to make amends, you can even go so far as to allow the child to return to the team if she's willing to apologize to you and the team and promise to be a model of good behavior. Kids can turn over a new leaf, and maybe a few days away from the team will make her realize how much she misses playing soccer. If she knows the door is still cracked open for her return, if she apologizes for her previous indiscretions, the potential exists for everything to work out in the end.

Taking a look at particular behaviors

While the kids you coach are vastly different, the types of problems you encounter are fairly commonplace. Some kids chat too much; others tune you out; and you probably have to deal with a child who always manages to show up halfway through practice. Take a peek at how to get through to these youngsters who test your patience.

The nonlistener

Some kids arrive at the field with a know-it-all attitude and they don't believe that they have to listen to your instructions. They tune you out and do their own thing. This inattentiveness can be especially troublesome if they employ techniques that, despite your continued instruction on how to perform them the right way, pose injury risks for other players. For example, they may continually take other players' feet out from under them when tackling. What can you do?

If you see that a child isn't listening to your instructions, sit him down in practice, and have him watch how the rest of the team follows instructions. After a few minutes, ask him whether he's ready to return to play and listen to what you have to say. Your nonlistener is likely to be much more receptive to your instruction after spending any length of time by your side while his teammates are on the field.

If the child isn't performing a skill correctly, and you suspect that she wasn't paying attention, ask the child why she isn't performing the skill like you demonstrated. Maybe she didn't understand your instructions and, out of frustration, tried doing it the way she thought it should be done.

When dealing with problems with your players, you always hold the trump card: playing time. It can be a great equalizer, attitude-adjuster, personality-changer, and attention-getter all rolled up into one. No one enjoys having his fanny stuck on the bench while his friends and teammates are out on the field during game day. Taking away playing time from a child who misbehaves is no different from a parent taking away TV, computer games, or treats from a child at home who misbehaves.

The nonstop talker

You may encounter some kids on your team who are more talkative than a used-car salesman and throw out one-liners like a stand-up comedian. That can create a lot of problems at times. Kids who are more interested in talking than listening to what you have to say can cause unwanted distractions. If the team is hearing only bits and pieces of your instructions because of a nonstop talker, your effectiveness as a coach may be compromised, along with the development of the rest of your squad. How do you curb the vocal cords of those kids whose mouths seem to be on the perpetual move?

At the first indication of a problem, remind the team that when you're speaking, all the team members need to remain quiet and listen to your instructions.

If that fails, you may have to call the player out. For example, say something like "Jimmy, please don't talk while I'm addressing the team. It's important that everyone hears what I'm going over. If you have a comment or question, please hold it until I'm done."

If the player's talking continues to cause problems, pull the player aside, and be firm in your stance that the child must abide by your rules or face the consequences — and then spell those rules out clearly for the child so she knows the penalties for her future actions. If you have to reprimand her again to be quiet, let her know that she's going to lose significant amounts of playing time. Usually, this threat is enough to get her attention — and close her mouth. This warning is basically the three-strikes technique (see "Using the three-strikes approach" section, earlier in the chapter).

The perpetually late player

Coaching youth soccer has negative aspects along with the positive, and one of the most annoying is the child who's consistently late for practice. He misses the warm-up and your pre-practice instructions, and shows up at your side halfway through a drill. Or, equally bad, he makes an appearance midway through the first half of your game, throwing your line-up out of whack and creating chaos with your substitution patterns. These late-arriving players are a nuisance, an inconvenience, and totally disruptive to the flow of your practice, distracting other team members in the process.

If the problem isn't rectified immediately and is allowed to drag on for weeks, the consequences can be even more severe than just a big headache for you. At some point, the child's late arrival at a game may force you to forfeit the game because you don't have enough players available. You never want one child's lateness to affect the playing experience of the entire team. The following are a few tips that you can incorporate to help get the kids to your practices and games on time:

✔ **Team talk:** As soon as you get a sense that late arrivals are beginning to create problems, talk to the entire team to reinforce your expectations on attendance. Stress that being part of a team is a commitment — one that needs to be kept at midweek practices and championship games alike. Make it clear that you're at the field — on time — for all practices and games and that you expect and deserve the same consideration from every one of your players. If the problem isn't addressed at the first hint of trouble, you slowly lose control of the season and the respect of your players who do show up on time. These kids are committed to you but frustrated by the lack of care and concern of other players who cut into the quality of the practice with their late-arriving habits.

✔ **Roll call:** Make a really big production out of attendance by taking roll call during warm-ups. Turn it into an entertaining exercise by calling out a funny nickname for a player or using an amusing voice that gets a chuckle from the kids. Even if you have only seven kids on your team, and a roll call isn't necessary from the standpoint of knowing who's there and who hasn't arrived yet, it can still be a fun moment that the kids enjoy being part of and won't want to miss in the future.

✔ **Fun games:** While you can't force players to arrive on time for practice, you can do a few things to help entice them to begin showing up on time. Throw in a fun little game before practice begins. You may be pleasantly surprised by the number of kids who suddenly show up at practice well ahead of time. Hopefully, they're pestering their parents to get them to practice so they don't miss out on the fun game with their friends.

✔ **Individual exercises:** When a player arrives late, don't immediately send her into the drill that you're running. This rule is especially important for an older player who hasn't gone through the proper stretching and warm-ups that the rest of the team completed. Instead, have her work on some individual drills, such as dribbling, on the sidelines before integrating her into the practice. If you're coaching a team of older players who are more susceptible to muscle strains and pulls, make sure the late player goes through proper stretching before you allow her on the field. Just because a player is late doesn't mean that she can overlook this important aspect of the game. You don't want to put her at unnecessary risk of suffering an injury that's easily avoidable.

✔ **Reduced playing time:** A youngster who's constantly late for practice should have his playing time in games reduced. Getting to play when you don't show up on time simply isn't fair to the rest of the team who shows up on time week after week.

Punishing a youngster who doesn't drive for the irresponsible behavior of her parents is difficult. As we discuss in Chapter 4, hopefully, you address the importance of everyone showing up on time for practices and games at your preseason parents meeting. Explain how crucial that is both for the season to run smoothly and for you to keep your sanity.

Any time you address being late for practice with the child, follow up with the parent. Many parents simply may not realize what a big disruption their being late to practice causes for the rest of the team. Hopefully, a brief conversation reminding them of the importance of having everyone at the field on time is all you need to prevent the problem from occurring during the remainder of the season. The following are a few things you may want to mention to the parents to ensure that the discussion goes smoothly and all parties are happy at the conclusion. Remind them about the

✔ **Team inconvenience:** Let the parents know that the late arrival is a disruption that inconveniences you and detracts from the time you have to teach the entire team. Stress that you really need the child on time at every practice for both his and his team's development. The more practice time he misses, the fewer number of touches he gets, which, during the course of the season, impacts his development.

✔ **Possible solutions:** You can perhaps help the parent find a solution that works for everyone. It could be as simple as having a teammate's parent who lives nearby pick up the youngster and bring her to practice.

✔ **Playing-time ramifications:** Remind the parents that playing time in games is distributed based on practice attendance and you'd hate to see their child penalized, but you have to be fair to the kids who are on time.

✔ **Child's compromised skills:** You're trying to build skills in players, so being late puts you and the child in a tough spot. Many of the skills you're teaching gradually build on those skills learned earlier. When a child is late and misses valuable instruction time, his development is compromised, and his practice of that particular skill is limited.

Chapter 20

Taking Your Show on the Road

· ·

In This Chapter

▶ Going over travel-team basics

▶ Tackling tryouts and picking players

▶ Providing a good experience for your players and their families

▶ Coaching off the field

· ·

As youngsters develop skills, some become passionate about soccer and look to take their games to higher levels and compete against stronger competition. And some coaches, after being around the sport for a few seasons, seek a more competitive setting. Enter select or travel teams.

These teams provide new coaching challenges: The players are more skilled, the teams are more talented, and the competition is more intense. Practices are highly structured, games are more frequent, and weekend tournaments are commonplace. The coach organizes tryouts, evaluates players, and puts together rosters. If you think you're ready, this chapter provides some useful information to help smooth your transition to the travel-team sidelines.

Hitting the Road

The travel-team environment is vastly different from your local recreation program. Games are highly competitive, and your team faces opponents from different communities, cities, and (in some cases) states. As long as you focus on providing for the best interests of all the kids, the travel-team experience can be richly rewarding for everyone involved.

What's a travel team?

Travel teams present opportunities for youngsters who are interested in focusing on soccer as their main sport and want to play against top-level competition on a regular basis. These teams play in highly competitive tournaments against other talented teams in out-of-town locations. They require a much greater commitment of time and money on the part of the children, parents, and coaches than local, recreational soccer programs. A typical travel-team week involves a couple of practices, and weekends are often swallowed up by traveling and competing in tournaments. Seasons typically run longer than those of recreational programs.

What age groups are travel teams appropriate for?

Generally speaking, travel teams are better suited for kids ages 12 and older who have a deep interest in and passion for the sport and who want to test their skills against other talented players. Because of the increased level of play, the added pressure that typically accompanies these teams, and a fuller schedule of practices and games, most experts say that kids under 12 shouldn't be involved with travel teams. That's a general guideline, because kids mature at different rates both emotionally and physically, and some 11-year-olds may be better equipped to handle the travel-team experience than some 13-year-olds, for example.

Because of the enormous time commitment associated with most travel teams, experts suggest that kids under 12 should be introduced to a variety of sports and activities that allow them to develop a wide range of skills — including balance, coordination, and agility — before specializing in one sport.

Each decision must be made on an individual basis. The best sports experiences are suited to the motivation and skill level of the individual athlete. The parents' desire to have their child play on a travel team isn't enough; the child must want it, too. The youngster must have the true desire and motivation to play more frequently. If his interest and motivation are suspect, he's better off sticking with a recreational soccer program. Parents can revisit the situation next season to see whether he's emotionally and physically ready. Families must also analyze whether the move is right for their child *and* for them, because the entire family must be ready if the travel-team experience is going to be a successful endeavor.

The Selection Process

Choosing players to field a travel team is challenging. Besides analyzing the skills and abilities of the players, you have the unpleasant task of breaking the bad news to the players who didn't make the team.

Holding a tryout

Orchestrating a well-run tryout speaks volumes about your coaching ability and makes choosing the players who are best suited to play on the team that much easier.

Starting off the tryout on the right foot

Spend a couple minutes at the start of the tryout introducing yourself and outlining how you're structuring the session. Giving kids an outline helps ease stress, allows them to focus on performing to the best of their ability, and eliminates any unnecessary surprises.

Kids are naturally nervous and probably a little uptight before tryouts begin. Be friendly when they arrive at the field; greet them with a warm smile; and exude a positive attitude at all times. Soccer is fun, and even though coveted spots on the team are at stake, don't turn the tryout into a negative experience that's more stressful than necessary.

Even though you may never see some of these kids again, keep their best interests in mind. That means approaching this session the same way you do an ordinary practice, which you start by having the kids stretch (check out Chapter 18 for some suggested routines). If you count on the kids to stretch on their own, some probably won't do an adequate job. Run them through a series of stretches so you know that their bodies are prepared for the tryout.

Avoid choosing players to lead the stretches. Even if you're familiar with some of the kids and know that they'd do a great job leading the stretches, that tactic sends the wrong message. The other kids may think that you're already playing favorites and that these kids are tabbed for positions on the team before they even try out.

Designing a well-structured tryout

Limit the tryout sessions to one hour for kids ages 12 and under. For older kids, you can bump it up to 1½ to 2 hours. If you need to hold multiple sessions to effectively evaluate all the kids, that's fine. You're better off holding a pair of one-hour sessions than one lengthy two-hour session. To make the best use of your time and adequately evaluate all the players, keep the following points in mind as you set up and conduct your tryout:

- ✔ **Use game situations.** Timed sprints down the field and dribbling the ball through a series of cones aren't good evaluation tools. For example, if one player dribbles the ball through the cones in 18 seconds, and another youngster takes 19 or 20 seconds to maneuver through them, what have you really learned about the talent level of these two individuals? Not a whole lot. A player can be fast and keep his head down the entire time he dribbles, which doesn't bode well when he's in a game setting and needs to be aware of where his teammates are and whether any defenders are converging on him.

The best approach to assessing talent is to put the players in situations that closely mirror game conditions and see how they respond to pressure and what types of decisions they make while playing both offense and defense.

✔ **Ensure plenty of touches.** Observing players in small-sided games of 2-on-2 or 3-on-3 provides a wealth of information on their abilities. Situations that allow them plenty of touches of the ball help you determine how they transition from offense to defense, how they recognize various situations, and how their thought processes operate in determining when attacking is appropriate and when regrouping with the ball is best. For example:

- Does the player cover a lot of territory, or is she content to stick to one area of the field?

- Does she look to pass the ball upfield, or is she more comfortable dribbling down the field herself?

- Is she good at spotting open teammates and delivering the ball to them, or is she more passive and fearful of turning the ball over?

- Is she good at reading and anticipating plays?

Taking in all this information and noticing these tendencies are vital for getting a true evaluation of a youngster's ability. Also, this information is valuable for the players you do end up choosing, because you can use it to help determine which positions they're best suited for.

✔ **Don't get station crazy.** If you use some stations, such as a shooting station to evaluate a goalie and the other players' shooting skills, limit how many stations you have going at one time. Having too many stations running simultaneously doesn't allow you to effectively monitor all the players. Plus, if the kids see that you're not at their station watching them, they may not be quite as focused on giving their best effort, which detracts from the effectiveness of the entire tryout process.

Don't get too caught up in coaching, because that takes away from the purpose of the tryout, which is to evaluate the kids' skills. But sprinkling your tryout with some coaching pointers isn't a bad idea. It gives you a chance to observe how the kids react to instruction, feedback, and even constructive criticism. You're going to coach some of these kids for several months, so gaining some insight into how receptive they are to your feedback is helpful. For example, if you have one roster spot left and a couple of players who are comparable in ability, how open each player is to receiving feedback is another factor that you can use in assessing who's the better fit for the team.

At the conclusion of the tryout, thank the players for following instructions and giving their best effort. Also, thank the parents for their willingness to get the kids to the tryout on time and adjusting their busy schedules to accommodate it. It's a nice touch that demonstrates how much you care.

Evaluating and selecting players

A well-structured tryout is the first step toward putting together your travel team (see the previous section). Now, as the kids are running, kicking, and competing, keep close tabs on them to determine who deserves the chance to play for you this season.

Get some assistance when monitoring the players. If you have a large turnout, having a few more sets of eyes watching the kids is helpful. If you're taking the place of a coach who handled the team last season, ask for his advice, or see whether he can come out to give you his input, because he has valuable experience on what types of kids it takes to play and compete at this level. If you have several adults helping you out, make sure that they get a chance to see all the kids; otherwise, their evaluations aren't as accurate and comprehensive as they could be. You can also ask your assistants to take care of the small details like setting up the cones for a drill, ensuring that each station has enough soccer balls, and so on. Doing so gives you more time in front of the kids for explaining drills, evaluating players, and building bonds.

Make a list of the skills you want your evaluators to monitor, such as speed, shooting, passing, receiving, trapping, shielding, aggressiveness, and 1-on-1 abilities, both offensively and defensively. If you have a large group and assistants helping you evaluate, give everyone a roster with the kids' names and numbers. Having scores and comments on each youngster from several sources can help identify the players most deserving of roster spots.

Evaluating skills is important, but be sure that you and your assistants take a look at these sometimes easily overlooked areas during the selection process:

- ✔ **Teamwork:** Assessing how players work with their teammates is crucial. A great ball handler is an asset to the team if he looks for open teammates, but he's a liability to the attack if he's reluctant to give up possession of the ball. A highly skilled player must be a team player in order to fit into the framework of your squad.

- ✔ **Demeanor:** Does the player get noticeably upset when a teammate fails to deliver an accurate pass to her that may have resulted in a good scoring opportunity? Does she get visibly frustrated when her pass isn't handled efficiently and results in the opposing team gaining possession of the ball? You want players on your team who are supportive rather than negative toward their teammates.

- ✔ **Mental muscle:** Don't neglect the mental aspect of the kids. Keep a close watch to see what type of competitors they are. For example, when they lose the ball to a defender, are they focused on regaining possession, or are they frustrated and lacking the competitive fire to go after it? Are they good sports who play within the rules, or do they resort to unfavorable tactics at times?

Keep in mind that these factors aren't automatic disqualifiers, because you have to evaluate each child on a case-by-case basis. If you choose a child who exhibits the occasional tendency to behave inappropriately, you have the responsibility to work with him and teach him the importance of behaving in a respectful manner. Otherwise, he's at risk of being dismissed from the team.

Breaking the good and bad news

You, and the players who gave you their best trying out, experience a wide range of emotions come selection time for the travel team. Seeing the smile on a child's face when you let her know that she made the team is one of the great things about coaching a travel soccer team. Unfortunately, at the other end of the spectrum is the unpleasant task of breaking the news to a youngster that she didn't make it. Take a look at some dos and don'ts when informing kids whether they will or won't wear a travel-team jersey for you this season.

Notify everyone in a timely manner

Sure, this ordeal would be easier on you if you had to deliver only the good news to the kids who made the team, but in fairness to everyone who sweated and performed to the best of their ability, you need to let all the children know whether they made it or not.

And make your decisions in a timely manner. Think about going on a job interview for a position you really want and how nerve-wracking the wait is. The same goes for kids trying out for your team. They're naturally eager to hear whether they made the team or not, so be as prompt as possible in your decision-making process.

Deliver the news in person

A letter telling a child he didn't make the team is the easy way out for you — but not the right way. The youngster gave the tryout his best, and he deserves to hear in person your evaluation of his play. If a large number of players tried out, and having 1-on-1 conversations in person simply isn't feasible, at the very least deliver the news over the phone.

If you're dealing with a small group of players, you may find it more comfortable paying a quick visit to all the players' homes to let them know whether they made it or not. With larger groups, set aside an evening to break the news. Check with your recreation department whose field you used for the tryout about using a room so you have privacy to speak to each child. Prior to the tryout, let everyone know the date and time for the announcements, and assign each player a time to meet with you. Conduct the meetings in five- or ten-minute intervals.

Be encouraging when giving the bad news

You don't want the child to regret that she tried out. Yes, she'll be disappointed when she doesn't make the team, but what you say (and how you say it) determines whether that disappointment lingers for a couple days or months and whether she uses your words as motivation to work on her skills.

The bad news can be crushing to a child's confidence and self-esteem, and you want to do everything you can to soften the blow of this setback. You don't want this news to quash a child's enthusiasm for the sport or derail his interest in playing. Be clear that not making the team isn't a judgment on the child as a person. Let the youngster and his parents know what areas of his game you were impressed with, and let him know those areas that he can devote a little more focus to. Offer recommendations on how he can go about improving those areas of his game, and encourage him to try out again next season. He may simply need one more season of recreation play to hone his skills before he makes the jump to a more competitive level of play.

The Season

Youngsters may need a little time to adjust to the travel-team schedule. After all, they have more practices and games to play in during the week than they're accustomed to; they have suitcases to pack and new locales to play in for out-of-town tournaments; and they have increased competition for playing time to adjust to because their teammates are quicker, faster, and stronger than a lot of the kids they're used to playing with from their recreation league teams. The following sections explain how you can help your players avoid being overwhelmed by the experience.

Try to recruit a parent or two to fulfill the role of team business manager. Your season will run more smoothly, and you'll be able to focus on coaching. These folks can be a huge help filling out tournament registration forms, making motel reservations, and locating restaurants for team meals, as well as taking care of a host of other responsibilities.

Avoiding burnout

Some travel-team seasons stretch on for several months, which increases the chance of players suffering burnout. *Burnout* occurs when players grow tired of playing, and it typically involves a combination of physical and emotional exhaustion. Even though kids love playing soccer, when you subject them to a heavy practice schedule that they normally aren't accustomed to, as well as an increased number of games, they're susceptible to suffering burnout. Here are some tips to consider to keep your team energized:

- ✔ **Keep it fresh.** With the extra practice load, providing kids with a wide range of drills throughout the week is more important than ever. The more variety you spice your practices up with, the less likely the kids are to become drained from participating. (See Chapter 6 for additional practice tips.)

- ✔ **Downplay winning.** The pressure to win can be a heavy burden on a team, and it can sap your kids' energy and cripple their enthusiasm, which are some of the first signs of burnout.

- ✔ **Know when to ease back.** If you have a heavy tournament schedule on the horizon, or if you know you're going to play a lot of games in a short time span, ease back on the practice schedule leading up to those games. This effort helps keep the kids' energy and enthusiasm at optimum levels. Taking this type of measure can help prevent potential problems, because after burnout settles in, the only real solution is plenty of rest and time away from the sport.

Keeping everyone in the game

Even though you give the bulk of the playing time to the most talented players at the travel-soccer level, don't forget that every child — whether she's the leading scorer or the least talented of the group — has an important role. Make sure the players are fully aware of that, too. When players are on the bench, they should be actively involved in cheering their teammates on and supporting them. Also encourage them to monitor the action closely; it keeps the kids' attention, and they may spot a defensive tendency displayed by the opposing team that you can exploit. Encouraging players to take an active role in all areas of the game, whether on the field or off, enhances their experience and further instills that they're valuable members of the team.

Making adjustments for weekend tournaments

Coaching in weekend tournaments is dramatically different from working the sidelines during a midweek game. One of the biggest differences you have to deal with is that tournaments typically involve several games played in a short period of time. Consequently, you do plenty of juggling and employ different strategies to ensure that you don't wear your players out. Try the following to keep your players fresh:

- ✔ **Rely on nonstarters more.** In games in which you're comfortably ahead, insert nonstarters to spell the regulars and give them valuable rest for the upcoming games.

- ✔ **Make adjustments to your playing strategy.** You may need to alter your playing strategy at times. For example, if you typically employ an aggressive attack that requires a large amount of running by all your players, and you're several goals ahead in a game, scale back and take a more defensive posture to ensure that your players have enough fuel in their tanks to compete in the next game, an hour away.

- ✔ **Adjust pre- and post-game routines.** You may have to adjust your pre-game warm-ups accordingly as you get deeper into the tournament to avoid exhausting your players.

- ✔ **Make sure your team is getting plenty of fluids.** In light of the heavy playing schedule, which often doesn't leave much recovery time between games, make sure kids are consuming adequate amounts of fluids.

Being on the Road

Coaching a travel team involves more than figuring out what type of offensive system best fits your team or who should start in goal in the upcoming weekend tournament. You must deal with a number of away-from-the-field issues that directly impact your and your players' experience.

Although what happens on the field is certainly your major responsibility, what takes place away from the field should also have your full attention. Safety is a huge consideration. Being in charge of a large group of kids for an out-of-town tournament that requires an overnight stay is an enormous responsibility. You have to ensure the safety of every child — not just on the soccer field, but also on the road to and from events and at the location where the team stays overnight. You're accountable for all the kids at all times. Besides being the coach, you're the chaperone who needs to closely monitor and know the whereabouts of every player at all times.

When you take a team of kids — and their parents — to a weekend tournament, a number of issues may pop up at some point, including the following:

- ✔ **Curfews:** Children naturally enjoy staying in motels and swimming in the pool, but to perform at their best, you must enforce curfews. The ages of the kids and the starting time of the game the following day should dictate the curfew. Let the kids and their parents know in advance what time the curfew is.

✔ **Extracurricular activities:** Competing in tournaments in different locations provides opportunities for sightseeing and participating in activities away from the field. Several factors must be taken into account when determining what activities, if any, you're going to do. You don't want your players to be so exhausted from sightseeing that they can't give you their best effort. Before departing for the event, go over the tournament schedule with the players and parents, and let them know whether they have any time for extracurricular activities. If you happen to be playing four games over a two-day period, the parents don't have enough time to arrange any activities for their kids.

If you have a break in the tournament schedule, decide whether you want to organize a team activity or allow the parents and their kids to do their own thing. Obviously, your group has varied interests, so organizing a team activity can be somewhat tricky. Also, keep in mind the added expense of these activities, because you don't want to put a financial strain on some parents or force them to participate in an activity that they can't afford. Always discuss these plans with the entire team before arriving at the tournament site.

✔ **Problems with partying parents:** For many busy families, weekend tournaments are the only vacations they have time for, so parents who want to enjoy themselves aren't uncommon. Of course, that's perfectly fine as long as the good times don't escalate into problems, such as excessive drinking or loud noise in the motel. Before departing for any overnight tournaments, let the parents know that you want them to have a good time and enjoy themselves but to keep in mind that they're at a youth soccer event and they need set a good example at all times.

Part VI
The Part of Tens

The 5th Wave   By Rich Tennant

"Okay – who told the goalie she could use her trampoline?"

In this part . . .

The Part of Tens introduces you to some unique ways you can go about making sure that all children on your team look back on their season with you and smile. If you use some of the ideas we present here, or if you use them to generate creative options of your own, your kids will carry fond memories of their season with you for the rest of their lives.

Chapter 21

Ten Ways to Make the Season Memorable

A child's experience in organized soccer can be a defining moment in her young life. Years from now, she isn't going to remember her team's record or how many goals she scored during the season, but she'll easily recall whether the time the team spent with you was a positive or negative experience. This chapter provides some methods you can use to ensure that your players have a memorable season that brings a smile to their faces for years to come and has them begging to play for you again next season.

Challenge the Coach Day

What do youngsters like most about playing soccer? Well, besides scoring goals and wearing the cool shin guards, they love opportunities to play — and beat — you, the coach, in any type of skill challenge. Reflect for a moment on your own sports experiences growing up and the first time you beat your mom, dad, or coach in a game. The feeling becomes entrenched in your memory forever. Kids genuinely love this type of challenge, so set aside one practice day at some point during the season in which each player on the team gets the chance to challenge you in some aspect of soccer.

With younger kids, give them plenty of options to choose among, because they probably haven't had this chance before with other coaches. Here are some fun options:

✔ Let them race against you the length of the field, dribbling a soccer ball.

✔ Dribble through a series of cones to see who can do it the fastest.

✔ See who can control the ball longest in a designated area, with the other person serving as the defender.

✔ Play a game of 1-on-1 in a scaled-down area with a cone serving as the goal that you must hit with the ball.

If you have players who are struggling to learn skills, letting them beat you may be the confidence boost they need. With some of the other kids, beating them by a goal or a couple of seconds can provide that extra motivation for them to work even harder in practice so they can win next time.

Bring Your Parent to Practice Day

In many schools around the country, kids have the chance to bring their parents with them for a day, and this idea works great in organized soccer, too. By having this day early in the season, you send the message that you really want the parents to be actively involved in their child's soccer experience. You don't want parents just showing up and reading a book or paying bills on the sidelines. Have them shadow their children during the entire practice and participate alongside them. They should go through the warm-ups with their youngsters and take part in all the drills. During this practice, run plenty of drills that involve 2-on-2 or 4-on-4 so that the youngsters team up to compete against their parents. Conducting this type of practice serves as a great bonding experience for both the parents and child, and it gives parents a better appreciation of what their child goes through during the course of a regular practice, particularly if they've never played soccer.

New Drills

Nothing sabotages fun and learning quicker than subjecting youngsters to the same boring practices week after week. Taking the time to introduce a new drill during every practice infuses your sessions with excitement and ensures that the kids never get in a mind-numbing rut. To give them something to look forward to at each practice, introduce the new drill at the same point in your sessions. You may find that unveiling the new drill at the start of practice, when youngsters are often the most focused and attentive, works best. Or you may discover that building the anticipation and saving the new drill for the last few minutes of the practice is a great way to conclude the session. After you establish a routine, you'll find that the kids eagerly anticipate the chance to participate in a fun new drill every time they step on the field.

Contest Day

One of the most effective ways to promote team camaraderie is to devote a practice session to a series of special contests. But instead of having the players compete among themselves, which only gives your better-skilled youngsters the chance to further showcase their talents while alienating the less-skilled kids, pair up the players ahead of time. By putting a talented child with a youngster who isn't quite as skilled, you force the kids to work together, which not only improves their skills, but also allows them the chance to get to know each other better.

As you know, the more familiar kids are with each other, the more they care about each other, and that translates into more inspired play on the field. The familiarity also leads to more supportive teammates who pull for one another to succeed and who step forward to offer encouraging words when things don't work out as planned. You can plant the seeds for long-term friendships, which are among the special benefits that come from participating in organized soccer. If you played soccer, or any sport, growing up, you probably can easily recall some of the friendships you forged with teammates.

Some samples of mini-contests you can do include

- ✔ Timing the pairs while they pass the ball back and forth a set number of times and run the length of the field
- ✔ Attempting headers where the players toss the ball to their partners, who must head it back to them (forcing the players to work together because the better the toss, the easier it is to head the ball)

Encourage the kids to support their partners, and you can even let them know before the contests begin that you award bonus points to those twosomes who demonstrate the most support for each other.

Midseason Report Cards

Remember your days in school when you'd bring home those progress reports with the smiley faces that said what a great student you were and how well you were doing? The report card gave you a sense of accomplishment and served as a springboard for continuing to work hard the rest of the term. Issuing midseason cards to your squad can accomplish much of the same and give players a real boost of confidence. Handwritten notes extolling the players' talents and recognizing what areas of the game they have really excelled in so far this season are nice touches that let players know that you appreciate the effort they put forth.

All players love to be recognized for their skills and hard work, and handwritten notes that players can look back at and read all season long often carry more weight than verbal accolades and serve as the motivation for them to continue giving you their best each time they step on the field. With older players, these handwritten notes can be just as effective. You can even go so far as to touch on an area of the game where you challenge them to make some improvements during the remainder of the season. Besides applauding those areas that they excel in, giving players goals to strive for gives them something extra to concentrate on during practice. This concentration helps maintain their focus through the second half of the season.

Bringing in New Faces

You're doing a great job of coaching, but every once in a while kids may enjoy a break from you, particularly if they're with you for several months. Bringing in a new face to talk to the kids about some aspect of soccer provides a new perspective that can be refreshing and reenergizing for them. You have plenty of possibilities within your community. A local high school soccer coach, a well-known high school soccer player, or coaches or players from a nearby college soccer team are all excellent resources.

Just giving the players on your team the chance to hear from someone who offers different tips on performing a specific skill, or some words of encouragement on what it takes to reach the next level, can be enormously beneficial in your youngsters' growth and development.

 Another option is bringing in a sports nutritionist, which is especially good for older kids, who are at an age where they're exploring all sorts of ways to improve their skills. Hearing the importance of eating right and drinking the proper fluids is much more effective coming from an expert in the field than it is coming from you.

Team Votes

One of the basic facts of growing up is that kids have to endure being told what to do much of the time. Between school, home, and other assorted activities, they're constantly being instructed, ordered around, and told how it's going to be. Once in a while, it's nice to let kids decide what they want to do. Giving them a chance to voice their opinions shows that you respect them as both soccer players and as people and that you value their thoughts and opinions.

If the league allows, let the players vote on the team nickname or the color of the uniforms. Even something as basic as letting them decide on the color of the team mouth guard builds camaraderie among the players and sends the message that what they think carries meaning with you. You can also let the youngsters work together to come up with a team cheer to do before they take the field for games. These types of exercises promote team unity and create a bond that isn't likely to be broken during the course of the season.

Team Captain for the Day

Rotating team captains every practice is a great way to give each child a little extra attention. At the start of each practice, let the team know who you designate as the team captain for the day. On the other hand, you may find that your kids are more receptive to being told at the end of practice who will be the captain at the following practice so they have something to look forward to.

Make the honor of team captain something that carries some weight. Besides the basics, like letting the designated captains lead the team warm-ups (see Chapter 6), allow the captains the authority to choose the first team exercise of the day or decide how they want practice to conclude. You can go so far as to have a specially colored jersey made that says "Team Captain" on the back that you give to the captain at the start of practice, or even something as basic as a colorful sweatband, armband, or headband that the kids will enjoy wearing. By listening to kids' ideas and then following through with them, you truly give each child the sense that he's an important and contributing member of the team. Unless you're coaching an older group of kids, it's best not to have a team captain on game days, with so much else going on.

Carnival Day

Kids love carnivals, games, and the chance to win prizes — and you can easily re-create that type of atmosphere by devising some off-the-wall activities at one of your practices during the season. For example, set up a soccer bowling station where a youngster has to kick a soccer ball and knock over a couple of plastic bowling pins or pylons. Or lay a Hula-Hoop on the ground and challenge kids to kick the ball from a specified distance and have the ball end up inside the hoop. At each of the stations, you can have a bucket of candy, gum, or little toys, and when the kids are successful, they earn a small prize.

Holiday or Birthday Themes

With young children, a practice centered on a holiday can be a fun way to mix up the routine. If your soccer season runs during the fall, Halloween is a natural for encouraging kids to come to practice in their costumes. Of course, you should adjust the exercises accordingly so you don't have youngsters running all over the field risking injury or damaging their costumes in a scrimmage, for example. Simply having the kids work on their shots on goal, for example, is a fun-filled activity for them. You can even show up in a costume yourself and play goalie, letting the kids take shots on you.

You don't have to limit your creativity to Halloween. If a child has a birthday during the season, give the kids birthday hats to wear during practice or some other type of party favors. Other holidays provide opportunities for you to get creative, too. For example, around Easter, set up an exercise in which the youngster completes the skill successfully to get the chance to look for eggs that you've hidden around the field. Of course, before doing anything of this nature, always check with the parents out of respect for their religious beliefs.

Chapter 22

Ten Ways to End the Season on a High Note

In This Chapter

▶ Passing out creative team awards

▶ Providing clever mementos

As your youth soccer season winds to a close, you should start thinking about concluding the season in a memorable way. Although throwing pizza parties and handing out participation medals are some of the more common routes many coaches take, you can go a step further and use your creativity to wrap up the season on a high note that will have the kids craving to return to the soccer field again next season. This chapter provides ten clever (if we do say so ourselves) season-ending ideas that will send the kids home with smiles on their faces.

Team Awards

Creating innovative team awards is a great way to recognize the contributions of the youngsters on your squad. Recognizing each player in some way is important when giving out any type of award. Singling out only a select few players leaves the others feeling isolated and hurt, and sends the message that they aren't valued and contributing parts of the team. Handing out special awards that you create on your own is a great opportunity to recognize the children for any special skills or attributes that meant the most to you during the course of the season.

We see no need to hand out the old standby Most Valuable Player award. First of all, everyone already knows who the best player on the team is, and second, presenting this type of award gives the impression that this individual is more important than any of the other team members. That's the last message you want to send at the end of the season.

With a little imagination, you can easily come up with ways to highlight each child's efforts during the season. For example, you can hand out a Most Likely to Block a Shot During a Game award. Giving this award is a great way to show your appreciation for the child who's always willing to do all the little things during the game in order for the team to be successful. Plus, this type of award is an ideal way to recognize a youngster whose contributions otherwise may have been overlooked. Such recognition is often enough to give that child a boost of confidence and the encouragement to return to the sport the following season.

The following are just some ideas of different types of awards you can present to your team. Use your imagination to come up with plenty of others that your players will welcome:

- Most Dedicated
- Best Sportsmanship
- Most Improved
- Hardest Worker
- Most Enthusiastic
- Model Teammate
- Best Defensive Player
- Best Passer
- Corner-Kick Specialist
- Penalty-Kick Specialist
- Best Dribbler
- Best Tackler

You can design the certificates and print them on a computer at home, or you can recruit an interested parent who has some artistic ability to do it for you. You can even collect a few dollars from each parent and order miniature trophies, with the players' names and the names of the awards engraved on them.

Team Videos

Videos are great for capturing the excitement of the season for the youngsters and their parents who will enjoy viewing them for years to come. Kids (excuse the pun) get a real kick out of watching footage of themselves and their teammates. If you have a parent who's experienced in using a camcorder, recruit him or her to shoot a video of the kids at different practices and games and put together a montage of the season. If you have a parent, or even a couple of parents, who shows interest and is willing to undertake this project, just make sure that he or she takes adequate footage of each child on the team. The last thing you want to do is have a child's feelings hurt because he doesn't appear anywhere in the piece or has limited appearances compared with the rest of his teammates.

Don't wait until your season hits the home stretch to organize a team video, because it may be too late. Gauge the parents' interest at the start of the season, and if they're enthusiastic, start making arrangements immediately.

You can also check with the parents to see if they're interested in chipping in to hire a professional videographer. You can bring it up at your preseason parents meeting, which we discuss in Chapter 4. A professionally done piece makes a great keepsake that the kids and their parents will treasure for years to come. You can cut down on the cost by having the professional come out for just a game or two during the season, but make sure that he gets footage of each child.

Individual Videos

If you have the financial resources to hire a professional videographer, or if a parent on your team has plenty of extra time on his hands, you can put together an individual video for each child that highlight the child's play throughout the season. Even a two- to three-minute video makes a great keepsake for the kids. If you decide to go this route, gather the team together before handing out the videos so they can watch them all as a team. It makes for a fun night, and everyone has a great time looking back at the team's play.

Team Trading Cards

Kids love trading cards of their favorite sports heroes with their friends, so working with a local photographer to design soccer cards with the kids' photos on the front and some interesting facts about them on the back goes over big with them. You can include basic information, such as date of birth, height, and weight, as well as fun information, such as the nickname you call the player during practice or a quote from you on what you admire most about his game. Give each kid a dozen or so that they can swap with their teammates, give to friends, or send to grandparents. You can discuss this idea with the parents prior to the season to see if they're willing to contribute extra money for the cards.

1-on-1 Meeting

A season-ending 1-on-1 meeting with each player is a great way to send the players into the offseason on a high note, motivate them to work hard, and have them looking forward to returning next season. This meeting is especially beneficial for the older kids. Talk to them about the area of their game where they made the most improvement this season and how proud you are of their efforts. Kids respond in a positive manner to the compliments and recognition, and it may just be the spark that ignites their enthusiasm to return to the field next season.

Keep in mind that the recognition doesn't even have to come in the form of praise for a specific soccer skill. For example, maybe the child wasn't much of a team player at the start of the season, but as the season progressed, she came around and started shouting encouragement to her teammates or congratulating them more enthusiastically for a goal or other excellent play. Or maybe she emerged as a better sport and no longer displayed any unsportsmanlike tendencies. You can highlight a variety of areas that all go into the youth soccer experience. Soccer is so much more than passing, shooting, and scoring. Being fully aware of that when evaluating each player's all-around game is important.

Be sure to talk with older children, particularly those who you know will be on your team next season or who are simply interested in improving their play. Discuss in a positive tone the areas of their game that they can concentrate on and improve during the offseason. Talk to them about how impressed you are with the strongest aspects of their game, and then follow it up by mentioning that if they devote a little extra attention to this other area of their game, they'll really be tough to stop next season. Remember, positive and encouraging words fuel their desire to want to improve and take their game to the next level.

When holding 1-on-1 meetings with your players, make sure that you're in an area without distractions. You don't want your complimentary words and feedback to go unheard or unrecognized by a youngster whose attention is diverted by kids playing nearby or by his teammates lingering around listening in to what you're saying.

Team Newsletter

A newsletter captures the excitement of the season and is a wonderful keepsake for any child's scrapbook and a fond remembrance of her time with your team. Some of the things that can be featured in the newsletter are

- ✔ Different action photos from various practices and games during the season

- ✔ Capsule summaries of each game (make sure that each child is mentioned at some point if you recap the season)

- ✔ Brief bios of the players, listing favorite television shows, school subjects, or how many brothers and sisters the players have

- ✔ A comment from you about each player, such as "Tommy is the team's hardest worker," "Susie displayed the best sportsmanship during the season," or "Billy had the best attitude"

You may be able to recruit parents to help in this endeavor by putting together some of the text for the pages or laying out the pages with the photos and headlines.

You can design a newsletter in a newspaper format and include a column about how much fun you had coaching the kids this season and how enjoyable it was to watch them learn and progress in the sport. Be sure to thank the parents for all their hard work and positive support, too.

Team Photo Album

A team photo album makes a great end-of-season gift that the children will enjoy looking at, and it's something that they'll hold on to and cherish for a lifetime. Before the season starts, designate another parent, or perhaps your spouse, to take photos during games. You can also choose a different parent each game to snap a roll of film of all the kids, which ensures that you have a wide variety of shots to choose among when putting together the albums. After you pick out the prints you want, simply make copies and make each album identical for all the players. If you or another parent has time, you can get really creative and make an album for each player that features a team photo and a variety of shots of that particular child participating in practices or games.

Crazy Practice

All season long, your practices have been well organized, efficient, and focused on helping the kids learn and improve a variety of skills. A great reward for the players who have shown up on time all season long and given you their complete attention is to stage a crazy practice during one of your last sessions with the team.

You can take a number of approaches for the crazy practice. For example, you can have the kids wear mismatched outfits to practice or have them wear their shirts and shorts backward. The younger the players are, the more excited they'll be to have the chance to be silly together and laugh with one another. Now, don't forget to join in the fun, too. The kids will probably get the most laughs seeing you and your assistant coaches dressed in strange outfits or wearing your clothes the wrong way.

Soccer-Ball Photo

All kids love receiving gifts, especially cool sports gifts related to soccer. A neat present is a soccer ball emblazoned with the team photo. These balls make great collectibles that the youngsters can proudly display on their bedroom shelves at home. The balls are also more eye-catching than the traditional team photo stuck in a frame. To have the balls made, contact well-known chain photography stores found in most cities, or ask the sports photographer your league uses for team photos. If he can't do it, he can probably steer you to someone who can.

Team Memento

If you want to hand out some type of participation memento, you can go with a medal shaped like a soccer ball or even a miniature soccer trophy, because all kids love receiving trophies to display in their rooms. Or you can give them miniature soccer balls that can be purchased at various sporting-goods retail stores. You can jazz up the balls by having the team name written on them or the team's record, if you coached in a competitive program and the team happened to win the league title or posted a good record.

Index